rode about 3 miles, thro' a shade forest of [...] Laurel, &c the Soil being very Rich.

We now assend the sand hills, & h[...] first observed growing) that very singular On[...] erfoliated, bearing a single yellow flower i[...] osom of the leaves. rode about 4 miles ariv[...] benezar, a very beautifull Village, chiefly in[...] the descensants of an antient colony of Germ[...] ofs, who chiefly imploy themselves in the [...] ture of Silk. The Town is laid out in large Sq[...] that every family has ground sufficient to p[...] Mulberry Orchard, a Garden & a Cornfield, & [...] ave been, & are at this time [...]ious & ten[...] heir little Plantations are [...]ated. The [...] Settlement, forms a delightfull Village incompass[...] with Gardens Orchid, Cornfields & Pasture ground[...] They likewise plant wheat enough for each fam[...]

The Great Naturalists

8

The Great Naturalists

EDITED BY ROBERT HUXLEY

With 198 illustrations

Thames & Hudson

CONTENTS

Half-title: Detail from Konrad Gessner's History of Animals.
Title page: Painting of a dandelion and stages in the
metamorphosis of a moth, by Maria Sibylla Merian.
Endpapers: Pages from the journal of William Bartram.

© 2007 The Natural History Museum, London
Layout © 2007 Thames & Hudson Ltd, London

First published in 2007 in hardcover in the United States
of America by Thames & Hudson Inc., 500 Fifth Avenue,
New York, New York 10110

thamesandhudsonusa.com

Library of Congress Catalog Card Number 2006940563

ISBN 978-0-500-25139-3

Printed and bound in China by C&C Offset Printing Co., Ltd.

'UNITY IN DIVERSITY'

Unity in diversity, and of connection, resemblance and order,
among created things most dissimilar in their form,
one fair harmonious whole...

Alexander von Humboldt, **Kosmos**, *1845–62*

WALKING THROUGH one of the world's great natural history museums today, the visitor marvels at the fossilized skeletons of giant reptiles, the iridescent wings of pinioned butterflies or the elegantly displayed gems and minerals. Some of those who are intrigued and absorbed by the specimens on view will know that they are just the tip of a vast iceberg of millions and millions of others stored in ranks of cupboards and ladders of drawers and shelves behind the scenes. Fewer, perhaps, will be aware of the fact that these collections represent the results of activity reaching back into the ancient civilizations of Greece and Rome and even beyond. They are the fruits of a phenomenal human endeavour that continues to this day, as an international army of scientists struggles to name, describe, classify and understand new discoveries, in what has become a rapidly changing environment. Modern natural science was built on the work of those who went before, who braved dangers from tempests and pirates to disease and political upheavals in their pursuit of cataloguing and understanding the natural world – these are the great naturalists.

What differentiates these people from modern scientists, and why do we begin a book devoted to them with Aristotle and end it in the age of Charles Darwin? To begin at the end, Darwin symbolizes a time when science changed from a broad-based and mainly amateur pursuit to the highly specialized profession that we know

A painting by Maria Sibylla Merian of the emperor moth (Arsenura armida). *Merian was fascinated by the process of metamorphosis and was one of the first to depict insects in all stages of their life cycle in the same image. She also painted creatures together with the plants or other organisms that they feed on, in this instance the coral tree* (Erythrina fusca).

7

today – a consequence in part of the huge increase in information concerning the natural world that resulted from European expansion overseas, as well as the development of essential tools such as the microscope. By the 19th century the scope of natural history had become so vast that private funding and amateur enthusiasms alone could not adequately quantify and encompass it. The scale of the challenge drove specialization, and the natural historian was replaced by the professional biologist and geologist, who then specialized further into geneticists, biochemists and systematists, for example, and then again into even more focused disciplines.

Unashamedly in this book, natural history is confined mainly to the history of the discovery, description, classification and understanding of whole organisms. Those whose main interests were in the details of the inner workings of living things or specific geological processes are generally not included, except where their studies had broader significance; hence pioneering work such as William Harvey's descriptions of blood circulation or Louis Pasteur's microbiological experiments do not fall within our definition.

Since humans are themselves an inseparable element of the natural world it is inevitable that its study will always have been of great interest to us from the earliest times. Pre-literate cultures since the dawn of humanity would have needed to classify plants into those that were edible, poisonous or of medicinal value, and to recognize animals as potentially dangerous or valuable. The precise reasons for studying and understanding the natural world have changed over the centuries – but, as with all human endeavours, the progress of this branch of science has been influenced by those constant factors that affect human beings. Religion and politics all play a part in the stories that follow, as do economic forces, superstition and war.

DESCRIPTION AND CLASSIFICATION

Evidence of a formal and more specialized interest in natural history came with the Sumerians in the 3rd millennium BC; they were literate and practised medicine, and recorded much of their lore. Herbal remedies were common, as was knowledge of minerals and their compounds, including iron, copper and mercury. The ancient Egyptians had a precise understanding of the Nile and its cycles, and their importance to agriculture, and they discovered much about anatomy and the preservation of organic materials through their mummification rituals. This knowledge was almost entirely empirical – that is, based on perception alone. The questions 'Why?' and 'How?' were not and perhaps could not be asked, since any development of science as such was hindered by the power of priests, who jealously guarded knowledge.

Aristotle teaching: an illustration from 'The Better Sentences and Most Precious Dictions' by al-Moubbachir, 13th century. Born in Macedonia in 384 BC, Aristotle's interests encompassed a vast range of scientific subjects, but as a natural historian he favoured zoology. As with many Classical scholars, his works survived by being translated and copied by later Islamic scholars.

The beginning of what we might now regard as natural science appeared with the Classical Greeks. It is remarkable how, without access to the body of knowledge that we have inherited, and given their limited accomplishment in scientific theories and the methods of experiment that we use today, they arrived at conclusions not far from those we now accept as safe. Much of Greek thought was concerned with the fundamental unchanging elements which made up the universe – earth, air, fire and water. The different schools of thought considered which of these was dominant, how they affected the working of the everyday world, and whether there was a fixed universe or an ever-changing one. It was in these times that the first attempts to describe and document the natural world were made, and, more significantly to this discussion, when the first endeavours to classify living things by their morphology rather than their practical uses emerged.

And so we begin with Aristotle as the first great naturalist. Aristotle stands out among others of his time for the scale and breadth of his study, and, more importantly, the lasting legacy of his work and its significance in the development of natural science. The great philosopher, among his many interests, collected together existing

9

The School of Athens, *a fresco by Raphael in the Vatican. Aristotle, in blue, is shown in discussion with Plato, while Theophrastus, in an orange robe, looks on. Theophrastus studied under both Plato and Aristotle, and succeeded the latter as the head of the Lyceum. Considered the 'father of botany', his surviving works on the subject are the most important we have from antiquity.*

descriptions of the plants and animals of his Mediterranean world, which he compiled in his great work, the *History of Animals*. To this he added his own descriptions, many no doubt based on the fauna and flora sent back to him from distant lands by his distinguished pupil, Alexander the Great. The key for Aristotle was to observe nature in order to understand it. In Aristotle's world, life was arranged on a scale from cold creeping 'vermin' at the bottom to warm mammals and man at the top. Such ideas were to remain largely unchallenged up to the 17th and 18th centuries.

Aristotle's mainly zoological works were complemented by the botanical interests of his pupil and friend, Theophrastus. Theophrastus's pioneering descriptions based on noting the presence or absence of particular characteristics in different plant species led to later botanists revering him as the 'father of botany'.

The pragmatic Romans were generally more interested in the practical application of aspects of the natural world in medicine and agriculture, rather than the theoretical basis of the subject. Their encyclopaedic approach is exemplified by the hundreds of animals, real and mythical, described in the *Natural History* of Pliny the Elder, or the catalogue of plants of medicinal value compiled by Dioscorides in his *De Materia Medica*.

From the fall of Rome to the Renaissance it is difficult to single out a natural historian who could be considered great; the so-called Dark Ages engulfed Europe, and mysticism and magic, with a few exceptions, took the place of reason.

EXPANDING KNOWLEDGE

The Renaissance rediscovery of the works of the great Classical civilizations had as great an effect in the natural sciences as in the arts. Although still tightly bound to the writings of Aristotle, Dioscorides and others, Renaissance scholars expanded their knowledge and understanding of plants and animals by dissection and comparison, and by recording them in much improved drawings and printed text. There were sound practical reasons for accurate drawing: the herbals of the time were guides to plants used in medicine and served as a reference for the herbalist and the physician, making their accuracy crucial. Centuries of copying, however, had produced a plethora of vastly differing versions of the ancients' work. The German physician and botanist Leonhart Fuchs stood over his illustrators as they worked to prevent artistic license rendering their drawings useless for identifying plants and animals – with potentially disastrous results. Fuchs went beyond the medical importance of his botanical subjects and described nearly 500 plants in detail, supported by the exceptionally detailed woodcuts that were ahead of their time.

If Fuchs saw that a good illustration was worth a thousand words then Ulisse Aldrovandi recognized that an actual specimen was worth a million. Aldrovandi, the first professor of natural science at the University of Bologna, created a museum of some 18,000 'natural things', from crocodiles to volumes containing pressed, dried plants; this was no mere cabinet of curiosities, but a large scientific collection of examples to use in the study and teaching of natural history, along the lines of our great museums today. Like Fuchs, Aldrovandi employed an army of woodcutters and illustrators whose work was strictly controlled to ensure accuracy.

Fuchs and his contemporaries organized their plant illustrations and descriptions by simple classifications based on medicinal uses and listed them alphabetically. However, the highly gifted Italian philosopher Andrea Cesalpino devised a system based on their physical form and structure. Although his systems used only a limited set of characteristics and did not bring truly related plants together, his was the first scientific attempt at a classification of the natural world.

In the 17th century the Western world entered the era known as the Enlightenment, or Age of Reason, and new ways of thinking stimulated by philosophers such as Francis Bacon in England and René Descartes in Paris changed natural history fundamentally. Experiment and observation replaced superstition and blind faith, and the study of nature became a respectable, desirable and even a fashionable activity.

The link between natural history and religion has been strong through the ages. Until the 17th century this had a primarily negative effect, as anyone who challenged the Church's accepted view of the world risked persecution or even death. Galileo stands out as a stark example of the dilemma faced by those who had to choose between science and faith. On the other hand, many practitioners of natural science were churchmen themselves, often seeing natural history studies as a means to understand God's works. The highly skilled Danish anatomist Nicolaus Steno was the first seriously to get to grips with the question of fossils and how fossil seashells could be found on mountaintops. Steno showed that what we now call sedimentary rocks had been laid down in layers, with the remains of once-living creatures – now fossils – buried within them. Furthermore, the Earth's crust had moved and pushed these layers up into mountains. As a devout Lutheran, Steno was able to reconcile this with the biblical account. He later converted to Catholicism and became a bishop, devoting the rest of his life to religion rather than the geology that had challenged its tenets.

New worlds, and their bizarre and wonderful creatures never before seen, were being discovered not just through perilous voyages of exploration around the globe, but also much closer to home, through the lens of a microscope. In 1665 Robert Hooke, a founder member of the prestigious Royal Society, a scientific institution based in London, published his *Micrographia*. For the first time the general public saw detailed images of a flea, a fly's eye and plant cells, revealed under a microscope. Hooke's work was to inspire a Dutch fabric merchant, Antony van Leeuwenhoek, to make a simpler but more effective device, with which he discovered a vast world in a drop of pond-water, teeming with inhabitants; he was also the first person to see bacteria. These two stand out as pioneers of one of the most powerful tools of the naturalist to this day.

One of the main activities of the great natural historians since ancient times was to try to bring order to the apparent chaos of the natural world. From Aristotle's day, attempts had been made to develop systems of classification by which to arrange the mass of known living things. The 17th century saw a move towards so-called natural classifications, which used a large number of characteristics to determine which species are related to each other. The most significant figure in this movement was the

The rhinoceros as depicted in Konrad Gessner's Historia Animalium, *copied from the famous print by Albrecht Dürer. It is the most enduring image of the rhinoceros, being used, for instance, in German science textbooks until the 20th century.*

English clergyman John Ray, whose highly methodical and thorough work introduced a scientific aspect to natural history that had not been seen before.

The elaborate systems of Ray and others were ahead of their time, but while they did bring together plants or animals with genuine relationships to each other, what was needed was a quick method to identify and categorize the many new organisms now being discovered through exploration around the globe. This was to be the accomplishment of one of the best-known of all naturalists, the Swedish doctor Carl Linnaeus. His simple – and at the time outrageous – sexual method for classifying plants meant that botany was now opened up to contributions from everyone, from the university academic to the country parson. Linnaeus's great legacy was the straightforward, easily applicable and unambiguous naming system that we use today.

While men such as Ray were studying nature as a means of understanding God's works, others were beginning to recognize its secular value as a potential source of wealth, power and revenue. This was particularly true in the expanding colonies in North America. In 1722 a talented young naturalist, Mark Catesby, had come to the Carolina colony as the replacement for an earlier surveyor who had been gruesomely killed in a native uprising – one of the many hazards facing the naturalist of these times. Catesby set about exploring, surveying and describing the wildlife and other

Eine Kamtschadalische Winterhütte von innen.

In their search for knowledge, naturalists were often intrepid explorers, making hazardous journeys to observe nature at first hand and to collect specimens. Georg Steller was a member of the Russian expedition led by Vitus Bering to Kamchatka and Alaska: this engraving of people overwintering in a hut comes from Steller's account of his travels, published after his death.

natural phenomena of the unknown interior. Though there was some scientific purpose to his work, it also undoubtedly provided useful information to the Governor of the state, one of Catesby's supporters on the trip, on the natural wealth of his territory. Catesby was an all-round naturalist of exceptional skill; in order to produce his great work on the natural history of the southeastern colonies he taught himself to make engravings. The resulting plates are startling in their lifelike representation of wildlife and unusually for the time he depicted birds and other animals in association with the appropriate plants, something that the intrepid Maria Sibylla Merian, who travelled to Surinam, had also pioneered. Their appreciation of the relationship between living things pre-dates the science of ecology by more than 200 years.

An economic interest in nature coupled with an entrepreneurial spirit and enthusiasm for the natural world are supremely brought together in Sir Joseph Banks.

A naturalist on Captain James Cook's first voyage, he was, with his colleague Daniel Solander, the first to collect and record plants and animals in the unknown regions of Australia and New Zealand, bringing back specimens and illustrations as evidence of this southern new world. Banks saw collections as tools of science, rather than merely as curios, much as we do today. He also emphasized the importance of good illustrations and commissioned artists to record the plants and animals of Australasia in a series of wonderful engravings which were only finally printed in 1988. This rich, self-funded young pioneer went on to promote the economic benefits of natural history in many ways, from the transport of breadfruit from the Pacific to grow in the Caribbean to feed slaves on plantations, to the introduction of merino sheep to Australia.

By the end of the 18th century, the ordering and classification of the ever-expanding natural world had moved away from Linnaeus's simple but unrevealing classifications to more natural systems, similar to ones devised by John Ray a century earlier that reflected real relationships. Natural systems were preferred by French scientists of the time – for instance Jean-Baptiste Lamarck, a severe critic of Linnaeus – and it is they who established many of the groups of organisms that we use today. Lamarck, like many others in this book, began his career in the Church, followed by the military, before devoting himself to natural science. He was an early proponent of the study of invertebrate animals (ones without backbones), a term he coined,

Many great naturalists were also great artists. William Bartram, who painted this depiction of a warmouth, or great yellow bream (Lepomis gulosus), *was a keen observer of plants and animals, combining an aesthetic appreciation of nature with scientific study.*

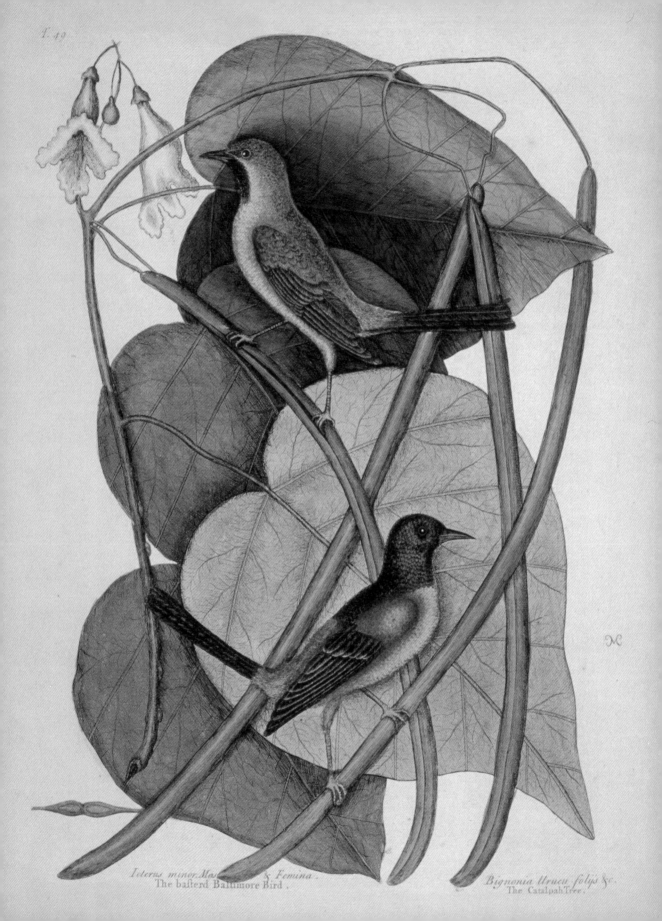

T. 49.

Ɯ

Icterus minor. Mas ...... & Femina.
The baßerd Baltimore Bird.

Bignonia Urucu folijs &c.
The Catalpah Tree.

and most of his classifications, for instance of crustaceans and arachnids, remain unchanged today. Lamarck is best remembered for his pre-Darwinian evolutionary theories, which, dangerously in Napoleonic France, implied that only time and favourable conditions, rather than God, were necessary to create the living world that we know. Lamarck belonged to a strong tradition in France of formulating a theory that encompassed the whole of the natural world – a tradition exemplified by the Comte de Buffon, whose 44-volume *Histoire Naturelle* eloquently documented the current state of knowledge. Buffon's work, although ridiculed by some of his contemporaries, was to influence naturalists, including Charles Darwin, for generations.

The activities of French naturalists at the dawn of the 19th century stand as examples of the rise of the professional in natural science. Interest in the subject had expanded rapidly in the universities, museums and botanic gardens after the French Revolution, and it was becoming a respectable field of academic teaching and research – a trend that was to continue across the world over the following century.

Across the Atlantic, in the fledgling United States of America, pioneer natural historians such as William Bartram were exploring and describing their country's natural wealth and indigenous peoples – both already under threat. Bartram and others wanted to establish an independent American tradition of natural science relevant to their own country, rather than mimicking the European model. Following in this tradition came the illegitimate son of a French sea captain and arguably America's greatest natural historian. John James Audubon's special interest was ornithology, and as a highly talented artist he not only described and studied birds, but was also able to capture the detail of their form, colour and behaviour. His greatest work, *The Birds of America*, is without modern parallel and illustrates in life-size images over 1,000 birds, organized in a naturalistic way rather than following established classification systems such as that of Linnaeus.

CHALLENGING ACCEPTED IDEAS

The 19th century was also the twilight of the rich, self-supporting amateurs who had dominated the subject for hundreds of years. Whilst these may have been the last, they were also some of the greatest. A prime example is Alexander von Humboldt, a German aristocrat who undertook a number of epic expeditions, fraught with danger, from the mountains and forests of South America to the frozen wastes of Siberia. His achievements as a natural scientist are many. As well as discovering, recording and

An illustration by Mark Catesby of Catalpa bignonioides, *a common ornamental tree which Catesby may have helped introduce to Britain; he has shown it with the Bastard Baltimore bird.*

collecting many species new to science, he also published monumental works in which he developed his theories of the world as a connected whole, and about the close relationship of the living and the non-living world and the influence of climate, geology and geography on the distribution of plant and animal species. His name is perpetuated in several academic institutions around the world and in the Humboldt Current off the coast of South America, which he studied and described. Humboldt was to be one of the main inspirations of the best-known of all natural historians and the end of our journey through the disclosure of the natural world, Charles Darwin.

Evolution was the hottest topic of the 19th century and one of the greatest and most challenging leaps in the understanding of the natural world. The key was the acceptance that not only was the Earth much older than anyone had dared believe, but that its age was sufficient to allow the planet itself and its living cover to have gradually changed through natural forces. It thus challenged people's faith in, and acceptance of, a Creation in the not too distant past. The idea of evolution had, of course, been proposed in various guises in the past, but all lacked sufficient evidence in support. Interestingly, it was Darwin's own grandfather, Erasmus, a leading intellectual and pioneer of the industrial age, who speculated on how species might change through time through sexual selection. He based his theories on observations of domestic animals, backed up by his broad knowledge of subjects ranging from geology to embryology, and published much of his work in the form of poetry.

While the young Darwin was inspired and informed by both Humboldt and, to some extent, his grandfather Erasmus, it was his friend Charles Lyell, a geologist, who was to provide a solid basis for his theories. Lyell had studied law at Oxford, but became interested in geology and devoted the rest of his life to the study of geological phenomena, from volcanoes to glaciers. His main interest was stratigraphy – the study of the layers of rocks and the fossils that characterized them. Lyell travelled widely, collecting fossils and recording exactly where and in what strata they were found, concluding that life had changed gradually on the Earth and not by a series of catastrophes such as the biblical Flood. As well as an influence on Darwin and his theory of evolution, Lyell was also later one of his greatest supporters.

And so we come to Charles Darwin and the evolutionary theory that was to provoke, stimulate and inspire generations of biologists, theologians economists, engineers and sociologists, to name but a few, to the present day. But he was not alone – it seems that the trend of scientific knowledge was moving in this direction, and naturalist and explorer Alfred Russel Wallace had reached similar conclusions based on his observations in the forests of Malaysia and elsewhere. He, like Darwin, was

Alexander von Humboldt was one of the last of the self-supporting amateur great naturalists. He made an epic journey around South America, by land and water. This image of a raft on the River Guayaquil was drawn after a sketch by him.

convinced that species could change and new ones evolve through environmental pressures, a process that Darwin called 'natural selection'. While Darwin proposed a joint publication of their theories, it is his name that is mostly remembered in connection with this world-changing concept.

After Darwin, the sciences of biology and geology were no longer the province of amateurs, but were to become increasingly specialized and professional, and a key element of the prevailing industrial society. Today we owe a debt of gratitude to the pioneers who described, experimented and collected, who gave us the means to order and understand the natural world and the potential not only to exploit it, but also to conserve it and ensure its future survival. The great collections of our natural history museums, universities and botanic gardens provide the tools for systematists and taxonomists to name, classify and work out the origins of a still largely unknown, but rapidly dwindling and endangered natural world.

THE ANCIENTS

THE FIRST NATURAL HISTORIANS whom we would recognize as such lived, observed and theorized in the city states of ancient Greece. In an atmosphere of relative freedom and prosperity, and unconstrained by religious authority, they had time to deliberate about matters beyond day-to-day survival. No longer held back by superstitions, the new thinkers of Greece could speculate on the causes of natural phenomena and the origins and workings of the universe. The application of reason to what they could see, hear or feel was the key to understanding, and the observations of the great philosopher-naturalists such as Aristotle and Theophrastus were to paint a picture of the natural world that was to persist for centuries, later passed on unchallenged to less free-thinking societies.

One of the earliest natural historians was Anaximander of Miletus (of the late 6th century BC) who believed that living things were formed from water and earth heated by the sun, and that humans were once fish that had shed their scales. These early proto-evolutionary thoughts were taken up by others such as Empedocles, in the 5th century BC, whose four elements of earth, air, fire and water were acted upon by forces of hate and love to produce life. In Empedocles' universe, the separate limbs, heads and bodies of animals appeared first and were then brought together by the force of love into fully formed animals. Not all were perfect – some monstrosities were produced as heads of goats coalesced with human bodies – but through a process of selection only those adapted to the world would survive. An early theory of evolution by natural selection perhaps?

The most significant of the Greek thinkers as far as natural history is concerned is surely Aristotle, a student of Plato and the first of our great naturalists. Aristotle had trained in Plato's Academy and wrote extensively on many natural phenomena; he is especially notable for making natural history a respectable scientific pursuit through his writings. He proposed that life forms sit on the rungs of a metaphorical ladder of life, from the lowliest and simplest creatures (plants in his view) at the bottom, to humans at the top, seeing this as a fixed and unchanging system. His general observations and descriptions of animals were exceptionally good for the time – he recognized dolphins as mammals, for instance, and described in great detail the elaborate feeding structure of the sea-urchin, still known today as 'Aristotle's lantern'.

Theophrastus specialized in plants rather than animals, describing over 300 plants and inventing his own terminology where words did not exist to express his ideas and concepts. Much of his botanical work has been preserved through the ages and has had a lasting influence: he established the basic methodology which still serves taxonomy to this day.

While the Romans, successors to, and in many ways inheritors of, Greek civilization, were highly pragmatic and as engineers outstripped their predecessors, they were less inclined to the theoretical study of natural history, preferring instead to create encyclopaedias and lists of known information. Pliny the Elder compiled descriptions of large numbers of animals, including many mythical and fantastic creatures. Tireless and highly industrious, he gathered together much of the knowledge that existed about the natural world in his time. He reputedly died from the effects of poisonous gases as he observed the eruption of Vesuvius in AD 79, while on a rescue mission in the Bay of Naples.

Another member of the Roman war machine, Dioscorides was a Greek employed as an army physician. He produced a work of real practical use that, although following the great botanist Theophrastus, concerned itself mainly with the uses and pharmaceutical value of plants rather than the nature of the plants themselves. His book, *De Materia Medica*, was to be extensively copied and translated for well over a thousand years.

With the fall of the Roman empire, the study of the natural world effectively came to a standstill – the state of knowledge as described by the Classical authors of the Mediterranean was not to be challenged or developed until the Renaissance.

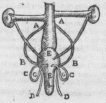

A A. *Initium ab aorta.*
B B. *Meatus descendentes.*
C C. *Applicati meatus.*
D D. *Reciproci meatus.*
E.　*Genitale.*
F.　*Vesica.*
G G. *Testes.*

TOP *A portrait of Dioscorides from an Ottoman manuscript of his work* De Materia Medica. *This remained in use for centuries, and was extensively copied and translated into many languages.*

ABOVE *A diagram explaining the workings of the body, from an early 17th-century edition of Aristotle's* History of Animals.

JULIA BRITTAIN

Aristotle

THE FIRST PHILOSOPHER-NATURALIST

(384–322 BC)

In all nature there is something of the marvellous.

Aristotle, De Partibus Animalium, *I*

OF ALL EARLY SCHOLARS, the ancient Greek philosopher Aristotle most deserves the description 'polymath'. His written works probably encompass a wider range of intellectual endeavour than those of any other naturalist featured in this book, and it is difficult to think of another historical figure who has surpassed his breadth of understanding and – more pertinently – of questioning. Ethics, literature, zoology, logic, psychology, meteorology, astronomy, metaphysics and politics all exercised his formidably enquiring mind, and he was a prolific and pioneering writer on all these subjects and more. His 30 surviving books are believed to represent only a fraction – between one-third and one-fifth – of his total output.

Aristotle was born in 384 BC, in the Macedonian town of Stagira, not far from modern-day Thessaloniki in northern Greece. His father, Nicomachus, was the royal physician in Macedonia, but died when Aristotle was a boy. At the age of 17 Aristotle was sent by his guardian to the Academy of the great philosopher Plato, in Athens, where he was to remain for 20 years, until Plato's death. It seems likely that the foundations of Aristotle's world view were laid during this period. While he later developed and challenged Plato's opinions, determinedly rejecting some of them, his eminent teacher's influence on his work, though often subliminal, was profound.

After leaving the Academy, Aristotle travelled for several years in Asia Minor, spending time in the coastal town of Assos, and on Lesbos, where he got to know the young botanist Theophrastus, a native of the island (p. 29). Aristotle's vivid descriptions of sea creatures probably had their origins in his first-hand observations and research here. In 343 BC he became tutor to the 13-year-old son of King Philip II of Macedonia, the future Alexander the Great. Returning several years later to Athens, Aristotle established his own school in the grounds of the Lyceum, which soon became known for its library and museum. Here, for 13 years, Aristotle taught and

Aristotle (right) and his influential teacher Plato, depicted in a detail from Raphael's 1510 fresco, the School of Athens, *in the Vatican. Aristotle later set up his own school, where, for the first time, natural history was taught as a subject of equal importance to other more traditional ones.*

studied a range of subjects which, for the first time, put natural history on a par with the traditionally 'respectable' sciences such as mathematics, medicine and astronomy. One of his pupils was Theophrastus, whose respect for Aristotle's methodical system of organizing knowledge undoubtedly influenced his own pioneering accounts of the plant world. Theophrastus became the head of the Lyceum when Aristotle ultimately retired, in 322 BC, to a property belonging to his mother's family at Chalcis, on the Aegean island of Euboea. There he died, a few months later, at the age of 63.

As a natural historian Aristotle covered many topics, but he favoured zoology, writing extensively on animal life in various works, including *Historia Animalium*, an ambitious nine-volume account of many zoological phenomena, which encompassed everything from fascinating tales of animal behaviour to graphic details of physiology. (Though sometimes translated as *History of Animals*, the Greek word *historia* in the original title is closer to 'research' or 'investigation'.) About a quarter of Aristotle's surviving work covers aspects of zoology, for instance *De Partibus Animalium* (*Parts of Animals*), *De Motu Animalium* (*Movement of Animals*) and *De Generatione Animalium* (*Generation of Animals*).

Those interested in the natural world can hardly fail to be absorbed and enchanted by Aristotle's observational writing, ranging from lively descriptions of marine life ('When the cuttlefish is struck with a trident the male stands by to help the female; but when the male is struck the female runs away' [*Historia Animalium*, Book IX]) to a comparative assessment of the different milks – and even rennets – derived from various mammals. More than 500 animal species feature in Aristotle's writings, and his fascination with his fellow creatures is unmistakable. On subjects ranging from the parental affection of dolphins and seals, or the 'dance-language' of the honeybee, to the intricate and complex mouthparts of a sea-urchin (still universally known as 'Aristotle's lantern' because, in *Historia Animalium* Book IV, he likens the five-sided structure to a lantern with the translucent panes of horn removed), he writes with a warmth and a liveliness that can only have come from many hours of close and sympathetic contact with the living world. Sometimes his observation led to significant discoveries. For example, he began to grasp the importance of the cardiovascular system as a result of watching, day by day, the developing heart and blood vessels in a series of eggs being incubated by a broody hen. He attached much importance to perceived phenomena, maintaining that credence should be given to observation before theory, and criticizing contemporaries who thought otherwise. Fundamental Aristotelian precepts like these have helped shape the course of science through the ages.

Science as we know it today did not exist in ancient times. The chemistry and physics of the 21st century would have been unrecognizable to the ancients in a way that modern philosophy, for example, would not. It was only with the advent of Galileo, Isaac Newton and other luminaries in the 16th and 17th centuries that modern experimental science had its beginnings. Clearly, the life sciences have come a long way too, but Aristotle's zoological works have an immediacy and, often, a surprising relevance all too rare in early scientific writings. His descriptions often read as though they were written yesterday, and indeed, in some cases his ground-breaking observations of the minutiae of animal behaviour were repeated and confirmed only many centuries later.

Aristotle himself was by no means the first notable scientist, and not all of his ideas were original. He was undoubtedly preceded, and influenced, by men of learning – some of them now anonymous

The European shag, Phalacrocorax aristotelis, *is the most familiar of several animal species whose scientific names commemorate Aristotle.*

– whose works have not survived. He also adopted and developed ideas formulated by known predecessors of the 5th century BC, such as the physicist and physician Empedocles, the medical scientist Hippocrates, and Democritus, who propounded an early form of atomic theory. Among Aristotle's more famous adoptions from the ancient world's popular scientific traditions were the belief that the Earth was at the centre of a finite universe, and the familiar theory of the four elements (fire, air, water, earth) and their defining powers or qualities (hotness, coldness, wetness, dryness). He also believed that living things existed in a seamless hierarchy, ranging from plants, through animals (from lower to higher), to man at the top of the ladder.

For centuries, much of Aristotle's thinking – the misguided as well as the vision-ary – was accepted with almost unquestioning awe and reverence. Subsequent scientists have often found fault with Aristotle's methods, complaining that he did not properly test the many theories and explanations he produced, or repeat experiments to confirm his evidence. He did not accurately record data in the form, for instance, of weights, measurements, temperatures and speed (in some cases he simply would not have had the technology to do so); and there have been famous grumbles about his non-mathematical approach and the eccentricities (by later standards) of his tentative taxonomy. Scientists have repeatedly argued that Aristotle's ideas in some respects held back progress in the scientific world.

However, it would be unjust to diminish Aristotle's significance on account of the unavoidable fact that his ideas do not match up to later expectations and knowledge. His influence on subsequent generations runs deep, and some of his key concepts and preoccupations have remained relevant to this day. He devoted much thought to the classification of different animals, exploring a host of distinctions such as blooded or bloodless (roughly corresponding to vertebrates and invertebrates), viviparous or oviparous (bearing live young or producing young by laying eggs), and solid-hoofed or cloven-hoofed, all still important today. And although our concepts of genus and species were developed by Linnaeus (p. 133) in the 18th century, they owe much to Aristotle's desire to identify, describe and sort the characteristics of different animals. (Sometimes he even used the Greek terms *genos* and *eidos* in roughly similar ways.) His observations, and the resulting descriptions, inevitably gave rise to occasional errors, but, in many more cases, they have seldom been bettered in over two millennia.

Aristotle's work certainly found favour with Charles Darwin (p. 267), who described him as one of the greatest observers that ever lived. There has been debate over which aspects of Aristotle's thinking so impressed Darwin, but it is reasonable to suppose that his seminal interest in a system of animal classification would have been among them. Darwin may also have seen an early version of evolutionary theory in Aristotle's so-called 'teleological' approach to science – that is, explaining the characteristics of animals in terms of their purpose or function.

A few months before Darwin died, he received a copy of Aristotle's *De Partibus Animalium* from his friend William Ogle, who had recently translated the work. On 2 February 1882, Darwin's considered response to the gift, in a letter to Ogle, was unequivocal: 'I had a high notion of Aristotle's merits, but I had not the most remote notion what a wonderful man he was. Linnaeus and Cuvier have been my two gods, though in very different ways, but they were mere school-boys to old Aristotle.'

Aristotle's major zoological works were translated into Latin by the prolific 15th-century Greek scholar Theodorus of Gaza, and published in Venice, in 1476, entitled De Animalibus. *This groundbreaking book, the title-page of which is shown here, was one of the earliest scientific texts to be printed in Europe.*

THEODORI:GRAECI:THESSALONICEN
SIS:PRAEFATIO:IN LIBROS:DE ANIMA
LIBVS:ARISTOTELIS:PHILOSOPHI:AD
XYSTVM:QVARTVM:MAXIMVM.

Ycurgum lacedęmonium qui leges ciuibus
suis constituit: Reprehendunt nõ nulli Pon
tifex summe Xyste quarte:ꝗ ita tulerit leges
ut belli potius ꝙ pacis rationem habuisse ui
deretur. Numam uero pompilium regem Romanũ laudãt
maiorem in modum:ꝗ pacis adeo studiosus fuerit:ut nulla
causa moueri ad bellum pateretur: quorum sententiam et si
alias probo:ut debeo (nihil enim pace commodius: nihil san
ctius) Tamen cum uita hominum ita ferat: ut bella uitari in
terdum nequeant.Sic censeo pręfiniendum consulendumꝗ
ut & bellũ interdum sit suscipiendum :si res urget:& pax ser
uanda sit semper:si fieri potest: nec belli ratõ unquã proban
da sit:nisi ut demum rebus compositis quieto tranquilloꝗ
animo uiuamus.Non enim ad pugnam & homicidia:nõ ad
discordias et bella nati sumus: sed ad cõcordiam & humani
tatem :Itaque principis istitutum atque officium id esse reor
ut pacẽ summa opera petat:seruet:& colat. Quod cum Ro
manos pontifices fere omnes fecisse quo ad potuerint:intel
ligam:laudo illorum animum:Q̃ neque ab istituto naturę
bonę recesserint:& pręceptum autoris diuini seruarint:quod
sepissime pacem conciliat:& commendat.Sed usum nõ nul
lorum ausim reprehendere. Pace enim qua uti debuerant ad
litterarum et artium bonarum studia:et uirtutum officia:illi
ꝗdem ad uoluptates parum honestas abusi sunt. quod cum
omni hominum ordini sit turpe: tum põtificis personę tur
pissimũ est.fuerunt tamen & qui recte pace uterentur:& põ
tificatum magna cum laude gererent: quibus te similẽ uideo
plane successisse. pręstas enim doctrina & moribus:quo sit
ut nomen tuum immortalitati mandandum censeas studio
potius litterarum quę nũquam peunt:ꝙ uel ędificiorum quę

a z

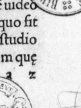

The Herball *by John Gerard is still one of the most famous English herbals. Gerard's debt to the 'Father of Botany' is shown in this title-page of the second edition of 1633 by the figure of Theophrastus in the middle row on the left (Dioscorides is on the right).*

Theophrastus

THE FATHER OF BOTANY

(*c.* 372–288 BC)

We must consider the distinctive characters and the
general nature of plants from the point of view of their
morphology, their behaviour under external conditions, their
mode of generation, and the whole course of their life.

Theophrastus, **Enquiry into Plants,** *I*

ONE OF THE MOST IMPORTANT of the ancient Greek philosophers and natural scientists, Theophrastus (originally called Tyrtamus) was born at Eresos on the island of Lesbos. His father was a fuller who processed woollen cloth for different purposes, and this perhaps gave Theophrastus an insight into the natural world and an understanding of phenomena in terms of real-world explanations, rather than some of the fashionable metaphysical concepts of the day. Theophrastus moved to Athens and studied philosophy, first under Plato and later under Aristotle (p. 23). It was Aristotle who both gave his favourite student the name 'Theophrastus', as an acknowledgment of the exceptional quality of his verbal skills and clarity of argument, and also, controversially, appointed him as his successor as the head of the Lyceum, which Theophrastus then presided over for nearly 35 years. As a further mark of his high esteem, Aristotle later bequeathed his library and original manuscripts to Theophrastus, as well as appointing him guardian of his children.

Like his teacher, Theophrastus wrote books on almost every sphere of knowledge. An astonishing 227 treatises are attributed to him, covering subjects as diverse as logic, ethics, natural history, mathematics, meteorology, astronomy, education, politics, music and religion. Most of this prodigious output is now lost, surviving mainly in fragmentary form as paraphrased quotations and references in the works of other Classical authors – Dioscorides (p. 33) was quoting him around 300 years later. In this way the writings of Theophrastus were passed on until the Renaissance.

Although Theophrastus broadly followed the philosophical teachings of the great Aristotle, he did not merely imitate them, but made his own empirical observations on the nature of the world. As an example of his experimental approach to understanding the natural world, Theophrastus is credited with the first recorded message in a bottle, in order to demonstrate that the Mediterranean was formed by the influx of water from the Atlantic Ocean. He also made the first known observation of pyroelectricity when he recorded in 314 BC that the mineral tourmaline becomes charged when heated – an observation that finds practical use today in anti-static hairbrushes, hair straighteners and hair dryers.

In fact, Theophrastus published a critique of Aristotle's generalized use of teleological (goal-directed) explanations of the natural world and also disagreed with his rationale for the existence of a 'Prime Mover'. Tried for impiety, Theophrastus was acquitted by the jury; indignant Athenians called for his accuser to be fined for his mistreatment of the philosopher. Known as a benevolent man, he was a central figure in Hellenistic intellectual culture and was held in high esteem by the Macedonian kings Philippus and Cassander and Ptolemy of Egypt.

It is for his contribution to botany that Theophrastus is perhaps best known, and his approach to the subject differed greatly from his predecessors. Of the surviving works of Theophrastus, two of the most important are on plants and both had a major formative influence on botanical science. Considered together, *Enquiry into Plants* (in Latin *Historia Plantarum*) and *On the Causes of Plants*, both comprising several volumes, constitute by far the most important contribution to botany during antiquity and even up to the Renaissance. Written originally in Greek, they were first translated into Latin by the 15th-century Greek-born Italian scholar Theodorus of Gaza, on the instruction of Pope Nicholas V, and published in 1483.

Theophrastus cited common names for more than 300 plant species, and the fact that similar names were quoted by contemporaries demonstrates that he was preserving elements of a widespread folk taxonomy based on the practical usefulness of plants to man. Though most of the plants he described were in cultivation, he was aware of many others that grew in the wild, but considered that they were unknown and un-named. He distinguished between the various means of reproduction of plants, and recognized the male and female parts of the flower. He also made the useful distinction between flowering plants that had centripetal inflorescences (the lowermost flower or the flower farthest from the terminal bud opens first) and centrifugal inflorescences (flowering starts with the terminal bud of a stem) – an important but technical difference that did not feature in plant classification until the 16th century. He was also interested in seed germination and was aware of the distinction between seedlings of the bean and wheat, representing the groups that we now call Dicotyledons and Monocotyledons.

His investigation of plants was handicapped by the insufficient terminology available at the time, and Theophrastus was obliged to introduce new technical terms

Masters and pupils at school in Athens, depicted on a Greek red-figure vessel of the 5th century BC. Theophrastus began his education on the island of Lesbos, but later moved to Athens, where he studied philosophy first under Plato and then Aristotle.

to communicate his observations. Another of his innovations was to classify plants using a hierarchical arrangement, similar to the dendrograms or cladograms in use today. In the field of botany, his attention to defining discrete characteristics of plants based on morphology (external and internal form), as well as understanding their life history, mode of reproduction and response to environmental factors earned him the further title of 'father of taxonomy'.

Theophrastus brought a systematic approach to the state of scientific knowledge in his time. His breadth of interests covered most areas of academic enquiry and he was the first philosopher both to look for the unifying concepts in science and to provide the theoretical basis for distinguishing the major scientific disciplines. His influence was prodigious, and the school over which he presided trained thousands of students. During his lifetime, Theophrastus became the pre-eminent popularizer of science. On his deathbed, he is said to have had only one complaint – that human life was too short and that it ended when some insight into its problems was only just beginning.

ROSA

Pedanios Dioscorides

RECORDING THE MEDICINAL USE OF PLANTS

(*c.* AD 40–90)

Phou … grows in Pontus, and it has leaves much like
elaphoboscon *or* hipposelinon, *with a stalk of a foot high
or more.… The root in its upper part is about the thickness of
the little finger and it has filaments … pale yellow, pleasantly
scented and resembling* nardus *in its smell, with a certain
poisonous kind of heaviness. Dried and given in drinks it
is warming and encourages urine, and a decoction
of it may do the same.*

Dioscorides, De Materia Medica, *I*

PEDANIOS DIOSCORIDES IS CONSIDERED the father of pharmacology and herbalism. His story is largely that of the publication and lasting influence of his greatest work, usually known by its later Latin title, *De Materia Medica*. This is one of the most enduring works of natural history ever written. Copied and translated from the original Greek into many languages, including Arabic, Persian and Latin, it formed the basis for Western knowledge of medicines for the next 1,500 years.

Dioscorides was born around AD 40 in the city of Anazarbos in Cilicia, which is now in southern Turkey but at that time was part of the Roman empire. Little is known in detail about his early life, but he later travelled around the eastern Mediterranean region with the Roman army as a physician during the reigns of the emperors Claudius and Nero, having joined as a *medicus* with responsibilities for treating soldiers wounded in battle. At the regional capital of Tarsus he had studied under Areios, who was the author of treatises on medicine (now lost), and although Dioscorides would acknowledge the important contributions to his work of a number of other earlier Greek scholars, including Creteuas (120–60 BC), and through him the earlier texts of Diocles of Carystus (*c.* 380–293 BC) and Theophrastus (p. 29), his own contribution should not be underestimated. He gathered information first-hand both by talking to local healers in the regions through which the army travelled and by

The Apothecary's Rose, Rosa gallica, *from a copy of Dioscorides'* De Materia Medica *made in 1460 and owned by Sir Joseph Banks (now in the library of the Natural History Museum, London). This rose was grown as an ingredient for perfumes and was regarded as a hangover cure from Roman times.*

direct observation of natural history and of the people under his care. While Hippocrates – acknowledged as the father of medicine – knew of around 130 medically active substances, Dioscorides listed over 1,000 natural product drugs, the majority of which came from plants. Dioscorides described medicines which are recognizable today as antiseptics, anti-inflammatory and anti-spasmodic agents, stimulants and contraceptives. In addition to a repertoire of genuine medically active compounds, he provided guidance on the preparation, dosage and treatment of specific conditions.

De Materia Medica was originally written as a number of separate volumes, the first focusing on plants that yielded aromatic oils and the ointments that could be produced from them. The second included animals, dairy products and cereals, while the third dealt with roots, seeds and herbs. In the fourth volume were other herbs and roots, and the fifth discussed wines and minerals. A sixth book dealing with poisons was occasionally included in versions of *De Materia Medica*. Two further books described venoms and the treatment of bites from animals. The unusual organization of the text arises from grouping materials by their effect on the human body, rather than by their relationships or a straightforward alphabetical sequence. Many of the medicines cited were concerned with contraception, abortion, fertility and the birth process, reflecting society's concerns at the time. While Dioscorides is not linked with any of the particular – often contradictory – theories about disease associated with his contemporaries, or with developing his own novel philosophy, his was an immensely practical and useful book. Regardless of the cause of a disease, once the problem was identified a cure could be sought in *De Materia Medica*.

THE INFLUENCE OF THE WORKS OF DIOSCORIDES

Unlike other Classical authors whose work was 're-discovered' centuries later in the Renaissance, copies of Dioscorides' book had been in continuous circulation and used in a practical manner since the height of the Roman empire. The book was copied in the Christian monasteries that promoted herbalism, and in addition to Greek versions there were at least seven different Latin translations and three Arabic, plus translations into a further eight or more languages. Within a century of the book's original publication, editions had appeared with stylized illustrations, probably derived from those of Creteuas who was cited by Dioscorides as the originator of this form of botanical publication. The first printed copy of a Latin version of the writings of Dioscorides appeared in 1478, a few decades after the invention of the printing press. One Latin translation of the 15th century was reproduced in another 49 editions in the 16th century. The printed herbals of early German botanists, including Otto Brunfels and Leonhart Fuchs (p. 48), owed much to Dioscorides, and many contemporary European authors were essentially imitators.

However, over the centuries manual copying and recopying in handwritten form had introduced errors during both the transcription and translation processes. Scholars now sought to resolve these either by comparison of the various versions or eventually by seeking the original plants that Dioscorides had described. As more authors sought to elucidate the work and make it accessible, two major groups emerged: those who provided commentary on Dioscorides and those who sought to produce more modern publications using local plants, but in the style of Dioscorides. As Dioscorides had based his book on plants and animals that he was familiar with in southeastern Europe, his descriptions were most appropriate to that region. Yet versions of his work were now used throughout Europe, from the North Atlantic to North Africa, and through the Islamic world to countries bordering the Indian Ocean and the Pacific. His readers tried to match the brief descriptions with local plants they were familiar with, sometimes with disastrous results.

Because plants provided by far the largest component of the medicines described by Dioscorides, botany and medicine were closely linked in the teaching of the early European universities. But the intensity of interest in the legacy of Dioscorides reached such a peak in universities in the 16th century that there was an inevitable

Mandrake (Mandragora officinarum) *from a copy of Dioscorides'* De Materia Medica. *Mandrake was reputed to have aphrodisiac qualities and legend has it that the plant screams when pulled from the earth.*

specialization into the discrete subjects of botany, pharmacy and mineralogy. By the 18th century, botanists were still paying homage to Dioscorides, even though scientists had by then developed a clearer descriptive form and used more realistic illustrations.

In the later 18th century, John Sibthorp, who succeeded his father at Oxford University as Sherardian Professor of Botany, began a quest for the plants of Dioscorides which would endure for the rest of his life. He travelled to Vienna to study the earliest

الصنف الرابع الذي يقال له الموس يوسن فاله ورق شبيه
بورق الاخر غير انه قريب الشط ر مزورق نقله الجفا الا انه ادق
منه واشناعنداك وله قضبان اربعة اوخمسه مخرجها من اصل

واحد طولها نحو من شبر ذفات طون مزلين وله ارب شبهة هذه رأس
الشبنت ومرثانه موضوع خ زدون رحمه هذا النبات
سقل مع اسقال الثمن ولذلك نمى البوسقويون ومعنا

Dioscorides' book De Materia Medica *was copied extensively from 100 years after he wrote it through to the Middle Ages and later. Many versions were published in Greek, Latin and Arabic, as well as eight or more other languages: this illustration of Dioscorides and an assistant collecting herbs is from a manuscript made in Baghdad in 1224.*

known manuscript copy of Dioscorides, the *Codex Vindobonensis*, and met the renowned botanical artist, Ferdinand Lukas Bauer. Together they travelled to Greece and Asia Minor in 1787 to collect and study the original plants that Dioscorides would have been familiar with. Bauer worked on illustrations, while Sibthorp collected and laid the groundwork for an ambitious new flora of the region. On a second expedition to Greece, Sibthorp contracted a disease and died on his return to England in 1796, aged just 38. He left his entire estate to the University of Oxford on condition that another botanist would be found to complete his work on the Greek flora. Sibthorp had left little more than notes, some 3,000 specimens, plus the magnificent illustrations of Ferdinand Bauer. The task of turning this into the *Flora Graeca* was finally completed in 1840 by John Lindley.

References to Sibthorp's quest for the plants of Dioscorides can be found in the names of plants. For example, *Valeriana dioscoridis* is considered the correct plant referred to by Dioscorides as 'phou' (also 'phu' or 'fu') and widely prescribed as an anti-spasmodic or anti-hysteric. The great man was also commemorated in other plant names. The genus *Dioscorea* in the *Dioscoreaceae* (yam family) was dedicated to him by Carl Linnaeus (p. 133) in 1754; fittingly, the genus is the source of some of the most effective contraceptive medicines available in Western medicine.

The influence of the works of Dioscorides extended from his own lifetime to the Renaissance and beyond. As well as being a major treatise on medicine, *De Materia Medica* is also an important document for the history of ancient chemistry; its significance to the botany of the eastern Mediterranean region continued into the 19th century, and it is still of relevance today in herbalism. Critics of Dioscorides are mainly critics of the medieval practice of unquestioning acceptance of ancient wisdom, which did much to stifle the development of science. The use of the work outside its regional context and errors introduced by manual copying and translation did much to bring it into disrepute, but the contribution made by this relatively humble and obscure physician in synthesizing existing information and adding knowledge based on his own observation cannot be questioned. In an era when many remedies were a mixture of superstition and hearsay, Dioscorides evaluated and codified the data, presenting them in a concise, consistent and rational framework.

Though he deferred to earlier Classical Greek authors, the scale and thoroughness of his work far exceeded them and anything else available throughout the Roman empire. His methods of observation, evaluation and formulation provided a sound basis for pharmacological science, and it would take 1,500 years before other scientists caught up with Dioscorides' methodology and moved beyond his remarkable vision.

Pliny the Elder

COLLECTOR OF KNOWLEDGE

(AD 23–79)

Greetings, Nature, mother of all creation,
show me your favour in that I alone of Rome's citizens
have praised you in all your aspects.

Pliny, **Natural History,** *37*

PLINY THE ELDER, or Gaius Plinius Secundus to give him his Latin name, was a Roman natural philosopher and author who is best known for his *Historia Naturalis*. This work, the title of which is usually translated as *Natural History* (though as already noted, *historia* means something more like 'research'), was truly encyclopaedic in scope, covering everything in the natural world. Born in Como in northern Italy in AD 23 into the relatively wealthy equestrian class, Pliny was educated in Rome by his father's friend, the military commander, Publius Pomponius Secundus. Pliny later refers to, and may have received tuition from, the rhetoricians Arellius Fuscus and Remmius Palaemon, and he certainly studied philosophy and rhetoric under Seneca the Younger. Intellectually Pliny was a Stoic, with firm beliefs in logic, natural philosophy and ethics. The primary purpose of a Stoic life was to live virtuously, according to natural law. In order to achieve this, it was necessary to understand the natural world. Stoic ethics were thus both informed by and grew out of a study of natural history.

As a young man, Pliny began to practice as an advocate, but at the age of 21 he left Rome for Gallia Belgica (now part of modern France), where he served as military tribune. For young men of the equestrian order this form of administrative office would have been a popular step in a political career, but Pliny demonstrated an aptitude for military life instead, and was promoted to commander of a cavalry unit (*praefectus alae*). From being an administrator he became a fighting officer and was stationed at Castra Vetera, a location that controlled the confluence of the rivers Rhine and Lippe in Germania Inferior. During the conquest of the Chauci, a

Detail of a closely observed Roman wall-painting showing a nightingale and roses, from a house at Pompeii buried in the eruption of Vesuvius that killed Pliny. Pliny had launched a mission to rescue friends from nearby Stabiae, but collapsed and died, possibly as a result of an asthmatic condition and the poisonous gases emitted from the volcano.

Germanic tribe, he observed the use of missiles thrown from horseback, a subject he chose for his first book, which included observations on the important characteristics of working horses.

Pliny travelled with the Roman army to what is today Spain and France, where he studied the language and visited sites associated with the Roman conquest of Germany. It is said that it was a dream that prompted him to compile a history of the German Wars, a work of 20 volumes that was cited by later authors. His final visit to Germany was with the future emperor Titus. Pliny also wrote a work on the popular subject of rhetoric, *Studiosus*, and one on grammar, in eight volumes, *Dubii Sermonis*. In AD 70, during the reign of his friend the emperor Vespasian, he took up public office and served as procurator in Gallia Narbonensis and later in Hispania Tarraconensis (now in France and Spain); he also visited North Africa and observed both agriculture and mining. Finally returning to Italy, he was appointed to a position working directly for Vespasian, whom he would visit before dawn for instruction and complete his duties promptly so that he could spend the rest of the day studying and writing. He was extraordinarily productive at this time, compiling both a history of the period from the reign of Nero to that of Vespasian in 31 volumes, and, more importantly, writing most of the *Historia Naturalis*, for which he had been planning and gathering information since the reign of Nero. Dedicated in the year 77 to Titus, it appeared in 37 books, though the notes and research originally filled almost 160 volumes. *Historia Naturalis* would be the only one of his works to survive to modern times, though we know of many of his other publications through references in his own writings and those of other authors.

Vespasian gave Pliny command of the naval fleet at Misenum, to the north of modern Naples. On 24 August in the year 79 he was staying at his villa in the city, accompanied by his 18-year old nephew Pliny the Younger, when his attention was

Title-page of an edition of Pliny's Natural History, *published in London in 1601. Pliny's great encyclopaedic work comprises 37 books, covering a variety of topics, from botany and zoology to agriculture and pharmacology.*

An illustrated initial 'E', depicting grape-picking and wine-making from the Natural History *of Pliny the Elder. As well as cataloguing animals and plants, Pliny described agricultural practices and left a snapshot of the technical and commercial exploitation of the natural world in his time, bringing together information from many writers and philosophers of the ancient world.*

drawn to an unusual cloud over a mountain across the bay. This cloud marked the beginning of the cataclysmic eruption of the long-dormant volcano Vesuvius, which would result in the destruction of Pompeii and Herculaneum. Pliny's appetite for knowledge and a desire to rescue friends led to him to take ships across the bay to Stabiae, some 5 km (3 miles) south of Pompeii – but the decision was to prove fatal. Pliny collapsed and died, perhaps as a result of an asthmatic condition and the poisonous gases emitted from the volcano, though he might have succumbed to a stroke or heart attack.

Pliny the Younger described the eruption and his uncle's death in two letters to the Roman historian Tacitus: 'Even the sea seemed to roll back on itself, pushed back by earth tremors. Many fish were beached on the sand. In the other direction gaped a horrible black cloud torn by zigzag flashes and masses of flames, like lightning but much larger.' Pliny the Younger also provides much personal information on the life of his uncle, describing him as a man who would begin work before dawn, reading every book he could obtain and making extracts of everything he read; a person who considered that any time away from study was time wasted. He only stopped reading during actual immersion during bathing, and had a book read to him while being rubbed dry; he also chose to be carried rather than walk so he would not lose precious minutes.

Plinio

Cionti fu ci comandarno adio

Plinio ilqualle u

A uella data aliuerno cuolti alafticha
Laffando di leuaopa ogni bel feno
Paffoamo tra la gente ccuda etrafficha
Era lo tempo lucido efereno
Alegro latte cco fuaue uento
El mare quieto edi ripofo pieno
Et era el fol poco piu giu chal mezo
Del montone ola luna uedea
Si uiua che cio mera un gra contento
E come lgiochi ala popa uolgea
Jouidi plinio iace fopra un letto
Secodo chin uerona ueduto hauia
Vte lui mi traffi etanto fu leffetto
Chio labracciai alluoco doue lgi era
Poi mi puofi afeder nel fuo cofpetto
O comel fol nafchoft la fua fpera
Cantare quei marinare falue regina
Si dolcie quato in fena mai lafera
Pareuta quella gente peregrina
Jo comenzai io dolce padre mio
Non perdiam tempo per quefta marina
Tu fai ol uolere tufai el mio difio
Perche rifpoft leuadoffi inpiei
In un penfier erauan tu et io
Poi comenzo lo zodiacho dei
Tuto imaginare dodeci fegni
De qualgi hor di fopra ne fon fei
Compfefi fon quefti dodeci regni
Da fete ftelle clone e capitane
Dolaltre perche ha ragi afai piu degni
Eluna fopra laltre in modo ftane
Che ciafchuna ha fuo fpera ouoi die ciello
Per loqual fempre con ordine uane

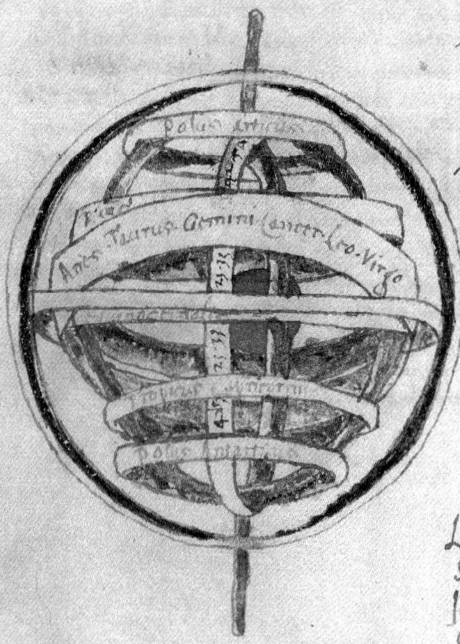

La octaua fpera e longi dala terra 1 millioni 1 millia 5 milgia
Saturno xlvii milioni xviii ccclxx millea
Jupiter xxxvii xlvii milgia
Solle mcccxl milgia
Venus ccccxiiii vii milgia
Mercurius cclxxxi 5 xlvi milgia
Luna cxviii xxxvii milgia secondo la pofitioe di alfagrno
lagl e piu uica dele altre

Pliny's legacy, the voluminous *Historia Naturalis*, is the first publication to encompass the whole of natural history – its boundaries generally being drawn between the natural world and the creations of man. It begins with an extensive list of the sources and authorities consulted by Pliny, with other books dedicated to astronomy, geography, human physiology, zoology, botany, the medicinal uses of plants and animal products, and metallurgy and mineralogy. It is a curious and eclectic mixture of second-hand commentary and superstition, with very little first-hand observation. Educated in rhetoric and grammar, yet a gossip, while Pliny favoured rational argument over the prevalent popular myths, he could not resist including some of the more fanciful ideas of the time. For example, he reported the belief that a porcupine could shoot out its quills; that frogs melt away into slime late in the year and come back together anew as frogs in the spring; and that diseased wheat turns into oats.

Not being trained in science or philosophy, Pliny presented a confused account of some of the more theoretical works, such as the botanical account of Theophrastus (p. 29). For botanical pharmacology he relied on the work of Creteuas, as did his more thorough contemporary Dioscorides (p. 33), and through these authors to even earlier ones. However, Pliny viewed botany as a complete subject in which plants were seen as intrinsically important, rather than just as a source of medicines or crops. Surprisingly for a work on natural history, he also provided the only contemporary account of the history of ancient art that has survived to the present, arising from his description of the use of natural minerals and biological materials in art. His comprehensive list of references and sources gives an insight into the breadth of literature of Rome and ancient Greece, much of which has not survived in its original form. The work also contains a perhaps unexpected amount of information on Roman society, including the technical and commercial advances of his time.

There are references to Pliny through to the 8th and 9th centuries and his work was considered important in the Middle Ages, with some 200 manuscripts surviving to the present day. Despite his uncritical inclusion of dubious information and the errors that he introduced through his lack of scientific training, Pliny's *Natural History* formed the single most important source of information on the subject until the revival of learning in the Renaissance.

An illustration by a 15th-century Italian artist showing Pliny the Elder, from the 'Dittamondo' by Fazio degli Uberti. In this poem, written around 1360, the author describes his imaginary travels and meetings with notable people from antiquity, including Pliny.

Cucurbita maior nostras urbana
fructu coloris Citrini ac subfla-
uescentis cum floribus . 1. 2. 3.

THE RENAISSANCE

FROM THE END OF THE CLASSICAL PERIOD until the 15th century, original thought and speculations about natural history were effectively stifled. The scholars who kept alive the traditions of Aristotle and Theophrastus were firmly bound by the Church's doctrines, and attempts to consider the deeper questions concerning the natural world were answered with mystical or religious interpretations for want of what we would now regard as a scientific explanation.

Much of the knowledge contained in the works of the ancient authors had been kept alive by scholars in the Islamic world, who translated and studied their writings. The main interests of such Islamic philosophers and physicians, however, were alchemy and pharmacology – the study of natural history was thus mainly confined to the medicinal uses of plants and minerals.

In the Western world few new works on natural history appeared. Instead, copies of the Classical authors that had been translated and transcribed and preserved in the Islamic world were still circulated, one example being the works of Dioscorides. A notable exception of the early 12th century was Hildegard of Bingen, known today for her abilities as a composer of sacred music, who used the Book of Genesis as a basis for classifying plants and animals in her *Causes and Cures.*

The copied and annotated works of the ancients – the originals of which were by now around a thousand years old – were inadequately filling a need for practical guides to plants for medical purposes. These herbals, as they are known, contained simple illustrations, which had usually been altered and 'improved' over time by many copyists. The morphological characters of a plant that might assist in its accurate identification were, on the whole, not described, with the legendary and magical properties of the plant given prominence instead.

In the mid-16th century, the deficiencies of these works were recognized by two German scholars. Otto Brunfels, who trained as a physician like many botanists after

A painting of a gourd, labelled, Cucurbita major, *from the vast collection of Ulisse Aldrovandi: he stressed the need for the accuracy of illustrations for the study natural history.*

him, set out to produce a herbal with accurate illustrations taken from real plants and not just copies of existing images. His great work *Herbarium Vivae Eicones* (*Living Pictures of Plants*) contained many beautiful illustrations, and while far from perfect was certainly a major step forward. It is likely that Brunfels's work inspired another German physician, Leonhart Fuchs, who described more than 400 plants in his *De Historia Stirpium* of 1542. Fuchs also added details of the plant's morphology, flowering time and distribution, and, unlike Brunfels, he made few references to the Classical botanists such as Dioscorides. Between them, Fuchs and Brunfels established a corpus of relatively well-illustrated and described plants for others to build on. It is likely that they also had collections of dried plants for their illustrators to refer to, but the credit for establishing the first known herbarium (collection of dried plants) is given to the Professor of Botany at the University of Bologna, Luca Ghini. Ghini was botanical tutor to another young physician-botanist, Andrea Cesalpino, whose contributions to botany justify his inclusion as one of the 'Greats'. While the works of Brunfels and Fuchs were inspired by the practical needs of medicine, Cesaplino studied plants for their intrinsic interest. His aim was to produce a classification of plants that reflected their real affinities, inspired by Aristotle's concept of essence. The results, based on a few characteristics of the fruits, were limited, but some of the groups he defined, such as the pea family (*Leguminosae* or *Fabaceae*), remain in use to this day. Botany was now established as a science and Cesalpino's work was to inspire later natural historians such as John Ray and Carl Linnaeus.

The zoological equivalent of herbals, known as bestiaries, were even more prone to flights of fancy. As well as real animals such as cats and dogs, they also included unicorns, griffins and sphinxes and they often contained an element of moral instruction, with particular qualities attributed to each animal – for instance the cunning fox. Bestiaries were popular reading throughout the Middle Ages, and up to the late 17th century they continued to serve as a means of moral education. For instance, the insect larva known as the ant lion was, according to fable, destined to starve, as its supposed ant nature would not eat meat and the lion part no plants – the equivalent of trying to serve god and the devil at the same time.

The first book that we might regard as primarily zoological was the *Historia Animalium*, published by the Swiss natural historian, Konrad Gessner in 1551–58. Gessner, like the German botanists Brunfels and Fuchs, understood the value of good illustrations and kept a close watch on his illustrators to ensure accuracy. He also realized the importance of using actual specimens to show exactly what plant or animal was being referred to by a particular name. He wrote and sent specimens to

Pierre Belon's most famous book was L'Histoire de la Nature des Oyseaux *(Natural History of Birds), from which this illustration of a man hawking is taken.*

a network of other natural historians, an early example of a tradition of correspondence which remains an essential part of science to this day.

The importance of collections of specimens and precise illustrations to the study of the natural world was demonstrated on a grand scale by another medical man, Ulisse Aldrovandi. Aldrovandi stressed the need for first-hand observation and was another scientist who insisted on the accuracy of illustrations – one of his greatest contributions to natural history. He used his collections of 18,000 objects to describe a variety of organisms and established a public museum in his native Bologna to bring these wonders to the general public.

The Renaissance had seen a great flowering of interest in the works of the ancients, coupled with huge advances in the accurate description and classification of the natural world. However, scholars remained shackled to the works of Aristotle, with both church and state threatening dire consequences to those who showed signs of breaking free from established ideas. Such attitudes, rooted firmly in the Mediterranean Classical past, were an impediment to understanding an expanding natural world as exciting discoveries were made in lands around the globe. A dramatic shift in ways of thinking and methods of inquiry was needed – and that was what emerged in the 18th century.

Leonhart Fuchs

THE VALUE OF ILLUSTRATIONS

(1501–1566)

*I do not need to expound at length the pleasure and delight
that the knowledge of plants brings, since there is no one who
does not know that there is nothing in life more pleasant and
delightful than to wander through the woods, and over
mountains and meadows, garlanded and adorned with these
varied, exquisite blossoms and herbs, and to gaze at them
with keen eyes. The pleasure and delight is increased not a
little if an understanding of their usefulness and
powers is added. For there is as much pleasure
and enjoyment in learning as in looking.*

Leonhart Fuchs, **Notable Commentaries on the History of Plants,** *1542*

L EONHART FUCHS TRAINED AS A DOCTOR and wrote over 50 books, mostly
on medicine. His most important work of natural history, *Notable Commentaries
on the History of Plants* (*De Historia Stirpium Commentarii Insignes*), published in
1542, was also a medical text – in it, Fuchs described plants, discussed their medicinal
virtues according to the Classical tradition and indicated the diseases they could
cure. However, by paying close attention to plant morphology and by including in his
book some plants with no known medicinal value, Fuchs contributed to establishing
botany as an independent discipline.

Born into a comfortable bourgeois family in the Bavarian town of Wemding,
Fuchs earned a bachelor of arts degree from the University of Erfurt when he was 16.
After a year as a schoolmaster, he went to the University of Ingolstadt, where he was
made master of arts in 1521 and doctor of medicine in 1524. He held a few short posi-
tions as a university lecturer and court physician before joining the faculty of the
Lutheran University of Tübingen in 1535, where he remained for the rest of his life.

*In Renaissance medicine, no sharp line separated food from simple medicines. Fuchs writes that
the shoots of asparagus (in Latin* Asparagus officinalis*; 'Spargen' in German), boiled in broth
and dressed with salt, vinegar and oil, are considered a delicacy. According to Dioscorides, cooked
shoots calm the stomach and promote urination; Simeon Seth adds that they are the most
nutritious vegetable and can be considered intermediate between plant and animal in their nature.*

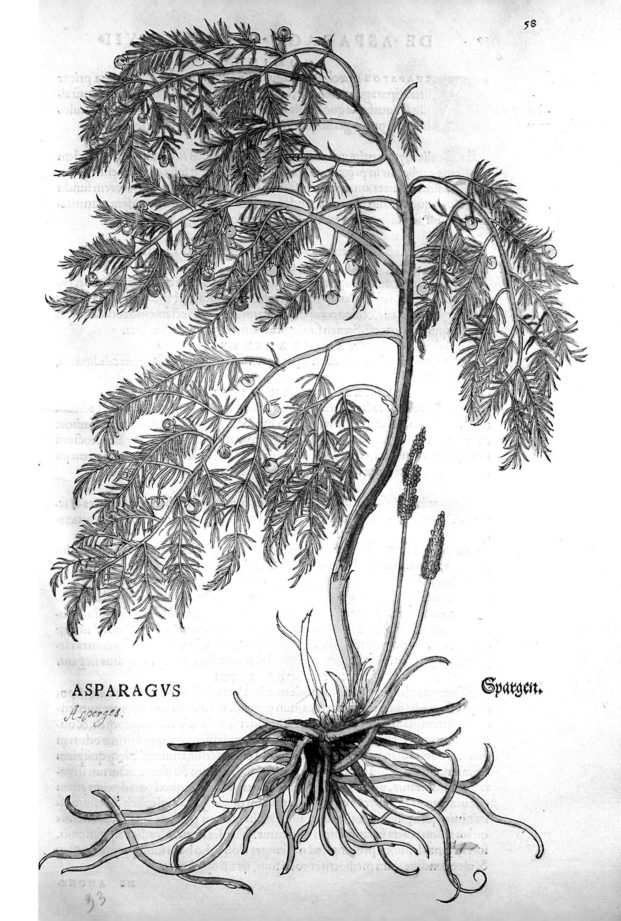

ASPARAGVS   Spargen.

Asperges.

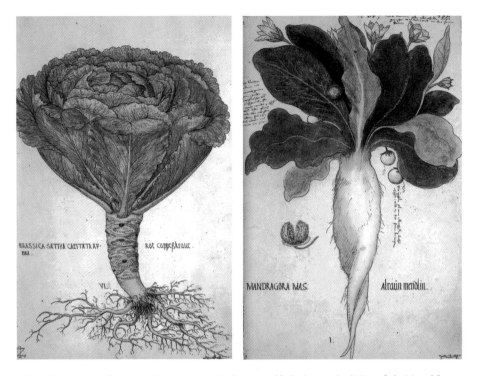

BRASSICA SATIVA CAPITATA RV-BRA.

Rot cappeßkraut.

VI.

MANDRAGORA MAS.

Altaün menlin.

1.

These illustrations from the Vienna Codex, Fuchs's unpublished second edition of the Notable Commentaries, *show the subtle detail of his artists' original drawings. The drawing of the mandrake* (Mandragora officinarum; RIGHT) *was the basis for the woodcut in the* Notable Commentaries; *the red cabbage* (Brassica oleracea *var.* capitata; LEFT) *was an addition. In his text, Fuchs warns his readers against counterfeit mandrake roots sculpted into human form (see also the illustration on p. 35).*

In Tübingen, as one of two professors of medicine, Fuchs taught theory, anatomy and medical botany.

Fuchs's approach to botany was inspired by a reform movement originating in northern Italy at this time. Niccolò Leoniceno, a professor at the University of Ferrara, was convinced that the names used by ancient medical writers for plants were not the same as those used by modern apothecaries. To put medical botany on the right footing, Leoniceno compared ancient texts with actual plants. His goal was to establish exactly which plant the ancients meant by each name. Then, doctors and apothecaries could use ancient medical recipes correctly.

Some of Leoniceno's German students then adopted this project as their own. Euricius Cordus wrote a short dialogue, *Botanologicon* (1534), describing an excursion into the German woods to hunt for plants in order to compare them with ancient texts. Fuchs knew Cordus from his student days at Erfurt, and he too was convinced that medical botany needed reform. His first medical publication, in 1530, on the errors of modern physicians, included an incisive critique of botanical mistakes, based on Leoniceno's method. His *Notable Commentaries* were intended to provide a definitive guide to plant names, descriptions and medicinal uses.

Fuchs was not alone in this aim. In Germany, he was preceded by his contemporaries Otto Brunfels and Hieronymus Bock – the three of them have been called, with some justification, the 'German Fathers of Botany'. Each emphasized a different aspect of botanical research, and it was Fuchs's work that, more than the others, shaped the later course of Renaissance botany.

ACCURATE ILLUSTRATIONS

The invention of printing in the mid-15th century revolutionized natural history illustrations. In Classical antiquity and the Middle Ages, every drawing of a plant or animal was unique. Each time a drawing was copied, it lost some of its original detail, becoming increasingly stylized. The woodcut, also invented in the 15th century, offered the possibility of making exactly reproducible copies of drawings. But naturalists were slow to pick up on its potential. Woodcuts of plants in early printed herbals imitated the crude, stylized pictures found in late medieval manuscripts.

The potential of the woodcut was finally realized in 1530. Brunfels, in his *Living Images of Plants (Herbarum Vivae Eicones,* 1530–32), placed short descriptions taken from ancient texts next to woodcuts by Hans Weiditz, a pupil of Albrecht Dürer. Weiditz's illustrations were stunningly different from anything that had been seen before. Working from original specimens, Weiditz produced bold, accurate drawings that could be easily transferred to wood blocks, allowing hundreds of identical copies to be made. The book's very title testifies to the effect that both author and publisher expected it to have on their audience. Indeed, the book appears to owe as much to Weiditz and to its publisher, Johann Schott of Strasbourg, as to Brunfels himself, whose earlier publications were on religion and education. Brunfels complained that Weiditz had depicted 'naked plants', those that had not been described by the ancients, whose medicinal properties were unknown. Yet Brunfels was a dedicated naturalist, as Bock testified in the preface to his own book, the *New Herbal* (*New Kreütter Buch,* 1539).

Bock's approach to natural history was diametrically opposed to Brunfels's. He decided not to include illustrations in his herbal at all. Instead, he wrote his own descriptions of plants, based on careful, repeated observations in the field and in his

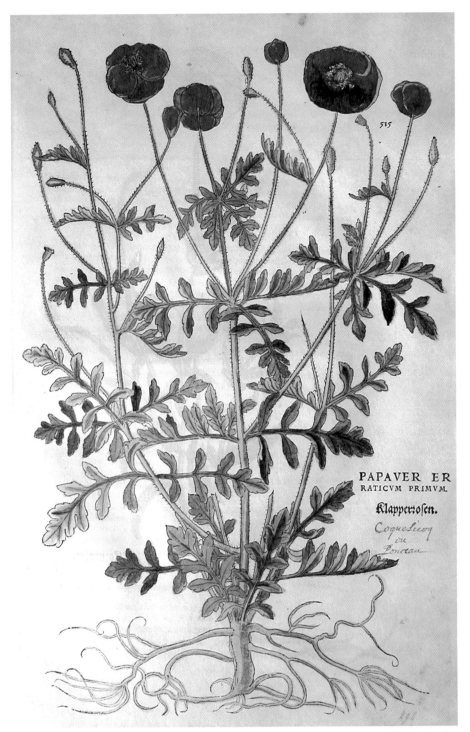

Corn or field poppy (Papaver rhoeas). *The bright colours in this woodcut were added by hand after the book was printed – many copies of Fuchs's* Notable Commentaries *were hand-coloured. Although the work was often done by women and children, who could be paid lower wages than men, a hand-coloured book cost many times more than the same one without colouring.*

Under the title 'Painters of the Work', Fuchs included this portrait of draughtsmen Heinrich Füllmaurer and Albrecht Meyer, and wood carver Veit Rudolf Speckle, at the end of his Notable Commentaries. It was unusual for illustrated Renaissance books to include portraits of the artists, but Fuchs knew that his book would owe much of its success to their talents.

own garden. Only after describing the plant as it appeared to him did he try to work out which ancient description applied to it. Instead of arranging plants alphabetically, as Brunfels had done, Bock organized them into groups based on similarity, though he did not adopt a systematic classification, and he separated 'foreign' plants, those introduced by merchants, from those that were native to Germany.

In the *Notable Commentaries*, Fuchs combined what he saw as the best elements of both Brunfels's and Bock's herbals. Alongside elegant, full-page woodcuts of plants, Fuchs gave their names in several ancient and modern languages, a description of their form, notes on when and where they grew, their temperament (a Renaissance medical concept) and their medicinal virtues according to several ancient authorities. Each part of this task involved innovative choices.

Unlike Bock, Fuchs was convinced that pictures were essential for his book. But Fuchs was not happy with Weiditz's approach either. Weiditz had used the artistic techniques of foreshortening and shadowing to increase the realism of his pictures. And he had depicted torn and wilted leaves, withered flowers and other characteristics of the actual specimen before his eyes. Fuchs thought that would not do. His contemporary, Sebastian Montuus, along with other philosophers, believed that pictures could tell a scholar nothing about the essential nature of a plant; at most, they could depict the peculiarities of individual specimens. Fuchs disagreed, but he saw the danger in Weiditz's approach. To overcome it, Fuchs insisted on carefully supervising the production of his pictures.

Fuchs employed a team of three artists; unusually, the book includes their group portrait at the end. Albrecht Meyer made the original drawings of the plant. Heinrich Füllmaurer copied each drawing on to a wood block, checking it against the plant itself as he worked. Finally, Veit Rudolf Speckle cut away the blank space from the block, leaving the raised surface that, inked and pressed on damp paper, would reproduce the image.

As the artists worked, Fuchs inspected the results. He corrected inaccuracies, but he also amended any part of the drawing that represented a peculiarity of the individual specimen that was not found in other plants of the same species. The result was a drawing that represented what a typical individual of the species might look like, but not necessarily what any individual plant did look like. In some cases, Fuchs showed flowers and fruits on the same plant, even when the two never occurred simultaneously in nature, so that the naturalist equipped with his book could recognize both. Despite the limitations of the medium, Brunfels's and Fuchs's example prevailed over Bock's: most 16th-century botanical books were lavishly illustrated.

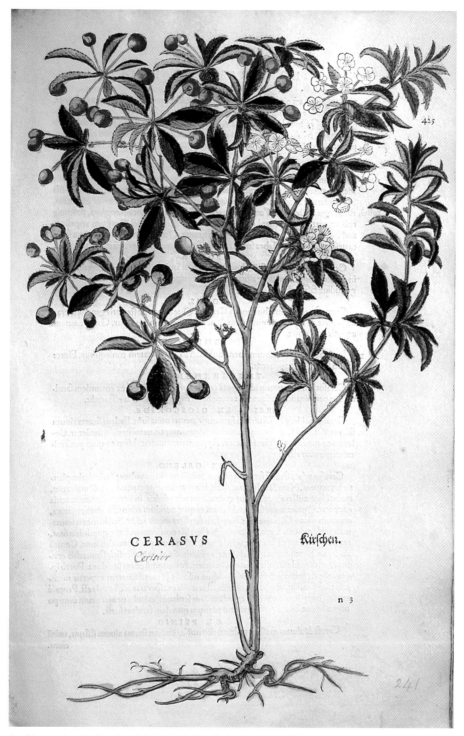

CERASVS   Kirschen.
Cérisier

n 3

425

241

In this woodcut Fuchs placed three varieties of cherry in one illustration (Prunus cerasus *and* P. avium); *the hand-colouring clearly distinguishes between them. The illustration shows the flowers and fruit at the same time, to aid in identifying the plant.*

EVPATORIVM
ADVLTERINVM.
Cursiges

Runigunt kraut.

265

z

Hemp agrimony (Eupatorium cannabinum):
Fuchs had no idea whether the ancients knew this
plant, and if so, what they called it. He complained
that the pharmacists of his day mistook it for true
agrimony. Germans called it St Cunegund's wort.

NAMING THE PLANTS

Fuchs's illustrations were striking, but they would have been useless to medical readers without the text that accompanied them. Following Leoniceno, Brunfels and Bock, Fuchs strove to establish the ancient Greek and Latin names of plants. Renaissance pharmacists often used ancient names for plants that were completely different from what the ancients meant. Such mistakes led to medicines that were weak, ineffective – or worse, harmful. Because Fuchs indicated the medicinal virtues of plants according to Galen, Dioscorides (p. 33) and other ancient sources, he had to ensure that he got the names right.

Fuchs was not always successful at this task. Plant geography was only just beginning to be studied, and he had never travelled beyond Germany. Unlike Euricius Cordus, who had studied in Italy, Fuchs had no first-hand knowledge of the differences between Mediterranean and German floras. Nonetheless, with effort and some luck, he successfully identified many of the plants known to the ancients. Even his failures spurred further research.

He began each chapter of the *Notable Commentaries* with a section on 'names': Greek, ancient Latin, modern Latin and German.

Purple violet, for instance, was '*Ion porphuron* to the Greeks, *Viola muraria* or *purpurea* to the Latins, *blau Veiel* or *Merzen violen* to the Germans; the pharmacists just call it *Viola*.' Coltsfoot, on the other hand, was known as '*Tussilago*' in Classical Latin, but '*Ungula caballina*' (literally, 'little horsehoof') to Renaissance pharmacists. Occasionally he included synonyms from other languages.

Fuchs organized his herbal in alphabetical order – according to the first letter of the plant's Greek name, or its Latin name when it was unknown to the ancients. But he prefixed the descriptions with four indexes of names: Greek, ancient Latin, pharmacists' Latin and German. That way, readers could go from any of the names to the plant itself. Sometimes, in the case of newly introduced plants with no ancient Greek or Latin name, Fuchs placed them near other, botanically related plants. He based his judgments of affinity on taste and smell, which were clues to a plant's medicinal virtues.

DESCRIBING PLANTS

Fuchs often referred readers to his pictures for an accurate description of a plant's form and shape. His verbal descriptions, unlike those of Bock and of Valerius Cordus

(Euricius's son), were brief, sometimes too brief, and often copied from Dioscorides. He contributed to standardizing botanical terminology by providing a list of difficult terms with their definitions. Even though many of Fuchs's terms are no longer used or have changed their meaning, the list was the first botanical glossary and helped contemporaries settle on names for the different parts of a plant.

Fuchs was more original in describing the places and times where plants grew and flowered, information that was essential for gathering medicinal plants and could also be used to help identify an unknown plant. He also described a plant's 'temperament', its balance of the ancient elemental qualities of hot, cold, moist and dry, that in Galenic medicine gave clues to how a plant would act as a drug. Following its temperament, Fuchs indicated the plant's actual medical powers by quoting liberally from Dioscorides, Galen, Pliny and occasionally other medical authorities.

Title-page of the Notable Commentaries. *The lengthy title emphasizes the exertion and expense that the book cost Fuchs. As a privilege, Emperor Charles V granted an early form of copyright (at the bottom), but the book was soon pirated in France.*

In describing plants, Fuchs aimed to reform pharmaceutical botany. Morphology was only a part, and not the most important part, of his descriptions. But through his pictures, and his attempts to distinguish different varieties of the same species, he also contributed to a growing interest in plant morphology in the 1540s and 1550s. Sparked in part by criticism of Fuchs and his contemporaries, this growing interest would lead the next generation of botanists to downplay medicinal botany in favour of the study of morphology and distribution. In this regard, Fuchs's book played an important role in establishing botany as an independent discipline.

AFTER THE *NOTABLE COMMENTARIES*

After the *Notable Commentaries*, Fuchs continued to gather illustrations and descriptions of plants. He and his publisher issued German and French translations of the *Commentaries*, as well as a volume containing the illustrations with minimal text for the use of students. By 1557, he had prepared two volumes for a new, expanded edition of the *Commentaries*, each with 400 illustrations and more accurate descriptions, and he was at work on a third. But his publisher died and he could not find another willing to take on the risk of publishing an expensive botanical book. At his death in 1566, it remained in manuscript. Fuchs's remarks in his new preface, and in his correspondence, reveal a man jealous of his reputation and suspicious of rivals, unlike the 1542 preface, in which he had been quite generous to his predecessors. He remained in Tübingen, where he continued to teach medicine. In his last three years he suffered from chronic illness. He died a disappointed man, frustrated in his ambition to revise and correct his great work of natural history. But his *Notable Commentaries*, flawed as they were in his own hindsight, marked an epoch in the development of Renaissance natural history.

Tomato (Solanum lycopersicum)*: this drawing from the Vienna Codex may be the earliest European illustration of a tomato plant. Despite its errors, it shows how Fuchs continued to seek out, describe and depict new plants.*

Ulisse Aldrovandi

OBSERVATION AT FIRST HAND

(1522–1605)

*I have never described any thing without first having
seen it with my eyes and done the anatomy of both its
external and internal parts.*

Ulisse Aldrovandi

ULISSE ALDROVANDI WAS AMONG THE GREATEST INNOVATORS of the
study of nature during the Renaissance, stressing the need for direct, personal
observation and the value of accurate illustrations in natural history books. At
around 17 years old, he began his university studies in his native city of Bologna, devoting himself first to the humanities and law and then to logic, philosophy, mathematics
and medicine. In 1553 he graduated in medicine, and in the following year began his
career as a university lecturer, teaching first logic and then philosophy. A chair of
natural philosophy was created specially for him in 1561, and he thus became the first
full professor of natural science at Bologna University. He later persuaded the city
authorities to create a public botanical garden, of which he was appointed director.
Although Aldrovandi did not practise medicine, he constantly endeavoured to improve
the health care provided to his fellow citizens, convinced that science should be 'useful'
to men and bring 'benefits' to them. Following his appointment as chief physician in
1574, Aldrovandi published the *Antidotarium*, the first official pharmacopoeia of
Bologna, to instruct apothecaries on the correct preparation of medicines.

Aldrovandi's aim in his long and tireless activity as a scholar was accurately to
identify and describe the largest possible number of animals, plants and minerals.
He was well aware that the descriptions found in the authors of antiquity (Aristotle,
Theophrastus and Pliny, among others) were often incomplete or inaccurate.
Moreover, the discovery of the New World and explorations in Asia and Africa were
constantly bringing new animal and plant species to light. He endeavoured as far as
possible to base his research on direct inspection of the 'things of nature', undertaking
several journeys in Italy for this purpose. But as he was unable to go everywhere, he
sought to recreate the world of nature in his home by bringing the specimens there
that he could not examine for himself in distant lands. His museum, and its collections
of specimens and images, were the instruments that enabled Aldrovandi to pursue his

Portrait of Aldrovandi from the University Library of Bologna, his native city.

grandiose project, and both were constantly enriched over a period of around 50 years, often by Aldrovandi's wide circle of friends and correspondents – which included university professors, physicians, apothecaries, nobles and churchmen, in Italy and abroad.

Towards the end of Aldrovandi's life, the museum, with the botanical garden as its open-air extension, rapidly became one of the most celebrated in Europe, receiving a constant stream of visitors. It contained 18,000 'natural things' (both actual specimens and depictions of them) and 7,000 dried plants bound in 15 volumes. In 1571, a visitor described it as 'a compendium of the natural things to be found below and above the earth, in air and in water.' Unlike the cabinets of curiosities and encyclopaedic collections typical of the time – often created merely to astonish the visitor – Aldrovandi's natural history museum served purely scientific purposes. It was a centre of study and research that enabled Aldrovandi to identify and describe animals, plants and minerals. He also used it in his teaching work to unite 'theory' with 'practice' by providing his students with concrete examples of the subjects discussed during his lectures and which they had studied in books.

The paintings, in watercolour or tempera, were essential tools for Aldrovandi. He eventually amassed around 8,000 of them (around 3,000 still survive, most conserved in the University Library of Bologna) and had them bound in numerous volumes. By means of these illustrations, Aldrovandi was able to examine species that he did not have actual or complete specimens of – sometimes his museum contained only individual parts, such as horns, feathers, tusks, tails. They also served as the models for the woodcuts used to illustrate his writings. Probably no scholar in the early modern age was more convinced than Aldrovandi of the usefulness – indeed the absolute necessity – of illustrative figures in natural history books. Only by means of such illustrations could readers see what the scientist had seen, check the accuracy of the descriptive text, and expand their knowledge of the natural world. Aldrovandi received many of these illustrations as gifts, but he also commissioned a large number of them himself. In order to create this impressive 'museum on paper', he hired and trained painters, draughtsmen and wood-carvers, who worked for decades under his direct and rigorous supervision. He exercised this close control in order to restrict the artists' freedom of expression and to ensure that they did not pursue exclusively aesthetic ends. Entirely uninterested in beautiful portraits of 'things of nature', Aldrovandi instead pursued accurate depictions of real objects.

*Aldrovandi set out to identify and describe as many 'things of nature' as possible and drew
on many different sources, which sometimes led him to include fantastical creatures in his works,
such as the Ethiopian dragon (top), from his* Serpentum et Draconum Historiae *(1640).
The realistic shark and a strange-looking sawfish are from* De Piscibus … et de Cetis *(1613).*

There is no doubt that these illustrations represent the most original and innovative aspect of Aldrovandi's works, for his written descriptions are often obscured under a thick mantle of erudition and encyclopaedism. Driven by an urge to provide the largest possible amount of information, to say everything about everything, Aldrovandi did not always restrict himself to describing the results of his observations and anatomical dissections; he also reported everything that had been written since antiquity about animals, plants and vegetables. The authors he cited were not only natural historians, but also fathers of the Church, theologians, poets, antiquarians, historians, emblematists and many others. This choice of expository method inevitably meant that Aldrovandi repeated – albeit often with caveats – many of the legends and fantastical beliefs about nature that had accumulated over previous centuries.

Aldrovandi focused his entire research on the publication of a great *Natural History*, but for various reasons, financial amongst others, he fulfilled this ambition only in part. During his lifetime he managed to publish only the three volumes devoted to birds, *Ornithologia* (1599–1601) and the one on insects (1602). The remaining nine volumes, which also included a *History of Monsters [Monstrorum Historia]*, were brought out by the Senate of Bologna between 1605 and 1667, but with a mixture of changes and additions by the editors. By completing the publication of Aldrovandi's works, the Bolognese authorities honoured the memory of an illustrious fellow-citizen, while at the same time publicly expressing their gratitude for Aldrovandi's bequest to the city of his museum, his collection of images and manuscripts, and a library of over 3,500 volumes. This large body of material, conserved in the Municipal Palace, constituted Bologna's first public museum.

Convinced of the value of illustrations, Aldrovandi amassed a huge collection of paintings of plants and animals, enabling him to examine species from the natural world of which he did not have actual specimens; this creature is labelled 'Coniglio dell'Indie' and was probably painted by Francesco di Mercurio Ligozzi.

Andrea Cesalpino

PHYSICIAN, PHILOSOPHER AND BOTANIST

(1519–1603)

*We look for those similarities and differences which
make up the essential nature of plants, not those which are
accidental; for things perceived by the senses become
comprehended primarily from their essential nature
and only secondarily from accidents.*

Cesalpino, De Plantis Libri XVI, *1583*

IN THE ANCIENT WORLD, plants were primarily studied for their medicinal or magical properties; Andrea Cesalpino, however, studied them for their intrinsic interest and is therefore considered as the world's first true botanist. In addition he was a physician and philosopher, and possibly one of the greatest intellects of his time. His breadth of knowledge and wide-ranging interests covered many realms, from blood circulation to mineralogy, but it was his workable classification of plants and an advanced – for the time – botanical 'textbook' that were his main legacy to natural science. His philosophical beliefs and writings won him the respect of church and state, but they also brought him perilously close to the attention of the Inquisition.

Cesalpino (also spelled Cisalpino) was born in Arezzo, in Italy, in 1519, and later studied at the University of Pisa, where his supervisors were Realdo Colombo for medicine and Luca Ghini for botany. After graduating, the highly gifted student worked at the university for the next 40 years, teaching philosophy, medicine and botany. Despite all his duties, he made botanical expeditions across Italy and wrote many great works on philosophical and botanical topics. This was a time when the first botanical gardens were being established, the earliest being at Padua in 1546. Luca Ghini established the second, at Pisa. Ghini was succeeded as director there by Cesalpino, from 1554 to 1558. Generally highly respected by the Catholic church, Cesalpino became physician to Pope Clement VIII and, when an old man, was professor of medicine at the papal university, La Sapienza. It is possible that he also became the Director of the Rome Botanical Garden, though this is not certain.

Among his many interests, Cesalpino studied the circulation of blood, correctly stating that the veins of animals originated in the heart rather than the liver – the commonly held belief since the time of the 1st-century AD Greek physician Galen.

Like many philosophers, Cesalpino considered plants to be very similar to animals and proposed that they too had a circulatory system, with a heart concealed somewhere at the base of the stem, and he also noted that when some plants are cut they 'bleed' sap. His conclusions suggest that Cesalpino was able to dissect plants in some way and examine their internal structure, and it is remarkable that he was able to make such accurate observations a century before microscopes were invented. These ideas and many others were included in his greatest work, *De Plantis Libri XVI*, published in 1583 and dedicated to the Grand Duke Francesco de' Medici. *De Plantis*, was a very different book from other works of the time, for instance it was unillustrated, unlike the popular herbals of the day.

Cesalpino's philosophy generally followed that of Aristotle, although he was also influenced to some extent by the great Andalusian-Arabic philosopher Averroes (Ibn Rushd). Averroes was the main translator of Aristotle's works, but his teachings went against Catholic doctrine, and so this association was a dangerous one that almost got Cesalpino into trouble with the Inquisition. Like Aristotle, Cesalpino was an 'essentialist', believing that a set of eternal and fixed essential characteristics can be used to recognize the 'essence' of anything. Cesalpino applied this belief to botany, proposing that by looking at a few characteristics of the fruit it was possible to identify the 'essence' of any plant. Aspects such as medicinal properties and taste were dismissed as 'accidentals', of no use in classification, although Cesalpino recognized, as we do today, that the natural groupings that he established often share common flavours and medicinal properties.

It was Cesalpino's aim to move away from classifications based solely on medical uses towards a more scientific system that could cope with large numbers of plant species. Through extensive observations made on his travels in Italy, together with his herbarium of dried plants (among the earliest known), he devised a classification of plants which, while still far from perfect, did go some way towards a natural system that grouped together plants with genuine affinities. Many of Cesalpino's groups remain to this day equivalent to modern plant families, such as the *Leguminosae* (bean family) and *Compositae* (daisy family).

Cesalpino's work was to live on long after he died in Rome in 1603, and was greatly admired by John Ray (p. 92) and Carl Linnaeus (p. 133). Ray used Cesalpino's classifications in his early works, before recognizing their limitations and devising his own system. Cesalpino's name lives on in *Cesalpinia*, a genus of woody leguminous plants named after the great botanist.

Ἀβρότονον	78.	Ἀγρόγλωσσος	156. 157.	Διὸς ἄνθος	151.
Ἀγάρου	76.	Ἄγος	141. 142.	Δίψακος	95.
Ἄγνος	18.	Ἀρρενόγονον	179.	Δορύκνιον	190
Ἄγχουσα	106. 107. 154.	Ἀρτεμισία	75. 76.	Δράβη	197.
Ἄγχουσα	53.	Ἄσαρον	229.	Δρακοντία	141.
Αἴγειρος	7.	Ἄσκυρον	227.	Δρυοπτερίς	263.
Αἰγίλωψ	104	Ἀσκληπιάς	185.		
Αἰθιοπίς	113.	Ἀσκάλαβος	9.	Ἐλάτη	10.
Ἀκαλήφη	61.	Ἀσπάραγος	139.	Ἐλάτινη	229.
Ἀκάρδιον	93.	Ἄσπληνον	264.	Ἐλαφόβοσκον	28.
Ἄκανθος	140.	Ἀσπὶς ἀττικός	71. 72. 73.	Ἐλελίσφακον	125.
Ἀκόνιτον	199. 200. 249. 250.	Ἀσφάραγος	167.	Ἐλένιον	71.
Ἄκορηα	94.	Ἀσφόδελος	215.	Ἐλένιον αἰγύπτιον	164.
Ἀλθαία	242. 243. 245.	Ἀπγακληλίς	98.	Ἐλεοσέλινον	25.
Ἀλικάκαβος	143.	Ἀτράφαξις	60.	Ἐλίχρυσον	79. 80.
Ἄλιμος	61.	Ἀψίνθιον	77.	Ἐλλέβορος	246. 247. 248.
Ἀλκέα	242.			Ἐλλεβορίνη	248.
Ἀλσίνη	55.	Βάκχαρις	45.	Ἐλξίνη	189.
Ἄλυπον	214.	Βαλλωτή	121.	Ἔμπετρον	43. 44.
Ἄλυσσον	196.	Βάτος ἰδαία	239.	Ἐπιμήδιον	229.
Ἀμβροσία	57.	Βατράχιον	250. 251. 253. 254. 255.	Ἐρείκη	7. 8.
Ἄμμι	21.	Βήχιον	81.	256. Ἑρπυλλος	129. 127.
Ἀμπελόπρασον	224.	Βλήτον	56.	Ἐρυθρόδανον	203.
Ἄμπελος ἀγρία	144.	Βολβὸς ἐμετικός	217.	Ἐρυθρόνιον	219.
Ἄμπελος λευκή	147.	Βόρρυς	57.	Ἐρύσιμον	195.
Ἀναγαλλίς	153.	Βούτομος	240. 241.	Εὐπατώριον	132.
Ἀνάγυρις	13.	Βούφθαλμον	70.	Εὐώνυμος	1.
Ἀνθόσμιον	228.	Βράθυς	8.	Ἐφήμερον	221. 226.
Ἀνεμώνη	252.	Βρύον θαλάσσιον	265.		
Ἄνθεμίς	69.			Ζίζυφα	19.
Ἀνθυλλίς	73.	Γαλίοψις	172.	Ζυγία	2.
Ἄνισον	31.	Γάλλιον	203.		
Ἀντίρρινον	174.	Γεντιανή	180. 181.	Ἡδύοσμος	127.
Ἀνωνίς	159.	Γεράνιον	36. 258.	Ἡλιοσκόπιος	214.
Ἀπάτη	89.	Γλαύξ	163.	Ἡλιοτρόπιον	50. 182. 207.
Ἀπόκυνον	186.	Γλήχον	127.	Ἡμεροκαλλίς	217.
Ἀρίσαρον	141. 142.	Γναφάλιον	154.	Ἡμέρων	70.
Ἀριστολοχία	231.			Ἡράκλιον	94. 95. 96.
Ἄρκευθος	10.	Δάφνη ἀλεξάνδρεια	136.		
Ἄρκειον	102.	Δαφνοειδής	135.	Θηλίπτερον	47. 49.
Ἄρκλιον	84.	Δαῦκος	32. 31. 34.	Θέρμος	166.
		Δελφίνιον	191.	Θηλύγονον	279.
		Δενδρώδη	210.	Θλάσπι	196.
		Δίκταμνον	129.	Θρίδαξ ἀγρία	91.
				Θύμβρα	128.
				Θυμελαία	135.
				Θύμος	129.

Cesalpino wanted to move plant classification away from one based on medicinal uses to one founded on physical characteristics such as fruits and seeds. This list (in Greek) at the beginning of his herbal of 1583 groups plants with physical similarities.

Portraict de la Giraffe.

Quand elle court, l
pieds de deuant v
semble. Elle se co
ventre contre terre
vne durté à la poic
aux cuisses côme
meau. Elle ne sçaur
stre en terre estant
sans eslargir gran
les iambes de deuãt
est ce auec grande a
té. Parquoy il est ai
re qu'elle ne vit au
sinon des branches
bres, ayant le col a
tellemẽt qu'elle pou
riuer de la teste à
teur d'vne demie p
Et l'ayants fait re
naturel, en auons b
lu icy mettre le por

D'vn moult beau petit Bœuf d'Afrique, que les ancien
Grecs nommerent Bubalus.
Chapitre L.

ALAN CUTLER

Pierre Belon

PIONEER OF COMPARATIVE ANATOMY

(1517–1564)

*Nature shows us the excellence of its work, declaring its
perfection and taking pleasure as each animated substance
executes its certain role; yet also desiring to employ in diverse
ways the same faculties and qualities that give animals
security on land, in the air and in the water.*

Pierre Belon, **L'Histoire de la Nature des Oyseaux,** *1555*

ONE EVENING IN APRIL 1564, a lone traveller passing through woods in the
French countryside near Paris was brutally murdered. His killers, whoever
they were, must have found little in his bags they recognized as treasure:
Pierre Belon had probably gone into the woods to collect botanical specimens. One of
the first explorer-naturalists, Belon rose from humble beginnings to find fame and the
favour of kings. His interests spanned all of natural history, but he made his greatest
contribution in the field of vertebrate anatomy. The modern sciences of comparative
anatomy and embryology trace their origins to his pioneering work. When he met his
tragic end that night, Belon was at the peak of his career and just 47 years old.

TRAVELS

In the mid-16th century, the French king Francis I was locked in a bitter rivalry with
Charles I of Spain, who was head of the Holy Roman Empire. Francis, seeking allies
wherever he could find them, made overtures to the Ottoman Turks, whose growing
empire covered most of the eastern Mediterranean. In 1546, Francis sent a diplomatic
mission to Constantinople; among the party was the 29-year-old Pierre Belon.

Born in 1517, Belon grew up in a small village near Le Mans, in northern France,
and was trained as an apothecary. With the help of a wealthy patron he studied in
Germany with the botanist Valerius Cordus. Cordus was an inspiring and unorthodox
teacher, encouraging his students to trust their own eyes and make observations of
nature, rather than rely on the usual authoritative texts. When Belon embarked on his

*An illustration from Belon's account of his travels through Italy, Greece, Asia Minor, Palestine,
Arabia and Egypt, published in 1551. This book gave European readers their first glimpse of
many exotic creatures, such as the giraffe shown here.*

journey to the mysterious East, he was well prepared to put these lessons to good use. Belon's travels lasted three years and took him through Italy, Greece, Asia Minor, Palestine, Arabia and Egypt. On his return he published a hugely successful book, *Les observations de plusieurs singularitez et choses memorables: Trouvées en Grèce, Asie, Judée, Egypte, Arabie, et autres pays estranges* ('Observations of many singular and memorable things found in Greece, Asia, Judea, Egypt, Arabia, and other foreign countries'). His eye-witness accounts of the plants, animals, people and places of this part of the world captured the imagination of European readers, who up to now knew about them only through the writings of ancient Classical authors. Separating fact from fable as best he could, Belon recorded his impressions of Greek ruins and Egyptian pyramids and made the first scientific descriptions of the giraffe and other exotic beasts. Not only were his writings about these regions considered definitive for many years, but his expedition set the pattern for later generations of scientific travellers, including Linnaeus (p. 133) and Charles Darwin (p. 267).

Studies of Fish and Birds

After Belon returned to France in 1549 he began the series of zoological studies for which he is most famous today. At the time, most writing on the subject of animals took a literary, religious or 'emblematic' approach – that is, their authors were more interested in animals as symbols or metaphors than as living, flesh-and-blood creatures. As a result, the books tended to be long on moralizing and literary allusion, and short on what we today would consider rigorous scientific description.

Belon was one of the first naturalists to break with this tradition. In 1551 he published *Histoire Naturelle des Estranges Poissons* ('Natural History of Some Unusual Fish'), in which he left out the poetry and focused on the facts as he found them. It was the first printed work devoted to fish, though to Belon a 'fish' was any creature that lived in the water. In fact most of the book was devoted to animals not classified as fish by modern biologists, such as cetaceans (whales and dolphins), hippopotami and the chambered nautilus. Of 55 pages in the book, only around 10 describe fish in the modern sense of the term. In later works, he expanded the list of fish species to over 100. The real strength of *Poissons* was not in Belon's taxonomy, however, but in his anatomical descriptions, which were largely based on his own dissections. Despite lumping them with the fish, Belon recognized that dolphins shared with land mammals air-breathing-lungs, mammary glands, a four-chambered heart and a placenta, as illustrated in a woodcut of a dolphin fetus. Belon's description of the fetal dolphin is often cited as the beginning of the science of embryology.

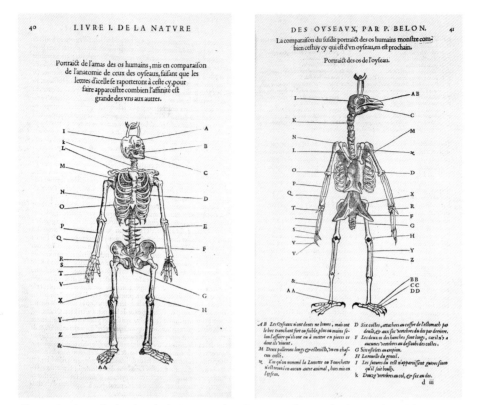

Illustration from L'Histoire de la Nature des Oyseaux *('Natural History of Birds'), published in 1555. Belon noted the homologies between bones in the human and bird skeleton. He drew no evolutionary conclusions, but marvelled at the unity of the natural order.*

Belon's last and most famous book was his monograph on birds, *L'Histoire de la Nature des Oyseaux* ('Natural History of Birds'), published in 1555, for which he dissected some 200 species of birds. Based on their life habits and anatomical features, Belon divided birds into six groups: birds of prey; water birds with 'flat' feet; water birds without flat feet; ground-nesting birds of fields; small birds inhabiting hedges and thickets; and birds that range among several habitats. Though his classification system only roughly parallels modern avian taxonomy, it was a decided improvement over the alphabetical listings by name of bird species used by previous authors.

HOMOLOGY

A picture is worth a thousand words, as the saying goes, and Belon's *Oyseaux* included a picture that probably had a greater impact on science than all his published words put together. The image showed the skeletons of bird and human side by side, with

Turkeys, both cock and hens, from L'Histoire de la Nature des Oyseaux, *in a hand-coloured version. This bird had only recently been introduced from the Americas.*

the corresponding bones of both labelled to show that, despite the outward differences of birds and humans, their skeletons were built according to the same basic plan; they were made up of the same parts, differently modified. This idea, known as homology, can be traced back to Aristotle, but it had never been so clearly and definitively presented. The homology of organs and body structures among different organisms was an important idea leading up to the evolutionary thinking of later centuries. But for Belon it simply demonstrated the unity of living things. There is no indication that he ever considered the possibility that one species could transform into another. That was a question for later thinkers.

Final Years

Belon's book on birds was literally his crowning achievement: King Henry II, successor to Francis, consented to have the book dedicated to him and promised Belon a royal pension (a promise he quickly forgot – Belon only received the money after several years of appeals). For the rest of his career, Belon turned his attention to practical applications of science. He received a licence to practise medicine and devoted much effort to experiments trying to acclimatize foreign crops to grow in France.

The circumstances of his violent death remain mysterious. He may have been the accidental victim of bandits, though some have speculated that, given his prominence and connections in the royal court, it was a political assassination.

Konrad Gessner

THE BEGINNINGS OF MODERN ZOOLOGY

(1516–1565)

*And what man withal his witte, can sufficiently declare and
proclaime the wonderful industrious minds of the little
Emmets and Bees, ... being silly things, and yet in[b]ued with
noble and commendable qualities ...*

Edward Topsell, **The Historie of Foure-footed Beastes,** *1607*

TODAY KONRAD GESSNER (or Conrad von Gesner) is remembered for his contributions in two fields: bibliography and natural history. In 1545 he compiled the *Universal Bibliography,* in which he set out to list all the titles of books ever written by any author since antiquity, an attempt for which he has become known as the pioneer of modern bibliography. In natural history, his best-known work is the compendious work, the *History of Animals.* Gessner also wrote about 'objects dug up from earth' (*fossilia* in Latin), which he noticed resembled other objects in nature: his was the first illustrated printed work that treated the subject of 'fossils'. Less well known perhaps is Gessner's extensive study of plants. A large number of sketches of plants (some drawn by Gessner himself), with extensive annotations, survive to this day, but he never succeeded in publishing his *History of Plants* in his own lifetime.

Gessner was born in Zurich in 1516, the son of a furrier. He had a gift for the Classical languages and studied at Strasbourg, Basel and Paris. He taught Greek at Lausanne for three years, visited Montpellier, where he met the French natural historians Guillaume Rondelet and Pierre Belon (p. 67), and obtained his doctorate in medicine from the University of Basel in 1541. From that year he taught Aristotelian philosophy at the Carolinum seminary in Zurich, where he was town physician from 1554. Apart from one major trip to Italy, his duties in Zurich prevented him from travelling extensively, but Gessner's house was filled with pictures of exotic animals and plants, dried specimens, gems, minerals and fossils. He also maintained a well-stocked garden, which he shared with a local surgeon and an apothecary. In order to supplement his income, Gessner wrote and edited many books. By the time he died of the plague, not yet 50 years old, he had edited or authored over 60 books.

Gessner's background as a physician is important, since the study of plants, animals and minerals at that time was mainly undertaken by physicians, as part of the study of naturally occurring medicines (*materia medica*). As a Renaissance scholar, Gessner also had great respect for the Classical civilizations of Greece and Rome, and he studied many subjects with equal attentiveness. His letters with his correspondents, several of whom were also medical practitioners, are full of news about books, the identification of plants mentioned by Dioscorides (p. 33), medicinal recipes, rare plants, animals and gems. These letters were often accompanied by actual seeds, pictures of plants and animals, dried specimens and books, as well as manuscripts.

HISTORY OF ANIMALS

The most famous of Gessner's works in natural history, the *History of Animals* (1551–58), was thus the product of a Renaissance scholar, philologist and physician, built on the foundations of an extensive network of correspondents. The title, *History of Animals*, alludes, of course, to Aristotle's work of the same name, and it follows his classification: the first volume dealt with viviparous quadrupeds; the second volume with oviparous quadrupeds; the third with birds; and the fourth with aquatic animals. The fifth volume on serpents was published posthumously (1587). But Gessner's enterprise included much more than Aristotle's work. He also wanted to collect everything extant that was ever *written* about animals. In this sense, Gessner was building on his earlier work as a comprehensive bibliographer. Gessner's *History of Animals* was not intended to be read from beginning to end as a systematic and original study of zoological taxonomy or morphology, but was to be used more like a dictionary or a reference work.

Each entry began with a picture and was divided into eight parts. In the first section Gesner enumerated the names of the animal in various languages: thus the

Each entry in Gessner's History of Animals, *called a 'history', was accompanied by a picture, here an elephant, and was subdivided into eight sections. The largest subsection was often that on philology.*

elephant is called 'elephas' in Greek and Latin, 'phil' in Hebrew and Persian, 'leophante' in Italian, 'helfant' in German, 'olyfant' in English and 'slon' in Illyrian. The second section concerned the places the animal was found, and how it differed according to the region it inhabited: Indian elephants are taller and stronger than African ones.

The third section described the animal's physical features and habits: an elephant has a hard, black-coloured skin which looks peeled and scabby; it uses the folds of its skin to catch flies; its voice is like a low sound of a trumpet; it eats barley, figs, grapes and onions, but if it eats a chameleon, it will die unless it is given an antidote of wild olives. This section often allowed Gessner to use his knowledge of plants. Thus of the 50 pages devoted to the wolf, 16 were used to discuss the true identity of the 'wolfsbane' regarded as poisonous to wolves by Dioscorides. The fourth section outlined the animal's

This picture of a bird of paradise was given to Gessner by the scholar and antiquarian Conrad Peutinger of Augsburg. Gessner reported that a bird of paradise was on sale in Nuremberg for 100 talers.

character: elephants love their own country, worship the stars, sun and moon, live in groups, are chaste, very gentle, loyal to their keepers, hate mice and are afraid of fire.

The fifth section covered the use of the animal other than for food or medicine. Gessner listed here, for instance, historical figures, including Hannibal, who used elephants in their military campaigns. The sixth section gave details of how to eat the entire animal, or parts of it. This section was understandably brief for the elephant, but extensive for the hare, pig, chicken and eggs, with ample references to Galen's verdict on their nutrition and citations from Apicius' recipes. The seventh section set out medicinal uses: the blood of the elephant, according to Pliny the Elder (p. 38), was good for rheumatics and sciatica; al-Razi taught that the dried flesh of the elephant soaked in vinegar and fennel seeds causes abortion; a paste made of ivory powder could cure whitlows, according to Dioscorides. This was a section that a physician could dip into, in order to find a comprehensive list of the medicinal uses of an animal.

The last section was philological: here Gessner listed all possible meanings and uses of the animal's name. It included headings such as etymology; epithets (an elephant is 'gentle', 'daring,' and 'enormous'); metaphorical uses of the name ('Elephantiasis' is a form of leprosy); images of the animal; creatures, stones and plants named after the animal (the 'elephantia' is a hare with hard black skin); proper names derived from its name (according to Strabo, a mountain in Arabia is called 'elephas'); and everything else about the use of the word 'elephant', including proverbs such as 'the Indian elephant cares not for the biting of a gnat'. This section was where Gessner was truly in his element, and is what made his work so voluminous.

Gessner's entry on the elephant typifies his approach in the whole of the *History of Animals*. On cursory examination, it appears nothing more than a mixture of factual and fictional accounts about the animal, listed alongside medical, zoological, philological and historical information. But Gessner's primary aim as a Renaissance scholar was to compile everything ever written about a particular animal. Viewed in this light, it is futile to try to assess his 'originality' in the study of natural history. For instance, his volume on birds relies heavily on the work of Ulisse Aldrovandi (p. 59), and his volume on fishes quotes extensively from the publications of Guillaume Rondelet, Belon (p. 67) and Hippolytus Salviani. Even the pictures were often borrowed from a variety of sources – the image of the reindeer is from Olaus Magnus' map, one of the pictures of the giraffe is from Bernhard von Breydenbach's *Journey to the Holy Land*, and most famously, the rhinoceros is copied from Albrecht Dürer's celebrated woodcut.

A COMPENDIUM OF SOURCES

Compared to the 197 folio pages Gessner took up on the eight sections on dogs, the entries on New World fauna were understandably shorter and incomplete. It is important to appreciate that not all the animals, birds and fish discussed by Gessner had been observed by him first-hand. Animals such as elephants and armadillos were very rare and exceedingly difficult and expensive to get hold of – as, of course, was unicorn's horn. So Gessner relied on his correspondents to send in pictures, descriptions and parts of a rare animal whenever possible. Given the difficulty of confirming the existence of such an animal directly, its identity was ultimately established through words. This is why, in Gessner's *History of Animals*, the elephant, the armadillo and the unicorn are given equal credence. Just as Gessner recorded in the section on the unicorn descriptions of single-horned beasts found in the Bible and in the works of Aristotle, Aelian, Pliny the Elder and Albert the Great, so he quoted from respectable contemporary physicians as to the morphology of the bird of paradise (feet-less) and its origin (from the Moluccas islands), and also reported the testimony of the imperial secretary Maximilian Transylvanus that the rulers of the Moluccas had sent these birds as gifts to the emperor Charles V. Such literary sources were quoted not simply to give authority to fauna rarely seen: even when Gessner himself had live specimens and could provide his own description – as in the case of the guinea pig – he still quoted a description from the donor, Johann Heinrich Munzinger, physician to the Fugger family, and added Peter Martyr's reference to the animal in his book on the New World.

Gessner recorded and reported the words of his contemporaries as carefully as he did those of the Classical authors. In some cases these descriptions formed the basis for establishing comparisons and similarities with known species. Thus, a four-footed creature with longer hind-legs found in Salzburg in 1531 was classified under the satyr, for which ample Classical and medieval descriptions could be cited. Here, then, is an example of how novel or strange animals could be assimilated into traditional categories of classification. Not all New World fauna could be treated in this way, but their number had not yet reached such a critical point that accepted schemes of knowledge could not accommodate them. Instead, this was a time when Gessner could hope to make sense of the world around him with reference to the words of past and present authors. It was a fundamentally bookish way of forming

The first printed picture of the tulip, 1561: Gessner saw a red tulip in April 1559, in the garden of Johann Heinrich Herwart at Augsburg. His friend, the Torgau physician Johannes Kentmann, had told him that the name Tulip came from the Turkish word for a Dalmatian cap.

knowledge, which modern historians of science have called 'erudite empiricism'. Gessner worked similarly with plants: when examining an unknown plant, he would regularly consult Classical and contemporary books on the 'materia medica'.

Gessner's *History of Animals* also demonstrates his obsession with words: as a Renaissance scholar, he understood the importance of *copia* – abundance of words and expressions – as a mark of civility. He was also interested in the variety of languages. For Gessner, language was a gift of God that marked humans out from other creatures. In fact he said that each history of an animal was a hymn to God the Creator. Gessner's natural history was thus a faithful enterprise, with a sense of history reaching back to the Classical world, adorned with the variety and wealth of human language.

THE ENLIGHTENMENT

THE NATURAL HISTORIANS OF THE RENAISSANCE had made important advances in the description and classification of the natural world free from a dependence on medicinal and other practical uses, but the discipline remained chained to the rock of the ancients. Even the more radical thinkers such as Konrad Gessner, who were naming and describing creatures from a drawing or even an actual specimen, were largely only clarifying Aristotle's concepts of, for instance, 'lion' or 'tiger', rather than critically observing them in their own right. Such backward-looking methodology was insufficient to handle the vast numbers of newly discovered and exotic plants and animals confronting Europeans for the first time. Attempts to shoehorn new beasts into the taxonomy of the ancients has left its mark in the common names of some North American animals – the cougar was called a Mountain Lion as only lions existed in the ancient world and the name was thus acceptable to the Church.

By the end of the 16th century, however, naturalists and philosophers were questioning the way the world could be understood and described. A new age of science and discovery was beginning, considerably influenced by the beliefs of two men: the English statesman, essayist and philosopher Francis Bacon and the French philosopher and mathematician René Descartes. Bacon's description of his Cambridge tutors as 'Men of sharp wits, shut up in their cells of a few authors, chiefly Aristotle, their Dictator' shows his rejection of the reliance on knowledge gained from ancient texts; instead he urged men to 'take the question to nature' and so learn about God's work by observation and experiment. Descartes, like Bacon, challenged the dominance of the ancients and also saw the importance of experiment in understanding the world, but in his case it was to support a pre-formed theory. His mechanistic philosophy stating that all living things in the universe are driven by clock-like mechanisms was to inspire later 17th-century scientists such as Robert Hooke and Sir Isaac Newton

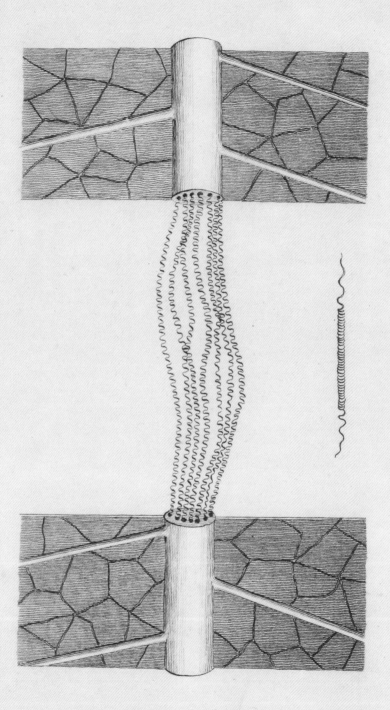

Erasmus Darwin, grandfather of Charles, was one of the leading figures of the Enlightenment in England. He was interested in a huge range of subjects, from mechanical devices to embryology, agriculture and evolution. This engraving of the detailed structure of a leaf is from his book Phytologia, or the Philosophy of Agriculture and Gardening *(1800).*

The landscape of Kamchatka, as encountered by Georg Steller on the Russian expedition to the arctic, led by Vitus Bering, and published in an account of his travels. Steller was one of the first naturalists to be employed on a large voyage of exploration and the first to describe much of the arctic flora and fauna.

These new ways of looking at and describing the natural world strongly influenced a group of scholars who began meeting in England in the 1640s, encouraged by the scientifically sympathetic regime of the Lord Protector, Oliver Cromwell. By the 1660s the group had (perhaps ironically, given their republican origins) received a Royal Charter, and so was born the Royal Society of London (or the Royal Society), which remains one of the world's most prestigious scientific organizations to this day. Many of the great natural historians of the Enlightenment were members and officers, and some achieved the esteemed rank of President.

One of the founder members of the Royal Society, Robert Hooke was appointed its curator of experiments and has been called the world's first professional scientist. Amongst his other achievements, Hooke was one of the pioneers of microscopy, and in his major work, *Micrographia*, he illustrated many wonders through his microscope, such as a flea in monstrous close up as well as many previously unknown structures, including cells. Hooke's work was an inspiration to a Dutch draper of little formal education, Antony van Leeuwenhoek, who, with his own simple but precision-made instruments, revealed a new world of tiny creatures in a drop of pond water. His effective establishment of the science of microbiology was one of the most significant advances of the 17th century.

COLLECTING AND CLASSIFYING

The most intellectually challenging problem that the scientific revolutionaries applied themselves to was the naming and classifying of the natural world. Without such a framework, any advances in biology would be impossible. Some progress had been made in the Renaissance by Cesalpino and others, but they still adhered to the Aristotelian belief in our ability to classify and understand relationships using a set of predefined 'essential' characters, such as certain fruit and flower parts in plants. This philosophy was challenged not only by naturalists, but also by philosophers such as John Locke, who denied the ability of humans to recognize such an essence. It was Locke's friend, the clergyman John Ray, who was the first to apply rigorous scientific methods to this problem. Ray devised natural systems of classification based on a whole suite of characters that would bring together species genuinely related to each other. Unfortunately, Ray's systems were cumbersome and difficult to apply to the huge numbers of new plants and animals confronting natural scientists at this time.

It was the Swedish doctor Carl Linnaeus (or Carl von Linné), who was, parodoxically, to both advance and retard the ordering of the living world. Linnaeus had a great respect for Ray's attempts to create a natural classification, but devised instead simpler, more utilitarian systems that would provide naturalists with a quick and straightforward means of identifying and designating new species. His systems recalled the 'essentialism' of earlier ones by using only a few flower characters to define groups, and although they were relatively easy to use, they assigned clearly related plants to different groups. Their simplicity encouraged a growth in interest in natural history in Britain and elsewhere, for which Linnaeus should be given due credit. However, his greatest legacy to modern science is his binomial system for naming things. Ray's generation had named plants with long Latin phrases (polynomials); for instance the Dog Violet was *Viola caule demum adscendente*,

A pharmacopoeia cabinet, forming the frontispiece of Materia Medica, Liber 1, De Plantis *by Carl Linnaeus (1749). Linnaeus, a Swedish doctor, developed a simple, workable system of classification for plants based on their sexual organs – which shocked and outraged many at the time.*

foliis oblongo-cordatis (describing its habit and the shape of its leaves). Linnaeus promoted a much simpler, two-name system, in which the first word represents the larger group to which the organism belongs, the genus – in this example *Viola* (Violets) – and the second part the specific member of the group that is being described – in this case *canina* (the Dog Violet); hence the name *Viola canina*, which can be applied only to this particular plant and no other. We, as modern humans, are *Homo sapiens*, while our extinct close relatives are *Homo neanderthalensis*, for example.

Linnaeus's proposed new methodology was largely rejected in France, where the search for natural systems continued Ray's work. It was in this highly intellectual ambience that some crucial philosophical advances were made. First, the Comte de Buffon hinted that perhaps groups such as families of organisms might reflect a common ancestry – a relatively low-key speculation that anticipated modern evolution-based systems by 200 years. Of more immediate benefit to the development of classification systems were the efforts to create natural methods of classification by the eminent botanical Jussieu family and their colleague Michel Adanson.

Adanson's observations on the strange and exotic plants that he collected in Senegal led him to conclude not only that it was necessary to study numerous characters of plants in order to produce a natural classification, but also that these should not be chosen until the plants had been completely studied and their structure understood. He was thus a fierce opponent of Linnaeus's method which selected only a few essential characters. At the time, Adanson's theories did not receive the attention they deserved and it was left to Antoine-Laurent de Jussieu to apply the new methodology in practice. Jussieu divided the plant kingdom into hundreds of families, most of which still stand today, and crucially recognized that not all characters were of equal significance – some were of more value in classification than others.

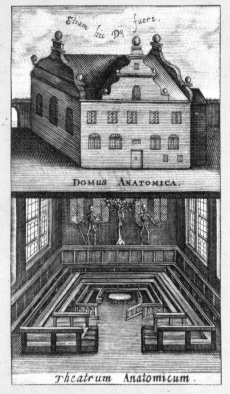

The anatomical theatre at the University of Copenhagen, where Nicolaus Steno received his medical training. A brilliant anatomist, Steno went on to become fascinated by fossils, which in turn led him to speculate about how rocks formed and were deposited in a sequence of layers.

The revolution in plant classification was mirrored in the insect world by the work of the Danish entomologist Johann Christian Fabricius. Like his tutor Linnaeus, Fabricius preferred to use a few essential characters to create his groups. His artificial classifications did not last, but he did become one of the most respected entomologists of his time – and perhaps all time – describing a remarkable 10,000 species, a vast achievement for one man.

EXPLORERS AND PIONEERS

Of course, the activities of all these classifiers and describers were dependent on the collecting of specimens. Sometimes they collected their own specimens, but more often they relied on the explorer-naturalists who risked their lives to gather and record an expanding nature. These pioneers came from a variety of backgrounds, and sometimes their interests involved them in surprising situations. William Dampier was famous for sailing three times round the world, and infamous perhaps for his association with the buccaneers who tormented the Dutch East India Company. As a naturalist he should not be underestimated, collecting plants in northwest Australia over 70 years before Cook arrived in Botany Bay. His journals were held in esteem by Charles Darwin, who referred to him as 'Old Dampier'. Perhaps one of the greatest collectors was Sir Hans Sloane. This renowned physician and scientist made his own collections, notably on a voyage to Jamaica, which he described in his major work *Natural History of Jamaica*, but he also acquired over 400,000 objects, not only from the natural world, but also prints, drawings, antiquities and coins. Sold on his death to the British nation, these formed the basis of the British Museum.

Robert Hooke is best known for his studies of nature through the microscope, but he was also interested in many other aspects of natural science. This is his 'instrument of use to take the draught picture of any thing', which he sent to the Royal Society in 1694.

Sloane was a wealthy and influential member of the Royal Society and willing to sponsor other young natural historians. One such young man was the pioneer of the American interior, Mark Catesby. With support from Sloane and others with vested interests, such as the Governor of the Carolina colony, Catesby established himself as

Mark Catesby, one of the first to study the flora and fauna of the American interior, published his painting of the Carolina Parakeet (Conuropsis carolinensis) *in his* Natural History of Carolina, Florida and the Bahama Islands *(1732–43). Around 100 years later John James Audubon also painted it (p. 234); it subsequently became extinct in the wild.*

one of the greatest naturalists, and is sometimes referred to as the founder of American ornithology. His exceptional talents left a legacy of fine collections and exquisite watercolours of birds and plants.

Although Catesby was born in England, he helped to establish a tradition of natural history in North America that would be taken up by pioneers such as William Bartram, the first 'home-grown' American natural historian of note. Bartram travelled extensively in the southern United States collecting, recording and illustrating the natural world. He published works on the flora of his fledgling nation and was held in great esteem by President Thomas Jefferson. His mixture of scientific enquiry and romantic description was to inspire many followers in America and elsewhere.

While Catesby and Bartram were risking their lives in the pursuit of knowledge of the North American interior, a young German scientist was suffering the hardships of the frozen north. Georg Steller was one of the first natural scientists to be employed on a large voyage of exploration, accompanying the Russian expedition led by Vitus Bering to chart potential new territories in Kamchatka and Alaska. Steller survived extreme conditions (Bering did not), collecting and observing, and became the first European to describe much of the arctic fauna and flora of North America, including the now-extinct Steller's sea cow.

Steller's journals were used by later explorers, in particular Captain James Cook on his arctic voyages. Cook is best known for his first voyage to the Pacific Islands, Australia and New Zealand. Ostensibly mounted to record the Transit of Venus for navigational purposes, his underlying mission was to discover the Great Southern Continent believed to exist in the South Pacific. Cook, like Bering, took naturalists with him, in this case Joseph Banks and Daniel Solander, who were to document and collect the flora and fauna of the region for the first time. Thus, like those enthusiastic young men Catesby and Steller before him, Banks could be seen as an instrument of a greater force – the expanding of the empires of the West. The economic and political potential of natural history was increasingly appreciated, and Banks was to become one of its greatest promoters.

The Background to Evolution

The classification and description of the living world was an intellectual challenge, but an increasing number of natural historians were also looking at the solid ground beneath their feet and questioning why there were different kinds of rock and whether the Earth had always been the same. Such questions brought them into conflict with the religious establishment and tested their own faith.

Archbishop Ussher had calculated from the Bible that the Earth was created on 26 October 4004 BC. But the evidence of eroded surfaces and deeply carved valleys suggested processes that had been active much longer. At the same time, the problem of the discovery of once-living things embedded in solid rock would not go away – the fossil question. Fossils intrigued the Danish physician Nicolaus Steno. He was convinced of the organic origin of fossils from his comparison of living shark's teeth with objects known as tonguestones (*glossopetrae*), which were clearly the stony remains of ancient sharks. He turned from anatomy to fossil hunting, and speculated that the various fossil shells he found were the remains of creatures buried in the mud of seas that had once covered the Earth, or the inhabitants of freshwater rivers and

Erasmus Darwin, from whose work this drawing comes, proposed that embryos were formed from 'molecules' from both parents, and made the connection between variation and sexual reproduction, providing some of the groundwork for evolutionary theory.

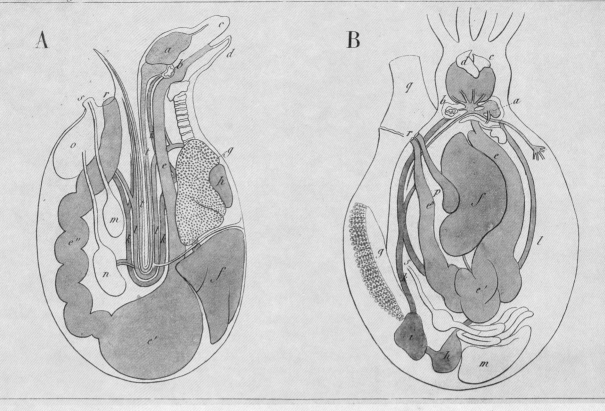

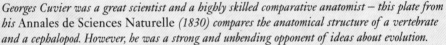

Georges Cuvier was a great scientist and a highly skilled comparative anatomist – this plate from his Annales de Sciences Naturelle *(1830) compares the anatomical structure of a vertebrate and a cephalopod. However, he was a strong and unbending opponent of ideas about evolution.*

lakes that had been washed into the oceans by Noah's Flood. Steno also recognized that rocks had been laid down in layers, and speculated that mountains were formed when these layers of mud collapsed into cavities.

Many other theories appeared at this time, some of which, like this one of Steno's, were later proved wrong, but were at least arrived at in a rational way, with less reliance on myth and legend. The ambitious Comte de Buffon applied himself to the whole spectrum of natural history topics, including the nature of the Earth. Buffon had calculated the age of the Earth as around 750,000 years, based on a theory of a once-molten Earth cooling down at a set rate. This brought him dangerously close to conflict with the Church, but Buffon cleverly tied his theory into the seven days of Creation, and the appearance of Man.

In the latter half of the 18th century two main theories of the Earth's origin came to prominence. The first, like that of Steno, was based on the power of water, and was promoted by the German geologist Abraham Werner. He envisaged a world once covered with water, in which rocks formed by the crystallization of minerals, and he dismissed volcanoes as unimportant belchings of coal burning underground. In opposition to Werner and the 'Neptunists', as they were known, were the 'Vulcanists'. The

Scottish geologist James Hutton believed the Earth to have been shaped by a combination of volcanic activity and erosion, and, most importantly, that the process was still taking place. Hutton was correct in his belief that the Earth changed through cyclical processes, but not about the mechanisms involved. Nevertheless his scientific approach and his significant contribution earn him a place among the great naturalists.

The advances made by Hutton were checked by the highly influential French anatomist Georges Cuvier. A brilliant but single-minded man, Cuvier dominated the stage with his theory of Catastrophism, which visualized a world and its life forms determined by a series of cataclysmic floods, the last of which was that of Noah described in the Bible. This powerful man all but stifled the development of geology for many years. He was also firmly opposed to any evolutionary ideas, but did accept that fossils were a snapshot of a world that no longer existed and explained them through his catastrophe theories: these extinct creatures had evidently met their end in the floods. Cuvier was, however, a highly skilled comparative anatomist and used his abilities to identify the large extinct sloth, *Megatherium*, as well as other fossils.

Whatever the merits of these various theories, they were at least all based on the premise that the Earth could change – although how and at what speed might still be open to debate. But what about the living world? The prevailing view of the early 18th century was one of a fixed existence, in which the same plant and animal species had populated the Earth since they were put there in the Creation. However, the accumulating evidence from fossils was making this less and less tenable.

Fittingly, it was Charles Darwin's grandfather, Erasmus Darwin, who first put forward a credible theory of evolution. A highly intelligent polymath, Erasmus Darwin published his theories not only in prose but also in the form of poems – an approach that would have found favour with the developing Romantic Movement. Although he did not refer to natural selection as such, he did use his observations of the natural world and embryology to suggest that through competition and sexual selection species could change through time

One of the best-known pre-Darwinian evolutionary theories was that of Jean-Baptiste Lamarck. Lamarck's speculations on evolution – the inheritance of acquired characteristics – are often unfairly misinterpreted, and he is remembered and judged for these, rather than his challenge as a credible scientist to the established views on the immutability of species, as well as his excellent taxonomic work on invertebrates. Both Lamarck and Cuvier were to influence Charles Darwin and, along with Hutton and others, provided the building blocks for the groundbreaking theory of evolution that was to emerge in the next century.

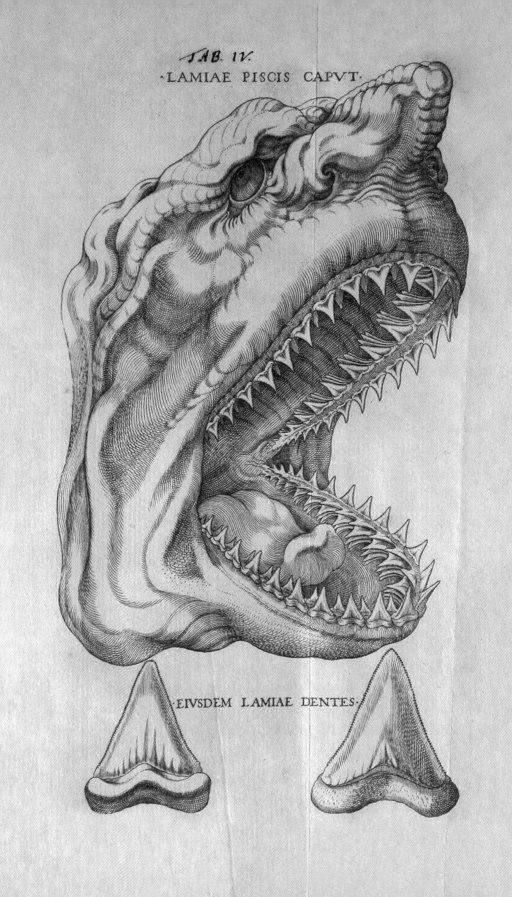

TAB. IV.

·LAMIAE PISCIS CAPVT·

·EIVSDEM LAMIAE DENTES·

ALAN CUTLER

Nicolaus Steno

UNLOCKING THE EARTH'S GEOLOGICAL PAST

(1638–1686)

*Our mind thinks that nothing can set a limit to its
knowledge, but when it withdraws to its own habitation it is
unable to give a description of it, and no longer knows itself.*

Nicolaus Steno, Discours sur l'anatomie du cerveau, *1669*

NICOLAUS STENO OPENED THE DOOR TO THE EARTH'S vast geological past. Often called the founder of the science of geology, he was the first to propose scientific principles by which students of the Earth could unravel its history by studying rock strata. But Steno, also known by his native Danish name, Niels Stensen, was much more than a precocious geologist. He was first an anatomist, supremely skilled at the art of dissection. His investigations debunked popular theories about muscles, the heart and the brain.

Born in 1638, Steno lived at a time when science was a new intellectual force in the world, and his passion and intellectual rigour helped refine its methods and determine its course. Yet he abandoned his own scientific career at the height of his fame to become a priest, ministering to the souls of the poor in northern Germany until his death in 1686, at the relatively young age of 48.

HEART AND SOUL

One day early in 1665 the intellectual elite of Paris gathered to hear a lecture by a young visiting anatomist from Denmark. Nicolaus Steno, son of a Copenhagen goldsmith, had won fame for a streak of new discoveries. He had a flair for dissection – a delicate touch with a scalpel that enabled him to tease out the subtlest anatomical features. As a Parisian journal noted, 'he makes most of what he presents so vivid that one is obliged to be convinced, and one may only wonder that it has escaped the notice of all earlier anatomists.'

Illustration from Steno's Canis carchariae dissectum caput *('A Shark's Head Dissected'),
published in Florence in 1667. Steno was impressed by the resemblance between the shark's teeth
and certain fossil stones known as* glossopetrae. *This led him to investigate the origins of
fossils and the rocks that enclosed them.*

At this time, the so-called scientific revolution was at its height. Galileo had died 20 years earlier, but his ideas still electrified minds across Europe. In Cambridge, England, a quiet student named Isaac Newton was beginning to ponder the riddle of gravitation. Natural philosophers, as they called themselves, sought mechanical rather than magical explanations for the mysteries of life. And for the greatest of these mysteries, they needed to look no further than their own bodies.

In the mechanical view it was impossible for physical matter to generate its own motion. Something, somehow, had to push it. But then how did muscles work? How could animals and humans cause their bodies to move? And what of the heart? What kept it beating? Steno's previous discoveries had made great leaps forward in these questions. After dissecting muscles in detail, he determined that they were bundles of contractile fibres, not, as others confidently asserted, balloons that puffed up when infused by an 'animating spirit'. His conclusions from his dissection of the heart also went against current thinking – the heart was not a cauldron of boiling blood, nor was it the dwelling place of the soul; it was made of no special substance. Close observation revealed that the heart was simply a muscle. According to the mechanical philosophy, however, this was impossible. A number of Steno's colleagues refused to accept the muscular nature of the heart, even after he demonstrated it to them personally.

Steno's lecture in Paris concerned itself with the other possible dwelling place of the soul: the brain. The brain's soft, pliable tissue made it exceptionally difficult to dissect. As a result, speculation about its structure and operation was rampant. René

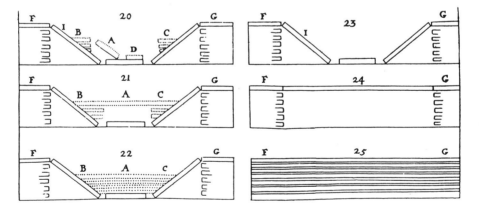

Perhaps Steno's masterpiece, De solido intra solidium naturaliter contento dissertationis Prodromus (*'Prodromus to a dissertation on solids naturally contained within a solid'*), *from which this diagram is taken, was published in 1699. Beginning at the lower right, it shows the stages by which the strata of Tuscany were laid down and the landscape was formed. It was the first published geological cross-section.*

Descartes, the French mathematician and philosopher, had concluded that the soul was located in the nut-like pineal gland. Sitting in the centre of the brain, he envisaged it twisting and turning, pulling cords of tissue and controlling the body like a puppet. But Descartes had reached this conclusion more through deductive reasoning than anatomical observation. The lecture audience hoped that the brilliant young anatomist, with his unmatched dissecting skills, would discover telling details that would settle the question at last.

A portrait of Steno in 1667 or 1668, while he was living in Florence and engrossed in geological work.

The lecture was a tour de force. Steno covered all that was known about the brain's structure and he wasted no time in debunking Descartes' theory. It made no anatomical sense. The gland had no freedom of movement; it simply could not gyrate as Descartes had supposed. Science, Steno cautioned his audience, had to be based on observations of nature, not pure reasoning, however elegant. It could not be bound by any set methods or predetermined philosophy; one had to follow where one's observations led. Too much remained unknown about the brain's basic structure to permit speculations about how it worked. As for the human soul, and its nature – perhaps this was not a question for science after all.

THE RIDDLE OF FOSSILS

The following year Steno found himself in Italy, as a guest in the court of Grand Duke Ferdinand de' Medici in Florence. Ferdinand had been Galileo's patron and sponsored an academy of his disciples devoted to experimental science. When a huge shark was caught off the coast of Tuscany, Ferdinand invited Steno to dissect it for the court. It was in many ways a routine dissection for Steno, but it led him to an observation that changed the course of his career, and the course of science. Steno noticed that the shark's teeth resembled in every detail certain medicinal stones called *glossopetrae*, or tonguestones. These stones were thought to grow within the earth or in some cases to fall from the sky during storms. But Steno saw that the resemblance between tooth and stone was too perfect to be an accident.

Stones in the form of shellfish and other marine creatures had been known since antiquity. They could be found high in mountains and at great distances from the sea. One explanation was that they were relics of a stupendous flood, possibly that associated with Noah in the Bible. But it was hard to explain how an inundation could cause the shells to become petrified, or why they would be so deeply embedded in the Earth's crust. And in some places they were so abundant that it seemed unlikely that they could be the result of a single, short-lived event, such as Noah's Flood.

Aristotle (p. 23) and other Greek writers had proposed that the land and sea had traded places over long periods of time, but that idea was unacceptable to most Europeans in the 17th century. According to biblical scholars, the creation of the Earth as described in Genesis had occurred no more than 6,000 years earlier. No one believed that mountains could rise or oceans dry up in such a short period. The most reasonable explanation for the fossil shells seemed to be that, despite their resemblance to marine creatures, they were simply unusual stones that grew within the Earth.

Steno could not accept this explanation, however. As an anatomist he had become convinced that every detail of an organ or tissue within an animal's body served a function. Perfectly formed teeth and shells didn't just happen by chance. But how did shells and teeth become embedded in solid rock? And what were they doing on land? The question fascinated Steno to the extent that he put his anatomical research on hold to investigate fossils full time. Ferdinand, too, was obviously intrigued, as he consented to finance Steno's travels around Tuscany to collect fossils and study its bedrock.

SOLIDS IN SOLIDS

The result of Steno's efforts was his masterpiece: *De solido intra solidium naturaliter contento dissertationis prodromus* ('Prodromus to a dissertation on solids naturally contained within a solid'), known as Steno's *Prodromus* or *De Solido*. It contained the rudiments of the science of geology. Steno noted the differences between the growth of inorganic solids, such as crystals, and organic solids, such as shells and bone. He recognized that the rocks containing fossils had originally been soft sediments, hardening into solid rock long after the shells or bones were buried. Although geologists now understand that not all rocks are formed from sediments – igneous rocks result from the cooling and solidification of liquid magma, and metamorphic rocks result from the transformation of other rocks by heat and pressure – Steno's conception of sedimentary rocks was a critical step in the development of geology.

In a further leap of insight, Steno realized that the same reasoning he used to interpret the incremental growth of a crystal or a shell, or the burial of a shell within sediment, could be applied to the larger scale of the Earth's strata. The strata were deposited layer by layer, in sequence, over a period of time. Geologists call this Steno's principle of 'superposition': in a sequence of sedimentary layers, the bottom layer is the oldest (laid down first) and those above it are progressively younger. The strata (and the fossils within them) are therefore a record of particular time intervals of the Earth's past. Steno also stated that water-deposited sediments are laid down in horizontal layers (the principle of 'original horizontality') and that they tend to spread laterally to form continuous sheets (the principle of 'lateral continuity'). Tilted or folded rock strata therefore indicate past movements of the crust, and truncated rock strata indicate shifting of faults or erosion of the bedrock.

Steno had no way of anticipating that later scientists, following his principles, would discover that the Earth was 4.6 billion years old, that the seas have waxed and waned many times, or that the Earth's crust consists of constantly shifting plates. From his observations of the strata of Tuscany he was able to deduce that the land had been covered by the sea at least twice, and that at least once the strata had tilted and shifted. At the time, the only commonly accepted record of the world's early history was the book of Genesis. While this account was authoritative, at least in the eyes of the faithful, it lacked detail. Steno saw his science as a way of filling in some of the blanks. The book of nature and the books of the Bible were complementary. Because both came from the same divine author, it was impossible that they could contradict one another. Steno seemed satisfied that, at least in a general way, scripture and strata carried the same message: God had the power to flood the Earth or raise mountains whenever He wanted.

STENO'S LEGACY

The geological ideas presented in *De Solido* were not immediately accepted by Steno's contemporaries. He had some high-profile supporters, such as the British scientist Robert Boyle and the German mathematician Gottfried Leibniz, but to most the concept of geological change remained unthinkable. Steno intended a lengthier follow-up work, but was soon consumed in a controversy of a more personal nature. In 1667, after years of spiritual anguish, he had foresworn the Lutheranism of his birth and converted to Catholicism. In the end, theology carried him away from geology just as geology had taken him from anatomy. In 1675 he took holy orders and became a priest. Just two years later he was made bishop and sent to northern Germany where he tended to the small Catholic population. Taking a vow of poverty, he lived a life of asceticism, the rigours of which destroyed his health. He died in 1686.

In the century following Steno's death, the need for coal and other resources to drive the Industrial Revolution stimulated interest in the structure of the Earth's crust, and Steno's geological ideas were ultimately vindicated. Honours for his religious career came later: in 1988 he was beatified by Pope John Paul II.

John Ray

THE ENGLISH ARISTOTLE

(1627–1705)

*Let it not suffice to be book-learned, to read what others have
written and to take upon trust more falsehood than truth, but
let us ourselves examine things as we have opportunity, and
converse with Nature as well as with books.*

John Ray, The Wisdom of God, *1691*

IN THE MID-17TH CENTURY, Britain was experiencing a period of political and religious turmoil which also coincided with a time of radical change in scientific thinking. Students of the natural world had to a large extent been reliant on the wisdom of the ancients such as Aristotle – regarded as the only authority by the established Church. The philosopher and statesman Sir Francis Bacon had challenged this doctrine, urging that one should 'take the question to nature' by experiment and observation, rather than slavishly and uncritically repeating the works of those who had gone before. On to this stage came John Ray, a religious man of humble origins, whose meticulous and logical approach set the understanding, naming and classification of the living world on a precise scientific basis.

Ray was born the son of a village blacksmith at Black Notley, Essex, in 1627. His mother, a herbalist, inspired him with an interest in the natural world, plants in particular. Ray's academic abilities were recognized early and, supported by a scholarship for poor students, he was admitted to Catherine Hall (now St Catherine's College), Cambridge, in 1644, with a career in divinity ahead of him. He soon transferred to Trinity College where the stronger emphasis on mathematics and languages suited his interests more closely. He received his degree in 1648 and, skilled as an orator, linguist and natural historian, he was appointed to a number of senior posts at Cambridge, always maintaining his role as a preacher. Ray was a popular and well-liked tutor and many of his students became close friends and fellow naturalists. One of these was a well-to-do young man, Francis Willughby, who was to have a profound influence on Ray's work. Between his teaching and preaching duties, Ray was able to pursue natural history studies, setting up a small botanical garden in the grounds of Trinity. Even during one of the many bouts of ill health that dogged his life, he used his time productively in collecting and studying plants in the Cambridgeshire countryside, publishing *The Catalogue of Cambridge Plants* anonymously in 1660, the first of many works on the natural world. It contained descriptions of some 671 plant species and was produced with the aim of stimulating interest in botany, the study of which was rather neglected at this time at Cambridge. Indeed, Ray and his friends were often ridiculed for their unfashionable pursuit.

In the preface to this book Ray wrote: 'My present purpose involved a measure of haste in order to revive the almost extinct study of botany.... There are larger prospects ahead. This little book may excite others to a similar survey of their own localities and so to a complete Phytologica Brittanica.' As is clear from this statement, the book was viewed as part of a much greater project to catalogue the flora and fauna of England. With this in mind Ray and Willughby made several excursions around the British Isles. On one expedition, in 1661, they came across the severed heads of the executed Earl of Argyll and the Reverend James Guthrie – grim reminders of the times in which they lived, and perhaps a portent of a dramatic change in Ray's life.

Ray's period at Cambridge coincided with one of the most eventful and turbulent periods of English history, with civil wars, the execution of a king and a religiously non-conformist republic put in place of the monarchy. These events had not troubled the puritan-inclined Ray unduly, but when the monarchy and established Church were restored, harsh laws and restrictions were introduced. One such law, The Act of Uniformity, required that all churchmen as well as Cambridge academics should renounce an earlier oath sworn under the republican regime.

Ray had not in fact taken this oath and had been ordained in the Church of England in 1660, but he strongly objected to a system that tried to force people to break a solemn vow. On principle, he resigned his post at Cambridge, thus losing access to its magnificent libraries and

A muse looks down on two children with fruits and flowers seemingly gathered in a botanical garden: the bookplate to Ray's Methodus Plantarum Nova *or New Method of Plants of 1682, in which he published his natural system of plant classification.*

intellectual environment, and also his livelihood. Ray was saved from destitution by his wealthy friend Willughby, who provided him with a modest income and a home at his family seat at Middleton Hall, Warwickshire.

Much of the next 10 years were spent by Ray travelling around Britain and on an inspirational tour of Europe. Ray, together with Willughby and a fellow student, set sail from Dover in 1663, visiting several countries, including Belgium, Holland, Germany, Italy and France. They collected and meticulously recorded the plants and animals they encountered in the countryside, described the fish they saw in markets and ports, and also met several of the leading naturalists of Europe. They were forced to return home in 1666 when the King of France ordered all Englishmen to leave the kingdom. Ray is said to have hitched a lift on a fishcart back to Calais, an appropriate mode of transport for the man who was later to become the world authority on Mediterranean fish.

Ray was now establishing himself as a significant force in the natural sciences and published a number of papers in the transactions of the fledgling Royal Society, to which he was admitted as a Fellow in 1667. A second major blow was to strike in 1672, however, when Willughby died at the age of 37. Ray was able to stay at Middleton for a short time with his new wife, but in spite of his personal charm, Willughby's widow was not well disposed towards him and he left, losing access to Willughby's notes and collections for many years. Ray eventually returned to Essex, with his wife and two daughters, and on his mother's death moved back to her cottage in Black Notley. Here he remained, continuing his works in declining health until his death in 1705.

THE CLASSIFICATION OF PLANTS

Although Ray applied his intellect and logical method to all aspects of the natural world, his main interest was in botany, in particular the classification of plants. By the late 17th century a major challenge was to name and classify the bewildering number of unknown plant and animal species arriving in Europe from newly explored lands around the globe. Most classification systems of the time dated back to antiquity, and relied heavily on real or imagined medical properties. Some earlier natural historians such as Andrea Cesalpino (p. 63) had taken a more scientific approach, but their classifications distinguished groups of plants by one or two characters only. These 'artificial' classifications fitted plants neatly into pigeonholes, but revealed little of their natural affinities and relationships. While Ray had attempted classifications in his early works, he had concentrated his efforts more on gaining a detailed understanding of the structure and biology of plants by observation and experiment, in this way defining a number of basic principles. For example, through dissecting and observing seeds he noted that plants fall into two major groups, depending on whether they have one or two seed leaves. Monocotyledons and Dicotyledons remain as fundamental groups today. This was followed by Ray's most significant and lasting contribution to science, the concept of species. Contemporary views on what defined the basic unit of classification were often bizarre, with some authors for instance believing that butterfly and caterpillar were different species. Ray defined his species as a group of individuals sharing a number of characteristics that would be perpetuated in their offspring. And he went further, listing other characters such as plant height that were actually of no use in classification and were therefore to be avoided. He wrote: 'no matter what variations occur in the individual or the species, if they spring from the seed of the one and the same plant, they are accidental variations and not such as to distinguish a species.'

Portrait of John Ray by an unknown artist. A devout Christian, Ray believed that the complexity of the natural world could not be the result of mere chance.

Ray believed that as many characters as possible should be used in classifications, thus producing what is known as a 'natural classification', one that brings together truly related plants in the same groups. Using these basic rules and a wealth of gathered information, Ray published his system in *New Method of Plants* in 1682. The system was not perfect – it placed trees, shrubs and herbaceous plants in separate groups for instance – but can fairly be said to have been the first credible natural plant classification. And now he had a workable system, he applied it on a grand scale in his greatest work, the *History of Plants*, published in three parts in 1686, 1688 and 1704. In his *History*, Ray described all plants known at the time, either from his own collections, from specimens collected by friends such as Sir Hans Sloane (p. 111) or from reliable documentary sources. Over 18,000 species were divided into 125 sections, many of which are equivalent to modern plant families. Part of this vast work was in effect a botanical textbook which included much of his experimental work on how plants are constructed, function, reproduce and feed.

SCIENCE AND RELIGION

From the late 1680s Ray turned his attention to zoology, geology and writings inspired by his religious faith. He had previously worked on several projects with Willughby,

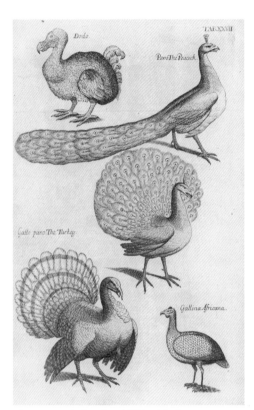

An engraved plate from Willughby's Ornithology, *published by Ray in 1676 after his friend's untimely death.*

and on his friend's death felt obliged to complete them. They appeared as *Willughby's Ornithology* (1676), *Willughby's History of Fishes* (1686) and the *Synopsis of Animals and Reptiles* (1691). A history of insects was completed by Ray in his later years using Willughby's collections, supplemented by insects collected for him in his infirmity by his wife and daughters, and was published posthumously in 1710. As with his botanical work, he gathered together existing literature and weeded out unnecessary names and synonyms, adding his own descriptions where they were wanting and aiming for a natural classification based on a range of consistent characters. In these works, which were supported by excellent illustrations, there was no room, as he says in the preface to *Willughby's Ornithology*, for the fanciful and mythological 'Phoenixes, Griffins, harpies, Ruk and the like'.

In his zoological writings, Ray took the opportunity to ridicule theories of spontaneous generation that were popular at the time – for instance, lemmings were believed to be generated from decaying matter or from the clouds, and this accounted for their sudden appearance in great numbers. As Ray pointed out with biting irony 'I reject all spontaneous generation not only of quadrupeds but of insects … but I cannot pass over the fact that recently eaten grass has been found by dissection in the bodies of these creatures rained down from the sky: so grass as well as mice are born in the clouds: curious that the sky does not ever seem to rain down hay.'

Ray can also be fairly regarded as one of the pioneers of geology in Britain. During his travels he collected and described a number of fossil species and became one of the earliest to adopt a scientific approach to their study. He had met the great natural historian Nicolaus Steno (p. 87) in France, and agreed with his theory that fossils were the remains of once-living organisms – most others at this time believed that fossils grew within the Earth or had been set there by God as a test of faith. Ray wrote: 'The first and most probable Opinion is that they were originally the Shells and Bones of living Fishes and other Animals bred in the Sea. This was the general Opinion of the Ancients, in so much as Steno saith.' Ray did not initially accept the concept of extinction, however, and so, for instance, believed that although he had seen countless species of ammonite fossils they might yet be found alive somewhere.

Ray's strong religious enthusiasm and commitment were to influence his science, and in 1691 he published a work that combined his faith and natural history. *The Wisdom of God* brought together his observations and a number of sermons from his time at Cambridge. Having established order by describing and classifying the natural world, he would now set about explaining how it worked. All this was set in the context of Natural Theology, or the knowledge of God derived from nature rather than through divine revelation. In Ray's view, the complexity of the natural world could only be the product of a powerful mind and hand, and not the result of mere chance; he also thought that all nature, even biting flies and wasps, was provided for mankind's benefit. 'There is no greater, at least no more palpable and convincing Argument of the existence of a Deity than the admirable Art and Wisdom that discovers itself in the mode and constitution on the Order and Disposition, the ends and uses of all parts and members of this stately fabric of Heaven and Earth.'

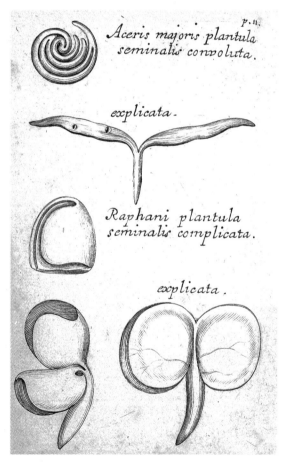

In his 77 years, Ray had moved the study of the living world on from mysticism and fable and set it on a firm scientific basis. He aimed not for self-aggrandizement, but to achieve a clear understanding of the works of God and provide the tools for others to do the same. His species concept remains little changed to this day, and although his rather cumbersome classification systems were replaced for many years by the simple but artificial systems of Linnaeus, in the longer term they were to inspire the natural systems based on many characters that are now in use.

In preparation for his work on systems of plant classification, Ray experimented with and dissected seeds, as illustrated in this plate. As a result, he identified the two major groups of plants: Monocotyledons and Dicotyledons.

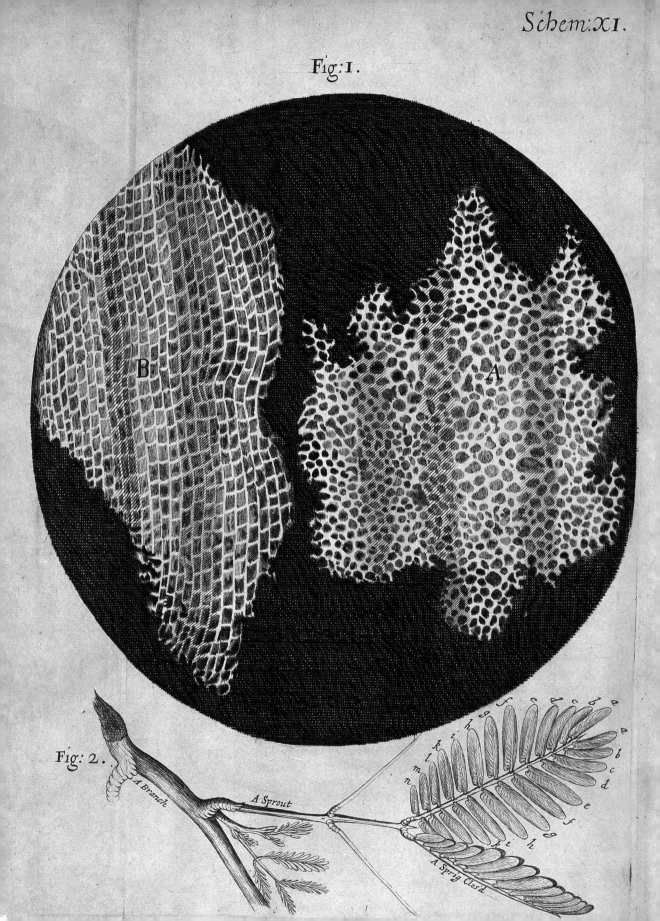

Fig: I.

B

A

Fig: 2.

A Branch

A Sprout

A Sprig Clos'd

Robert Hooke

NATURAL HISTORY THROUGH THE MICROSCOPE

(1635–1703)

*I have often thought, that probably there might be a way
found out, to make an artificial glutinous composition, much
resembling, if not full as good, nay better, than that
Excrement, or whatever other substance it be out of which, the
Silk-worm wire-draws his clew.... This hint therefore, may,
I hope, give some Ingenious inquisitive Person an occasion of
making some trials, which if successful, I have my aim, and
I suppose he will have no occasion to be displeas'd.*

THIS PERCIPIENT PROPHECY of the invention of artificial fibres comes from one of the greatest books in early science. It was a large folio volume entitled *Micrographia*, published in 1665. The author, Robert Hooke, was the first professional scientist, being instructed on 25 March 1662 by the Royal Society of London to present microscopical demonstrations at each of the Society's meetings. His book was full of wide-ranging speculations and descriptions of subjects – from lunar craters, needles and a razor to textile samples. Most of the pages were devoted to natural history through the microscope: Hooke produced breathtaking studies of ants, lice, fleas and gnats. The book became a best-seller and was reprinted two years later. *Micrographia* marked the dawn of popular science, and its repercussions have echoed on through the centuries. And it is even possible to buy a copy of this ground-breaking book today, for facsimiles have been published over the years and are still readily available.

Robert Hooke was born on 18 July 1635 at Freshford on the Isle of Wight and was a sickly child, initially unable to attend school. Young Robert had a penchant for making scientific toys at home – including sundials and clocks – and learned Greek well enough to go to Westminster School. Even as a schoolboy he was said to have

Robert Hooke's best-known illustration shows a specimen of bottle-cork cut in longitudinal (left) and transverse (right) section. Hooke noted that cork was made up of tiny rectangular boxes, like small rooms – hence his coinage of the term 'cell' that is with us to this day. He demonstrated this specimen at a meeting of the Royal Society of London on 13 April 1663, and later included it as Scheme XI of his great book, Micrographia *(1665).*

In March 2006 this 635-page bound set of copies of Royal Society minutes, which Hooke had written out for his own reference, came up for auction in London, but was secured before the sale by the Royal Society for £1 million. The papers, posthumously indexed by Hooke's editor, William Derham, had remained in the Derham family for over three centuries.

invented 'thirty different ways of flying'. Later, at Oxford University, he came to the attention of the great Robert Boyle, who took him on as a research assistant. In 1660 Boyle helped found the Royal Society, and in November 1662 Hooke was appointed Curator of Experiments.

MICROSCOPICAL REVELATION

Contrary to popular belief, *Micrographia* was not the first book to be devoted to the microscope. That was Pierre Borel's *Observationum microscopicarum centuria* of 1656. Borel's was a small book of only 45 pages, however, whereas Robert Hooke's impressive volume was what we might now call a 'coffee-table book', with large pages and fold-out plates. Hooke's most famous microscopical observation is of cork, which on 13 April 1663 he showed to be made up of tiny square rooms or cells. This was how the term 'cell' entered biology – but Hooke was not observing living cells in cork, rather the dried walls of dead cells. Curiously, he had already seen living cells the week before, for on 8 April he had examined the tiny leaflets of a moss growing on a wall. The published plate shows the cells clearly, and deserves to be recognized as a milestone in natural history.

After the demonstrations of moss and cork, which he showed with samples of Kettering-stone, came a succession of other revelations: leeches in vinegar and mould on leather on 22 April; diamonds in a flint and a spider with six eyes on 29 April; male and female gnats (6 May); the point of a needle, the head of an ant and a fly (20 May). On 24 June, Hooke was told to work 'with Dr Wilkins and Dr Wren' to broaden his programme of demonstrations. John Wilkins was the Bishop of Chester and was Secretary of the Society, while Christopher Wren was a physician, although he is far more familiar now for his architecture, in particular St Paul's Cathedral in London.

Hooke's insights set in train much of the science that came later. For instance, his concept of the nature of light as a 'very short vibrative motion transverse to straight lines of propagation through a homogeneous medium' was the starting point for the work that was to make Isaac Newton famous. Hooke came to regard Newton as a plagiarist of his ideas, and would be incensed by the modern term for the rainbow-coloured fringes visible when two sheets of glass are pressed together – 'Newton's rings'. They were first studied by Hooke, and he really deserves to have his name attached to the phenomenon. His invention of the hygrometer and his study of capil-laries ('small glass canes' he called them) were equally innovative.

Hooke's Legacy

Our knowledge of the breadth of Hooke's ideas has recently been extended by the rediscovery of a set of his hand-written notes from meetings of the Royal Society made between 1661 and 1682. These papers were due to be sold at auction in 2006, but at the last moment were bought for the Royal Society. Among the pages are descriptions of Hooke's design for an accurate timepiece, proposals for an experiment to demonstrate the Earth's rotation and accounts of his early work with the micro-scope. Hooke's interest in mechanics pervaded his life, and he applied his beliefs to the world of natural history too. Throughout *Micrographia* there is a mechanistic theme of the way in which physics could account for natural history.

Although the world of natural history dominates this impressive book, other fascinating and innovatory discussions lie within. It was Hooke who looked seriously at the fossilized remains of plants and animals, and recognized their true origins. Ammonite fossils, for example, were colloquially known at the time as 'serpent stones' and were believed to be snakes that had been cursed and turned to stone. Hooke discerned the truth. He wrote that, in his view, a deluge, earthquake or storm

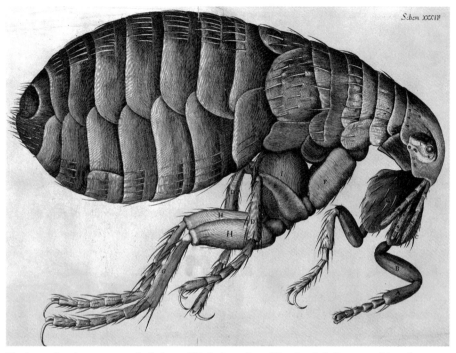

Hooke produced two spectacularly large folded plates for publication in Micrographia. *Almost as though in irony, these great plates showed two of the tiny parasites most familiar to his readers – a louse and a flea.* Pulex irritans, *the human flea, appeared as Scheme XXXIV, facing page 201.*

had thrown them together and that 'mudd, or clay, or petrifying water' had 'in tract of time … settled together and hardened in those shelly moulds' found in the modern world. It was a pioneering and surprisingly prescient insight into how fossils form.

Robert Hooke is remembered today for the law named after him, stating that a spring lengthens in proportion to the force applied, but he has also left a far greater, and more concrete, legacy – for example, he became Chief Surveyor of London after the Great Fire of 1666 and worked with Wren to rebuild the city. In later life his feud with Sir Isaac Newton grew increasingly bitter; as a result Newton did all he could to remove Hooke's name from the records. In the end, however, Newton's campaign came to nothing; Hooke is rightly recognized as a great pioneer and the first person to bring the microscopic sights of nature to an astonished public.

More remarkable is the fact that his book is still widely read in facsimile by modern students of the natural world. Tucked away in the unnumbered pages of the Preface is a description of how to make a single-lens high-power microscope. This was clearly consulted by the Dutch draper Antony van Leeuwenhoek (p. 104) during

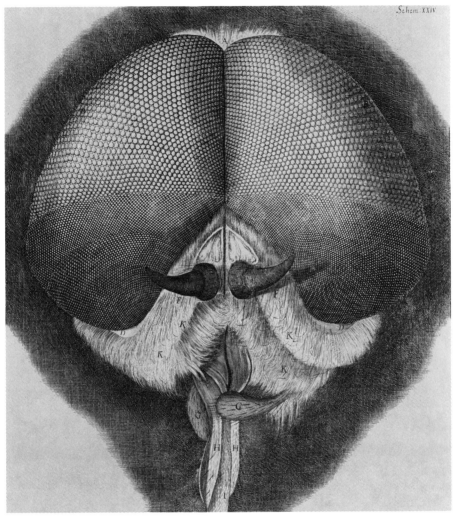

Schem XXIV.

The compound eye of insects had first been pictured by Francesco Stelluti in 1630. Hooke produced a striking impression of the head of a house-fly, with its spectacular compound eyes, for publication as Scheme XXIV in Micrographia.

his visit to London in 1668. When Leeuwenhoek began his career as a microscopist of the natural world, it was Hooke's observations he replicated – and Hooke's design of microscope that he made.

It would please Hooke to know that his words are read by people today much more often than those of Newton. And although we now have the discipline of non-Newtonian physics, Hooke remains a constant. After a lifetime of tribulation and battling to establish his name, his reputation is assured.

Antony van Leeuwenhoek

THE DISCOVERER OF BACTERIA

(1622–1733)

*Looking at this water … the motion of most of these
animalcules was so swift, and so various – upwards,
downwards and round about, that 'twas wonderful to see.
And I judge that some of these little creatures were more
than a thousand times smaller than the smallest ones
I have ever seen upon the rind of cheese.*

WITH THESE WORDS the modern science of microscopical biology was launched. They were written in Delft, the Netherlands, in September 1674, by an untutored draper and civic official; the author of the letter, Antony van Leeuwenhoek, is the father of microbiology. By discovering micro-organisms he took the greatest single step in biology of the entire 17th century, and one of the most fundamental in the whole history of natural science. His interest in the natural history of life beyond our normal vision was unique and proved to be crucial to the development of our understanding.

There are more microbes in a spoonful of soil than the total human population of the Earth. Their variety is astonishing, and their importance is still little understood; more research than ever before is being done into the realm of these ordinarily invisible organisms. Yet until that momentous day when Leeuwenhoek put a glass phial of lake-water in front of his microscope lens, no one had any idea of the extent of the world's microbial populations.

Leeuwenhoek was born in Delft on 24 October 1632 and was christened on 4 November that year, his name appearing on the same page of the baptismal register as Jan Vermeer, who became Delft's greatest painter. Curiously, when the young Vermeer died, Leeuwenhoek (who was by that time a local civil servant) was appointed executor to Vermeer's estate, though there is no evidence that they ever met. After his father died and his mother remarried, Leeuwenhoek was sent away to school, aged six, and later went to live with an uncle. In due course he settled in Amsterdam to learn the drapery trade, but in 1654 he returned to live in Delft, where he was to stay for the rest of his long and distinguished life. In 1668, Leeuwenhoek visited London in the course of his work and while there he came across an extraordi-

This pencil drawing by Leeuwenhoek's limner shows duckweed and microbes from a Delft canal. It was sent to the Royal Society of London with Leeuwenhoek's letter of 25 December 1702. The elongated structure in fig. 8 is the root of a duckweed plant seen under the microscope. Also clearly portrayed are rotifers, Hydra *and* Vorticella. *The drawing was engraved and published in* Philosophical Transactions *(vol. 23, p. 1291) and* Collected Letters 1939–1999 *(vol. XIV, pl. IX).*

nary book filled with pictures of fleas and lice, bees and seeds, flies, midges and mould as seen through microscopes. The book, already in its second edition, was called *Micrographia*, and it was bursting with information about the amazing sights this new instrument could reveal; its author was the young Robert Hooke (p. 99). Both men were then in their 30s.

Micrographia was the talk of the town, and so it is no surprise that it came to the notice of this visitor from the Netherlands. Also, it contained fine engravings of fabrics seen through the microscope. Leeuwenhoek would have found these compelling, as drapers regularly used lenses to magnify cloth to assess its quality. After he returned home, Leeuwenhoek must have thought about Hooke's *Micrographia* and its astonishing revelations. Eventually, he began to develop a design for a simple microscope, exactly as set out by Robert Hooke in the Preface to his book, and soon others began to take notice. The physician Reinier de Graaf wrote a letter to the Royal Society in London in 1673, reporting that: 'a certain most ingenious person here named Leeuwenhoek has devised microscopes which far surpass those which we have hitherto seen.' That was in April. In August came another missive, this time from Constantijn Huygens, who wrote in support of 'our honest citizen Leeuwenhook ... a diligent searcher'.

LEEUWENHOEK'S FIRST OBSERVATIONS

Leeuwenhoek's first microscopical investigations were of mould, a bee and a louse – all of which were featured in Hooke's *Micrographia*. By June 1674 he was cutting superbly fine sections of biological materials and sending them to London, where I rediscovered them, still in excellent condition after 308 years, in the archives of the Royal Society – testimony to his extraordinary dexterity.

In each letter Leeuwenhoek wrote to the Royal Society he took issue with Hooke's descriptions in *Micrographia*. Hooke had made observations of the appearance under the microscope of cork, elder pith and the shaft of a feather, and in response were Leeuwenhoek's own descriptions of exactly the same choice of specimens, using Hooke's design for a high-power microscope.

And then came his momentous letter of 7 September 1674. Leeuwenhoek described, in the homely and vernacular style he always used, how he had been crossing

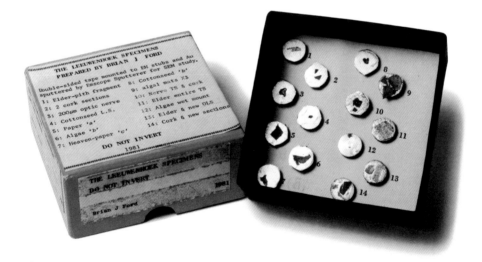

The discovery by the author of original specimens prepared by Leeuwenhoek, and dating back three centuries, is one of the landmark revelations in the history of the microscope. A small portion of each was fixed to an aluminium stub, coated with gold to render it electrically conducting, and examined by the author at Cardiff University under an electron microscope, with the agreement of the then President of the Royal Society, Sir Andrew Huxley (himself a noted microscopist).

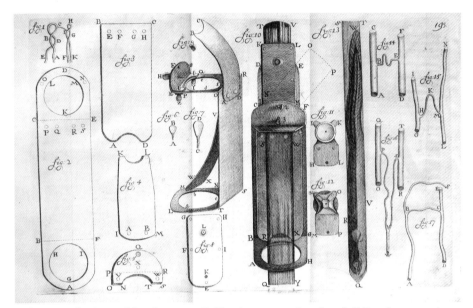

When Peter the Great of Russia came to Delft to learn more about boat-building, he arranged to meet Leeuwenhoek, who gave him one of his microscopes. This diagram (published as plate 193 in the Arcana Naturae detecta ab Antonio van Leeuwenhoek, 1695) *shows the kind of instrument that the Dutch microscopist gave the tsar, who took it back to St Petersburg with him.*

a lake named Berkelse Mere, and had paused to consider the lake water. In winter it was clear, he wrote, but as the summer drew on small white or green growths began to appear. The locals told Leeuwenhoek that they were caused by the evening dew, but he was not convinced. 'I took up a little water in a glass phial', he wrote, 'and examining it next day I found floating therein diverse earthy particles ….'

Some he said, were like a human hair, but with green spirals inside. There is no mistaking his description: this was the chlorophyte alga *Spirogyra*. This species contains its chlorophyll – vital for photosynthesis – inside spiral strips that run the length of the cells, looking like a green spring; these are the 'green spirals' about which he wrote. Some were round, he said, and others were oval; he saw some with 'two small legs near the head, and two small fins at the hindmost end of the body.' These were surely the wheel-animalcules we now call rotifers. They are tiny creatures, just visible to the naked eye, that move about propelled by circles of beating hair-like cilia, looking much like wheels, or projecting horns. 'Others,' he wrote, 'were green in the middle and white in front and behind.' You might find that description familiar – it is the green alga always popular in school books on biology, *Euglena viridis*.

During the following year, Leeuwenhoek began systematically examining samples of freshwater, and soon reported seeing small creatures with minute limbs moving ceaselessly about. They were clearly not water fleas: 'those little animals appeared to me ten thousand times smaller than those represented by M. Swammerdam and by him called water-fleas ....', which, Leeuwenhoek wrote, could be perceived by the naked eye. His organisms were too small by far for that.

He sent a full account to Henry Oldenburg, secretary of the Royal Society, on 9 October 1676, and extracts were presented at the fortnightly Society meetings throughout February 1677. A section of the letter was printed in *Philosophical Transactions* dated March 1677. Another summary of Leeuwenhoek's startling discoveries was sent to France and appeared in *Journal des sçavans* in 1678. His observations were by now being widely discussed by natural philosophers – Leeuwenhoek was observing microscopic life as nobody before had ever done, and his discoveries were set to revolutionize natural history.

THE MAKING OF THE MICROSCOPES

How could someone make a microscope at home sufficiently powerful to observe bacteria, fungi and minute algal and protozoan cells, as Leeuwenhoek did? The secret lies in the simplicity of the design. Generally, the microscopes of the mid-17th century (like those of the modern era) were tall, grand designs with separate lenses to approach the specimen and to focus the image. Lenses generate aberrations in which spurious colour, and irregular fields of focus, distort the reality of what is observed. When lenses are fitted together, they magnify the aberrations.

There is a simple way to overcome this problem – use one lens instead of several. A single tiny lens, about the size of a pin-head, can create images that are magnified hundreds of times and yet show remarkably little distortion. Leeuwenhoek used to grind a single tiny lens and fixed it in between two metal plates with apertures – the lens fitted securely between them. A system of screws attached to the plates allowed the user to move and focus the specimen. It was an ineffably simple solution to the problem, and allowed Leeuwenhoek to turn out hundreds of microscopes without any complex instrument-making. Two questions immediately arise. First, why did Leeuwenhoek not use a compound microscope, like the other

Portrait of Leeuwenhoek by Jan Verkolje, 1686; he is shown holding one of his famous microscopes.

microscopists of his day? Secondly, since Leeuwenhoek's design was clearly based on that described by Hooke in his preface to *Micrographia*, why did Hooke himself not use a simple microscope, especially if the results were so impressive? Using single lenses, Leeuwenhoek made microscopes that could magnify up to 300 times; most of the drawings in Hooke's book were enlarged only one-tenth as much.

Hooke preferred a compound microscope because it was impressive, beautifully tooled and professionally produced. In addition, his was purchased for his work at the Royal Society. Leeuwenhoek knew no instrument manufacturers and could not have afforded a microscope even if he had. He was an amateur with scarce resources yet with a burning enthusiasm to make micro-scopes. As for Hooke and the simple microscopes, the truth is that he did use them. His studies of lice and fleas were certainly made with a compound microscope, but this kind of instrument cannot resolve the fine details that Hooke includes in his magnificent engravings, which must have been observed through a simple microscope. Clearly, Hooke used his compound microscope for general views, but filled in the fine details with a simple one.

Utrecht University Museum holds this brass microscope, no bigger than a postage stamp, made by Leeuwenhoek. Unusually, the lens is blown rather than being ground.

It was Leeuwenhoek's determination, stubbornness and single-minded enthusi-asm that drove him to use a simple microscope for the fifty years of his career in microbiology. Hooke had given up after just a few years, mainly because hand-held simple microscopes were difficult to use. Such a practical difficulty was no obstacle to Leeuwenhoek.

DESCRIBING MICROSCOPICAL NATURE

Leeuwenhoek's descriptions are vivid and natural. In the middle of September 1675, he sat with his microscope in hand and with a tiny glass tube held in position with a small blob of wax. He wrote with a quill pen, stopping and starting as his observations progressed, eagerly watching everything that went on inside this diminutive micro-bial universe.

> *They sometimes stuck out two little horns, which were continually moved in the manner of a horse's ears. The part between these little horns was flat, their body otherwise being rounded, save only that it ran to a point at the rear end; at which pointed end it had a tail, nearly four times as long as the whole body, and looking as thick, when viewed with my microscope, as a*

spider's web. At the end of this tail there was a pellet, of the same size as one of the globules within the body, and I could not perceive this tail to be used by them in the open water. ... I have seen several hundred little creatures, caught fast by one another in a few filaments, lying within the compass of a grain of coarse sand.

It would be difficult to misunderstand such clear descriptions, or to fail to be enraptured by the sheer sense of excitement and determined enthusiasm that drove his meticulous investigations of the microscopical communities that met his astonished eyes. Leeuwenhoek was breaking new ground, and knew it; by 1686 he felt he was of sufficient distinction to acquire a 'van' in his name, and was known as Antony van Leeuwenhoek thereafter. Royalty were aware of him, statesmen came to visit him; he was elected to the Royal Society.

BREADTH OF ENDEAVOUR

During his incomparably productive life Leeuwenhoek turned his microscope on virtually everything he could find. However, it was his extensive studies of living micro-organisms that underpin his reputation. His descriptions are clear, and properly balanced by a capacity for self-criticism and objectivity. He has always had his detractors, however. A generation ago, students were being taught that Leeuwenhoek could not possibly have observed what he claimed, and he has frequently been regarded as a dilettante who imagined much of what he wrote. So is it possible to see the diminutive organisms that Leeuwenhoek claimed to observe? Using modern replica microscopes with a single lens and also with the Leeuwenhoek microscopes that still survive, including the original microscope preserved at the Museum of the History of Science at Utrecht University, experiments by the author have shown that single lens microscopes can indeed resolve the algae and protozoa Leeuwenhoek described, and can even reveal living bacteria. A study of blood revealed the erythrocytes (red cells) with clarity, and even the lobed nucleus within a leucocyte (white cell).

Although he did not begin his career in microscopy until he was already 40, Leeuwenhoek went on to give half a century to unremitting research and made a host of crucial revelations. When he lay dying, aged 90, he was still engaged in microscopy, examining gold-bearing sands for clients in the East India Company. The respiratory condition he suffered at the end of his life was so well described that it still bears the name Leeuwenhoek's Syndrome. Nobody could have imagined that so much insight would be triggered by a chance observation of cloudy lake-water ... not even Antony van Leeuwenhoek himself.

Sir Hans Sloane

THE GREAT COLLECTOR

(1660–1753)

*I cannot again but admire your industry in collecting so great
a number of species in so short a time, and not only collecting,
but so exactly observing and describing them.*

John Ray in a letter to Hans Sloane, 28 February 1693

IN HIS 93 YEARS, the noted physician, scientist and collector Sir Hans Sloane amassed one of the greatest assemblages of plants, animals, antiquities and coins, and many other objects, of his time. It was to be the founding core of the British Museum and later the Natural History Museum in London.

Born in Killyleagh, Northern Ireland, in 1660. Sloane was the son of an agent to the local land owner. A keen observer of nature from his childhood, he later recalled how he had 'from my Youth been very much pleas'd with the study of Plants and other Parts of Nature'. He noted, for instance the local habit of chewing dulse (a seaweed) as a cure for scurvy, a disease caused by vitamin deficiency. In 1679 Sloane moved to London to study chemistry at the Apothecaries Hall and to pursue his favourite interest – botany – in the Physic Garden at Chelsea. He was soon to befriend some of the most influential natural scientists of the day, including the celebrated 'English Aristotle', John Ray, and Robert Boyle, the great physicist, chemist and inventor.

Like many young men at this period, Sloane left England to study and gain experience abroad, moving to France in 1683. On his travels he studied anatomy, medicine and botany, and met some of the great contemporary botanists and physicians, such as Monsignor Magnol, after whom *Magnolia* is named. Sloane was inspired by the passion of these leading scientists to discover, describe and name new plants and animals, and on his return to England in 1684 he was able to put this enthusiasm to good use.

In 1687 Sloane was appointed as physician to the Duke of Albermarle, the new Governor of Jamaica, and sailed for the West Indies armed with lists of specimens to collect for his fellow natural historians Martin Lister and John Ray. He wasted no time in gathering information; on the three-month sea voyage he made observations of the natural phenomena and wildlife that he encountered, and the entire voyage was to establish him as both a collector and accurate describer of the natural world. During his 15-month stay in Jamaica natural science was his major preoccupation and he made

1184. An occidentall Bezoar brought from Mexico & given
L 183. to me by Mr Gruntzman. Lapis Bezoar Germandelbr

1185. A fossil elephants tooth given by the Governors lady of
Siberia to Mr Bell a surgeon & curious traveller
there. Mammotovoi Kost. Henr. Wild. Ludolf. gramm
Ruff. p. 92. where wee are told that they are Elephants teeth the wh[i]ch of the delugo. Some of the
Ruffians beleive it to be the teeth of the largest anim
=al of the earth yt it lives underground. Mamanto A strange fort
of bone like ivory found near Jenisitzka & Mangasca of
Lange travels to China. State of Ruff. vol. 2. p. 15. a fort
of horne foffild Behemoth. Job. cap. 40. found in the holes
occafioned by the fall of the earth & banks of the river the
Horns jawbones & ribs of it have fometimes fresh blood &
flesh striking to them. a whole skeleton to be gathered
Mamant of Muller. Jofer. Oghacks. State of Ruff. p. 90. vol.
2. Obur fossils thought to be, by some, others an animal
living upon mud in the moraffes, when they come to faid in
wch they lye it rowles so fast upon them that they cannot turn
being unwieldy but perish faid by some to have seen the animal
in Boreafowa. find molar teeth of 20. or 24. th weight.
Elephants teeth of Mr Le brun on the river Don twelve
verfts from Veronitz p. 411. So by the Czar to come from
Elephants brought by Alexander the great when he
paffed the Tanais to Kostinza. An unknown fort of huge
bones dugg out of the earth in Siberia of which they turn snuff
boxes. State of Ruff. p. 12. part 1.

213 e 1186. Officula auris vitulini.
1187. Metatarfus of some quadruped?
213 e 1188. The dens molaris of some very large quadruped
22 y fossil. an. 129.? from Markham
229

1189. A tophus faid to come from a fwine in Amboina
220 d weighs Ʒ4. Ʒiij. from Dr Kempfer.

OPPOSITE: *A hand-written page of Hans Sloane's Catalogue of Fossils, Vol. 5.*
ABOVE: *(Top) A dried and pressed specimen of cocoa* (Theobroma cacao), *collected in Jamaica by Sloane, accompanied by illustrations by Everhard Kickius and the Reverend Garrett Moore. Moore was a local artist in Jamaica and made the initial sketches, which were completed and supplemented by Kickius on Sloane's return to London. (Below) Sloane's herbarium pages of 'wild ginger', now known as* Renealmia antillarum. *As with cocoa, Sloane observed and noted how the locals used the plant. The herbarium of specimens collected by Sloane amount to 365 large volumes, which are still consulted today.*

A
VOYAGE
To the Islands
Madera, Barbados, Nieves, S. Christophers
AND
JAMAICA,
WITH THE
Natural History
OF THE
Herbs and Trees, Four-footed Beasts, Fishes,
Birds, Insects, Reptiles, &c.
Of the last of those ISLANDS;

To which is prefix'd An
INTRODUCTION,
Wherein is an Account of the
Inhabitants, Air, Waters, Diseases, Trade, &c
of that Place, with some Relations concerning the Neighbouring Continent, and Islands of America.

ILLUSTRATED WITH
The FIGURES of the Things describ'd,
which have not been heretofore engraved;
In large Copper-plates as big as the Life.

By HANS SLOANE, M.D.
Fellow of the College of Physicians and Secretary
of the Royal-Society.

In Two Volumes.   Vol. I.

Many shall run to and fro, and Knowledge shall be increased. Dan. xii. 4.

LONDON:
Printed by B. M. for the Author, 1707.

The title-page of Hans Sloane's Natural History of Jamaica *volume 1, published in 1707. In his 15-month stay in Jamaica Sloane amassed information and made collections on many aspects of the island, from natural history to indigenous culture.*

extensive notes and collections on many aspects of nature, from fauna and flora, to climate and indigenous culture. His major work based on this voyage did not appear in print until 1707, with a second volume appearing in 1725. Commonly known as *Natural History of Jamaica*, it contains accurate and highly readable descriptions of the plants and animals Sloane encountered, as well as accounts of how the island's natural resources were used by its inhabitants. Sloane did not restrict his observations to the physical attributes of the animals and plants, but he also describes their behaviour and distribution. For instance, he wrote of one species of ant: 'This is of a dark brown Colour, very small, and hath two very long Antenna. They devour every thing; I attempted to preserve the Skins and Feathers of Humming Birds, and was oblig'd, to keep them from these Ants by hanging them at the End of a String from a Pully fasten'd in the Cieling and yet they would find their Way by the Cieling to come at and destroy them.'

As he makes clear in this quote, preserving specimens in the hot and humid Jamaican climate was extremely difficult, and Sloane was careful to provide a good pictorial record, recognizing that many specimens would lose their colour or completely decompose before they could be returned to England. He employed a local illustrator, the Reverend Garret Moore, to make initial drawings, and a Dutch artist, Everhard Kickius, to work on them later.

Back in London, Sloane continued in the service of the Duchess of Albermarle before setting up practice in Bloomsbury in 1695, establishing himself as a successful society physician. He had been made a Fellow of the prestigious Royal Society in 1685, and in 1727 was to succeed the great Sir Isaac Newton as its President. In parallel with his medical work, Sloane was also developing a reputation as a highly competent scientist and collector, joining an informal group of Royal Society Fellows and others with an interest in botany – the Temple Coffee House Botanical Club. Here he swapped descriptions and specimens of new plant species with regular attendees such as the Bishop of London and the Queen's Botanist, Leonard Plukenet. Plukenet was a difficult character, often publicly and crudely critical of his fellows, and Sloane frequently found himself at odds with him. Sloane distrusted Plukenet's identifications and there were suspicions that Plukenet was not above describing a known plant as a new species. In contrast, Sloane's descriptions were competent, and his attitude

An illustration of birds from Sloane's Natural History of Jamaica. *The smallest is probably the Jamaican tody* (Todus todus), *which Sloane called the 'green sparrow' or 'green hummingbird' and described as 'one of the most beautiful small birds I saw'.*

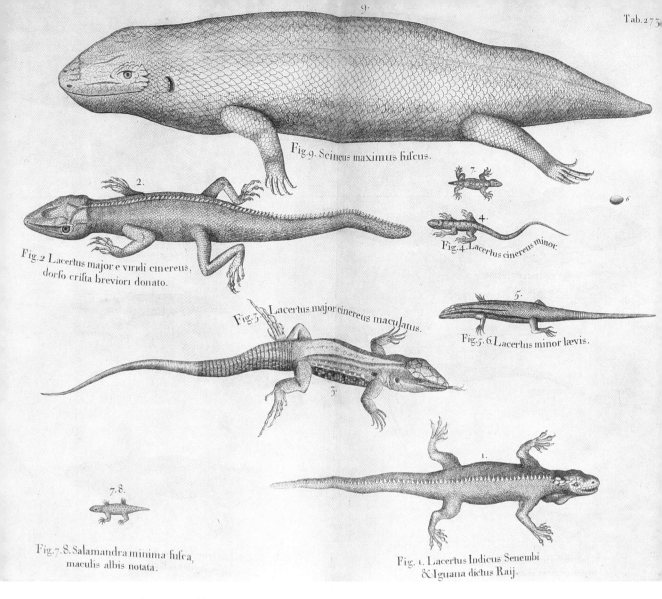

An illustration of lizards from Sloane's Natural History of Jamaica. *The largest is the Giant Galliwasp* (Celestus occiduus), *believed to be extinct since the 19th century.*

towards naming new species was both advanced and free from the egotistical competitiveness of his contemporaries. He would readily accept that plants he had thought to be new might, on comparison, be the same as plants already described by other botanists. The exactness of his descriptions of plants make them useful to this day.

Unlike many of his contemporaries, Sloane also tended to avoid empty theorizing about the 'hows' and 'whys' of the natural world, preferring instead to describe and classify. As he wrote 'Knowledge of Natural history, being Observations of matters of Fact is more certain than most Bothers, and in my Opinion, less subjected to Mistakes than Reasonings, Hypotheses and Deductions are.' However, he was struck by the similarity between living plants and animals that he had encountered in Jamaica and fossils found in Britain and surmised that the geography and climate of Britain had changed in the past, remarking that this was 'pretty strange'.

Sloane was to become a wealthy and influential man, partly through marriage but also through his success as a physician and promoter of new remedies. Always shrewd, he was not averse to capitalizing on his observations, and having tasted a native concoction of cocoa in Jamaica he adapted this as a remedy 'For its Lightness on the Stomach and its great Use in all Consumptive Cases'. He found the native drink 'oily and nauseous', but discovered that a pleasant and marketable product could be made by boiling it with milk and sugar – and so was born drinking chocolate.

As Sloane's collections grew rapidly through the purchase of other collections, exchanges with his friends and correspondents, and bequests, they filled a large part of his house and he was obliged to employ a full-time curator and assistants to manage them. The collections were a microcosm of the known living world, with North America, southern Africa and Japan among the regions represented by specimens. They became a valuable resource for future natural historians and the great Swedish natural historian Carl Linnaeus (p. 133) was later to describe and name many new species of plants on the basis of specimens or drawings in Sloane's 'museum'.

At his death in 1753 Sloane's will made provision that his curios: '… may remain together and not be separated and that chiefly in and about the city of London, where I have acquired most of my estates and where they may by the great confluence of people be most used.' His collections were offered to the British nation for £20,000, a large sum in those days, but probably much less than their real worth. Money was raised by a lottery and Sloane's collections thus formed the basis of the British Museum at Bloomsbury, as well as its later offspring, the Natural History Museum at South Kensington.

It is mainly Sloane's botanical collections that have survived intact to this day, although there are also significant ones of insects, shells and other objects. His 365 book-like volumes of dried plant specimens remain an important part of the collections of the Natural History Museum, and are still regularly consulted by scientists and historians alike.

Skull of the rhinoceros hornbill (Buceros rhinoceros), *just one item from among the huge collections amassed by Hans Sloane which ultimately formed the basis of the Natural History Museum in London.*

Maria Sibylla Merian

THE METAMORPHOSIS OF INSECTS

(1647–1717)

It has occurred repeatedly that the most beautiful and most
peculiar caterpillars transformed themselves into the
simplest animals and the most simple caterpillars
into the most beautiful ... butterflies.

Maria Sibylla Merian, Metamorphosis, 1705

IN MODERN TERMS, Maria Sibylla Merian may be best characterized as an amalgam of natural history illustrator, naturalist and, to a certain extent, entrepreneur. She left behind an extensive painted record of plants and animals, notably insects, along with some specimens, now mostly lost, and a few texts, descriptions and letters. Merian's life and work have attracted considerable attention for three reasons: first, because she was a female natural history illustrator and naturalist, thereby intruding into a traditionally male-dominated sphere; secondly she developed a lasting interest in metamorphosis, in particular in butterflies and other insects, making her an early entomologist; and thirdly, by spending several months in Surinam she became a pioneer student of tropical fauna and flora.

Merian's life was unconventional. She was born 2 April 1647 in Frankfurt am Main, the daughter of the well-known engraver and publisher Matthäus Merian the Elder, but he died when she was three. Her mother remarried, and Merian's step-father, Jacob Marrell, a pupil of the artist Georg Flegel and painter of flower pieces and still lifes, became her principal mentor, promoter and supporter. Aged 18, Merian married Johann Andreas Graff, a painter of architectural scenes, and later gave birth to two daughters, Johanna Helena and Dorothea Maria. The family moved to Nuremberg, where Merian's first work was published, but later returned to her mother in Frankfurt. Following marital discord and separation in 1685, the four ladies joined a dissenter group and moved to castle Waltha near Leeuwarden in the Dutch Republic, where they lived in a pietistic, monastic community.

It seems Merian was obsessed from an early age by the diversity of insect life, with a focus on metamorphosis. She is known to have experimented with silkworms at the age of 13 – no doubt fascinated by the astonishing transformation of the caterpillars to masses of silk and then into moths – and had learnt in her step-father's

Painting by Merian of flowers in a Chinese vase with butterflies, a beetle and a fly; watercolour on vellum, c. *1680.*

This painting by Merian of two butterflies from Surinam (watercolour and gouache on vellum, painted before 1706) is almost certainly the model used by her to illustrate the two butterflies in plate 2 of Metamorphosis, *shown on page 122.*

studio in Frankfurt the art of drawing and painting, the preparation of pigments – in which she is known to have traded later – the engraving of copper plates and the printing process. At the age of 32, in 1679, she published *Der Raupen Wunderbare Verwandlung* ('The Miraculous Transformation of Caterpillars') in Nuremberg. Two more instalments followed, in 1683 and, posthumously, in 1717. Merian showed a special interest in the food plants of caterpillars, conjecturing the special requirements of some. She was sent insect larvae by correspondents and followed their subsequent development, keeping and feeding them in small boxes, while describing their different stages in detail and illustrating them. Plant diversity was another of her favourite topics, and she portrayed a long procession of garden plants. Her first printed work, *Florum Fasciculus Primus*, published in Nuremberg in 1675 and consisting mostly of adaptations from the natural history painter Nicolas Robert, was intended to provide models for embroidery and, with two later fascicles, contained a total of 36 copper engravings.

By now divorced from her husband, Merian, who never remarried, took up residence in 1691 in Amsterdam, and entered the circle of naturalists based there, among them Caspar Commelin and Antony van Leeuwenhoek (p. 104). In 1699, together with Dorothea Maria, she then made an intrepid journey to the Dutch colony of Surinam in South America, where they spent 21 months in a religious community near what is now Paramaribo, observing and recording tropical fauna and flora, mainly butterflies. Sick with malaria, Merian was forced to return to Amsterdam, where she is reported to have exhibited her trophies in the town hall, and continued her work as a natural history illustrator. She depicted a broad spectrum of natural history objects, published in G. E. Rumphius's posthumous *D'Amboinsche Rariteitkamer* ('The Ambonese Curiosity Cabinet'), which came out in Amsterdam in 1705. In the same year her famous *Metamorphosis Insectorum Surinamensium* appeared, comprising 60 coloured engravings, in a Dutch and Latin version. For this magnificent work, Merian prepared portraits of tropical plants together with a profusion of insects, spiders and other animals, recorded during her stay in Surinam, which she combined into individual plates. In accordance with the tradition of her time, the scale of magnification of the elements within individual plates varies greatly. Both the images and Merian's texts are a mine of information, and among the many later scientists to consult and refer to this work was Carl Linnaeus (p. 133).

However, because of the limited commercial success of this project, the declining quality of her later works and a stroke, which confined her to a wheelchair,

Provence Rose; watercolour on paper by Merian, 1675. It is inscribed by her 'Deß Menschen Leben ist gleich einer Blum' ('Man's life is like a bloom'). This work comes from an album formerly belonging to Professor E. C. Arnold in Nuremberg.

Plate 2 from Metamorphosis Insectorum Surinamensium, *published in Amsterdam in 1705:*
this coloured engraving shows a pineapple, two butterflies (see page 120) and other insects.

Merian lived her final years in poverty and died, aged 69, on 13 January 1717 in Amsterdam. On the day of her death, a very substantial part of her painted work was bought by an agent of the Russian tsar Peter the Great for 3,000 Dutch guilders.

Merian's work includes flower pieces and still lives, but interpretation and accurate attribution are often difficult – she signed only some of her works, almost never dated them and produced copies; on the other hand, many anonymous illustrations attributed to her may not be from her hand. In addition, Merian's natural history drawings – mostly gouache on vellum, rarely watercolour on paper – are now widely scattered. The Russian Academy of Sciences, St Petersburg, and the Royal Library, Windsor, hold major collections. While she lived, only a selection of her work was published in small editions as copper engravings, forming, together with her descriptions, three illustrated books now exceedingly rare and much sought after on the art market. Of these only very few were coloured by her. Later editions of inferior quality published after her death blur the picture.

This coloured engraving, plate 56 from Merian's Metamorphosis, *shows a water hyacinth and the metamorphosis of a frog and an aquatic bug. The scale of magnification of the different elements varies greatly, as was the custom at this time.*

Much less well known are Merian's activities as an entrepreneur. She collected and traded in insects, of which a few specimens may survive in Karlsruhe, and brought back insects, spiders, crocodiles, snakes and turtles from Surinam intended for natural history cabinets. She was also her own publisher for *Metamorphosis*.

As a person Maria Sibylla Merian remains elusive; her descriptions and letters deal primarily with technical and financial matters and offer limited insight into her personality. The subject of an extensive feminist literature, she was no doubt a woman of exceptional qualities, a keen observer and a highly productive natural history illustrator, combining accurate scientific documentation with a tendency to ornamental improvement. Her magnum opus, the *Metamorphosis*, is rightly regarded as a milestone in the history of entomology.

Mark Catesby

COLONIAL NATURALIST AND ARTIST

(1683-1749)

*As I was not bred a Painter I hope some faults in Perspective
and other Niceties, may be more readily excused, for I humbly
conceive Plants, and other things done in a Flat, tho' exact
manner, may serve the Purpose of Natural History, better in
some Measure than in a more bold and Painter like way ... and
where it would admit of, I have adapted the Birds to those Plants
on which they fed, or have any relation to.*

M. *Catesby,* **Natural History of Carolina, Florida and the Bahama Islands,** *1732–43*

A N INHERENT PASSION FOR NATURAL HISTORY combined with strong self-motivation led Mark Catesby to become one of the most influential naturalists of the early 18th century. His most famous work, the two-volume *Natural History of Carolina, Florida and the Bahama Islands* (1732–43), remained the most authoritative work on American natural history, particularly birdlife, for over 100 years after its publication, and Catesby is often described as 'the founder of American ornithology'.

Catesby was much more than a botanist, ornithologist or natural historian, however, and his works covered a much broader arena. He studied the relationships and associations between the organisms he observed in the field, and also made observations and formed hypotheses on the origins of the native people he met on his travels. It could therefore be said that Catesby was also an ecologist and anthropologist. In addition, he had a passionate interest in the development of plants of potential horticultural and economic importance, particularly those which he believed might be transported from their native range in North America and cultivated back in England.

Mark Catesby was born in Castle Hedingham, Essex, southern England in 1683, but early on in his life the family moved to Sudbury, where his father was to become mayor for a time. Catesby's uncle, Nicholas Jekyll, was a local historian and friend of the famous botanist John Ray (p. 92). Another of his uncle's friends was the botanist Samuel Dale, who lived close by, and it was Catesby's meeting with Dale that was

Liquidambar styraciflua, *otherwise known as the sweetgum tree, a commonly grown ornamental tree today and a species possibly introduced to Britain by Catesby. Here he depicted it in association with the green lizard of Carolina.*

T. 65.

Lacertus

Shrax acerie folio

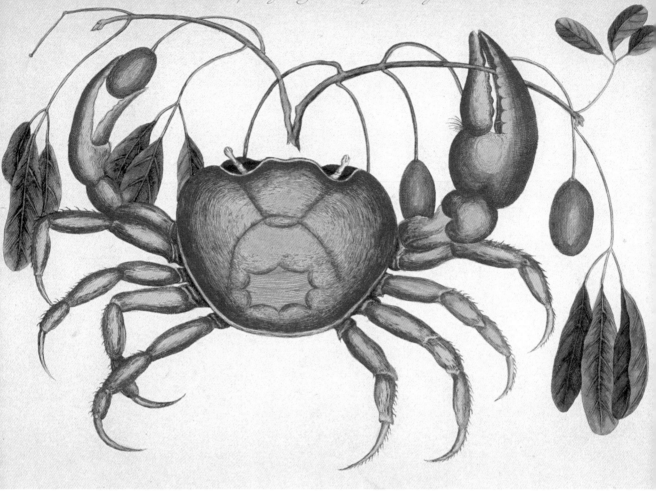

Land crab, from the second volume of Catesby's work, holding part of a Tapia *tree in its claws. Catesby said of this tree: 'Of these fruits amongst many others, these crabs feed'.*

perhaps to have the greatest influence on his development as a natural historian. Through Dale, Catesby gained access to the new intelligentsia of British natural history, who were ultimately to support his burgeoning career.

TRAVELS IN THE AMERICAS

Catesby's first opportunity to realize his ambitions in natural history came in 1712, when he left England for America to visit his sister, who had married and settled in Virginia. He was to remain in the Americas until 1719, and during this time collected many botanical specimens, which he sent back to his uncle Nicholas Jekyll, and to Dale. Significantly, Catesby also sent plants to Thomas Fairchild, a London nursery-man with whom he had earlier studied horticulture. On this first expedition to America Catesby also visited Jamaica, most likely inspired by the work of Sir Hans

Sloane (p. 111) as published in his *Natural History of Jamaica*. While Catesby himself described his time in the colonies as unproductive, these first seven years collecting and observing nature were in fact the perfect apprenticeship for more intensive study, something that did not go unacknowledged by his mentors in England.

In the early 18th century, the American colonies were a new and exciting source of scientific information for academics in England. Prior to Catesby, the foremost published work relating to the natural history of the colonies was John Lawson's *A New Voyage to Carolina* (1709). Under the patronage of James Petiver, an apothecary and botanist, and acquaintance of Sir Hans Sloane, Lawson then undertook a further, more comprehensive study of the natural history of southeast America, but was unfortunately killed in 1711. This tragedy was followed in 1718 by the death of Petiver, at which point William Sherard became the leading advocate of the exploration of the American colonies. Sherard, a former British consul at Smyrna and fellow of the Royal

The ivory- (or white-) billed woodpecker, which was sadly later to become extinct in North America, although one was reportedly sighted in the wild in Arkansas in 2005. Here the bird is shown in association with the willow oak, Quercus phellos.

Society, later founded the Chair of Botany at Oxford University; he was a patron of several naturalists and was a man of influence. Samuel Dale, intimately involved in Catesby's first voyage to the area, now introduced the young naturalist to Sherard, who immediately saw him as the ideal replacement for Lawson and elicited patronage for a second journey to America. Amongst Catesby's supporters for this new expedition were the then Governor of South Carolina as well as Sir Hans Sloane, Charles Dubois of the East India Company, and Sherard himself.

After a difficult three-month sea voyage, Catesby arrived once again in America on 23 May 1722. On this occasion he ventured further than the by-now relatively well-known state of Virginia, to the Carolinas, which were at that time little explored. Catesby was an industrious and skilled fieldworker, often working alone for many

The red-winged starling; Catesby said of this bird, in conjunction with the purple-daw, with which it is often seen, that 'They seem combined to do all the mischief they are able'.

days at a time. He undertook numerous journeys, often to remote areas, and endeavoured to visit the same locations at different times of year in order to observe the full range of natural history found there. As on his first expedition to America, he rewarded his patrons' support with specimens he collected on his field excursions, and many of these can still be seen today in the collections of the Sherardian Herbarium in Oxford, and the Sloane and Dale herbaria in the Natural History Museum, London. Catesby's botanical collections also survive in the form of many of the illustrations in *Hortus Elthamensis* (1732), Johann Jakob Dillenius's important pre-Linnaean work. William Sherard's brother, James, lived at the time at Eltham, southeast of London, and Dillenius was employed to describe and illustrate the plants growing in his garden, many of them cultivated from seeds sent to Sherard by Catesby.

Samples of living plants were also sent to various nurserymen in England, including Fairchild once more. This interest in the horticultural potential of plants found in the Americas was to continue throughout Catesby's life. Many plants commonly grown in England today as ornamental species may well owe their introduction to Catesby, including the Indian bean tree, *Catalpa bignonioides*, and the sweetgum, *Liquidambar styraciflua*.

PROBLEMS OF PUBLICATION

The patronage of Sherard and others provided Catesby with connections to the leading men of natural history of the day, and these were to prove invaluable on his return to England when he set about publishing his seminal work. Despite earlier pressure from Sloane, Catesby insisted on retaining his own sketches and artwork made while in the colonies. He had a clear vision of the work he wished to produce, all he lacked was the funds. He proposed to publish his work in 10 fascicles, each containing 20 plates, the revenue from the sale of one fascicle helping to facilitate the production of the next. Even this practical plan would have proved beyond the means of Catesby, however. Fortunately, he was able to gain the support of Peter Collinson, a wealthy draper and patron of natural history, who also helped finance John Bartram, father of William (p. 165). Collinson made several interest-free loans to Catesby to help finance production of his book. In addition, Catesby also partly financed himself by working at several leading nurseries in London, and had friends in the Americas continue to send him material for potential commercial cultivation.

There were still other problems to overcome, including the fundamental one of how to produce the plates for the work. As pragmatic as ever, Catesby formulated a novel plan – he undertook to learn how to make the engravings himself, a painstaking and difficult process. Catesby's engravings in his *Natural History of Carolina, Florida and the Bahama Islands* were notable for several reasons. Rather than adopting the traditional method of cross-hatching, Catesby instead followed the natural lines of feathers in his bird paintings, for example, a laborious method but one that produced a more natural look. Another innovation was to depict his birds in association with the plants upon which they fed or where they nested or were otherwise seen. This approach was pioneering in ornithological illustration, and in most cases both the associations and depictions of the birds themselves are accurate. It is perhaps for this reason that although Catesby was a botanist, his

The fieldfare of Carolina, depicted by Catesby as dead, and in association with the snakeroot plant of Virginia, Aristolochia *sp., supposedly a remedy for snakebite, an assertion which Catesby doubted – this image was perhaps intended to make such a point to his peers.*

most famous book became celebrated for its paintings of birds. The first volume was completed in 1732 and presented to the Royal Society in the same year (despite bearing a publication date of a year earlier). Catesby was then proposed, and elected, a Fellow of the Royal Society. For the following decade Catesby continued work on his book while also undertaking some artistic duties for the Society, and the second volume was finally completed in 1743. It was to be a work of enduring quality and wide appeal, with two further editions produced – the third in 1771. Its success was in no small part due to the beauty of the illustrations. Although Catesby's botanical paintings were largely cited by Linnaeus (p. 133) only as secondary references, the great botanist took many of his names for birds directly from Catesby's work.

Rightly famous for his achievements in ornithological illustration, Catesby's role in the dissemination of knowledge of natural history through his membership of the Royal Society should also be recognized. In addition to his artistic work for the Society he also took part in many meetings, reading out letters from friends and fellow botanists. Catesby's other notable contributions to scientific knowledge include his essay entitled 'On the passage of birds' (1747), in which he was the first to describe details relating to bird migration. Although in some aspects Catesby revealed the naivety common at the time with regard to this phenomenon, he was also in advance of many more famous contemporaries in his understanding, and this is not the only area where Catesby's thinking was ahead of his time. When first visiting the American colonies he observed similarities between the facial features of native people there and people of Asiatic origin. On the basis of this he hypothesized that there must have been an ancient land bridge between Alaska and Asia, something we accept is true today, but which could not possibly have been known in Catesby's time. Even after his death in 1749, Catesby continued to influence horticulture, largely through the posthumous publication of his only purely botanical work, *Hortus Britanno-Americanus*, published in 1767 and dedicated to useful and ornamental American plants.

Not only was Catesby an outstanding observer and recorder of natural history and a tireless fieldworker, his studies also prepared the way for many later, perhaps more famous natural historians.

The American bison, of which Catesby declared that, whilst he had already described this animal in the first volume of his work, he had but then only an inadequate sketch, whereas now he was able to 'exhibit a perfect likeness of this awful creature'.

Carl Linnaeus

THE MAN WHO BROUGHT ORDER TO NATURE

(1707–1778)

God created – Linnaeus arranged.

Carl Linnaeus

CARL LINNAEUS (OR CARL VON LINNÉ) was a Swedish doctor and naturalist whose belief that God had ordained him to bring order to nature inspired him to develop a straightforward system of classification that could be applied to all living things. In particular, his binomial system of nomenclature, consisting of genus and species, provided scientists with a tool for identification that was simple to use, easy to remember, and could be universally applied and understood. It is perhaps hard to comprehend now why such a seemingly simple system could have such far-reaching consequences, but it should be remembered that at this time there was no one single, accepted system in use; rather there were several different ones across Europe. Furthermore, Linnaeus's famous sexual system for the classification of plants, based on his detailed knowledge of their anatomy, manifested his rather earthy sense of humour and showed that he was not just a dry academic scientist but a man of the world.

Linnaeus was born into a pious religious family in the town of Råshult in rural Småland, Sweden. His father, a minister, had created a large garden in the parsonage, where he introduced his son Carl to botany. Linnaeus was obsessed with different organisms, especially plants, and so decided on a career in natural history, despite his parents' wishes that he would follow his father into the Church. In 1727 he went to the University of Lund to study medicine. In the following year he moved to Uppsala, which had both a much greater reputation for medicine and a botanical garden containing many native as well as various rare foreign plants. He studied under, and enjoyed the patronage of, the botanists Olof Rudbeck the Younger and Olof Celsius, both of whom shared in equal measure Linnaeus's passion for plants.

Linnaeus was able to maintain himself sufficiently, if modestly, through his position as curator of the university's botanic garden and by giving private lessons. In

Linnaeus cited the illustrations by Mark Catesby (p. 124) as secondary references in his naming of some plants. This is Catesby's painting of a magnolia, which Linnaeus named Magnolia virginiana var. acuminata, *now known simply as* Magnolia acuminata.

An 18th-century portrait of Linnaeus, dressed in the local costume of Lapland (Saamiland), after his visit there in 1732, and holding a shaman's drum.

this way he continued his researches, and in 1730, incorporating his practical familiarity with the numerous existing systems of botanical classification, particularly those of Joseph Pitton de Tournefort, the 17th-century French botanist, and John Ray (p. 92), Linnaeus wrote an essay on his proposed new classification method based upon his theory of plant sexuality. He later developed these ideas in published form – with such momentous consequences.

In 1732 the Uppsala Science Society provided funds for Linnaeus to travel to Lapland (now known as Saamiland), where he made numerous drawings and observations that led him to an appreciation of the immense value of local floras. In 1734 he travelled around the Dalarna region of central Sweden. A year later he set off again, travelling to the University of Harderwijk, in the Netherlands, where he intended to stay for a week to defend his doctoral thesis on the symptoms and treatment of 'ague'. In fact he spent the next three years there, as well as visiting other European countries and corresponding with leading botanists of the day. In the 1730s the Netherlands was the major educational and publishing centre of Europe, and several of the universities were home to academics of great erudition. Linnaeus enjoyed the patronage of the physician Hermann Boerhaave and the botanist J. F. Gronovius at Leiden, and with their help he turned his manuscripts into an impressive series of books. In 1735, shortly after his arrival, Linnaeus published *Systema Naturae,* the first of a number of publications in which he presented his new taxonomic arrangement of nature, introducing his binomial nomenclature and the sexual system for classifying plants. This provoked a ferocious reaction: Johann Georg Siegesbeck, a botanist in St Petersburg, was outraged, on both theological and moral grounds – a view that was shared by the English naturalist William Good-enough, who was appalled by Linnaeus's 'disgusting names, his nomenclatural wantonness, vulgar lasciviousness, and the gross prurience of his mind'.

Linnaeus returned to Sweden in 1738 as an established and accomplished biologist, and married Sara Elisabeth Moraea, whose income provided financial support for Linnaeus. He became physician to the Admiralty in 1739 and a leading figure in the formation of the Swedish Academy of Science. In 1742 he was appointed professor of practical medicine at Uppsala, a position he later exchanged for the chair of botany, dietetics and *materia medica*. He remained in this position for the rest of his life, an arrangement that allowed him to pursue his botanical interests and his concern with classification.

LINNAEUS'S KEY WORK

In 1751 Linnaeus published *Philosophia Botanica*, a revised version of his *Fundamenta Botanica* (1736), in which he established the principles underlying his binomial nomenclature, defining the terms used and setting out his methods. Linnaeus believed that a natural system of classification could be derived from God's original, immutable creation, one that would place plants in their true relation to each other, rather than one based on medicinal properties or superficial human perceptions. But this would only be possible if all the species of plants on the Earth were known. Until this complete state of knowledge could be achieved, Linnaeus put forward his artificial system, based on a few specific characters that could be easily recognized and compared in any organism. For plants, in particular, Linnaeus's taxonomic scheme was extremely simple, consisting of counting the number of stamens (male organs) to determine the class, and the number of pistils (female organs) to determine the order. This system provided an easy, practical and usable tool for sorting and identifying plants that even amateurs could use with ease, stimulating a general interest in botany (and inspiring Erasmus Darwin [p. 159] to write his long poem *The Botanic Garden*).

It was two years later, in 1753, that Linnaeus published *Species Plantarum*, in which he set out his system of nomenclature for naming plants. At the core of Linnaeus's method was the binomial, or 'two names': the genus and the species. This was intended to replace the polynomial, in which an extensive name consisted of a string of descriptive terms for each species. Linnaeus's system was one by which all living things could be classified and distinguished using just two basic Latin names; they were easily memorable and universally applicable. Linnaeus was not in fact the first to suggest such a system, and in this, as in other aspects of his work, he was building on the theories of others. Gaspard Bauhin, a Swiss botanist and anatomist, had proposed the concept of the binomial convention in his seminal work *Pinax Theatri Botanici*, as early as 1623. The use of Latin, the scientific language of the time, replaced the use of names in the individual languages of each country, so that botanists could now be certain that they were all talking about the same plant. At first, Linnaeus regarded the second part of his binomial nomenclature as the *nomina trivialia*, or trivial name, for a species, but he was quick to see the advantages of a label that could be attached once and for all and need not be altered in the light of further discoveries of new species. Current naming schemes still use Linnaeus's binomial nomenclature (the genus beginning with an upper case letter, the species with a lower case), but classify species on the basis of their systematic relationships, as determined from characters examined using DNA, biochemistry and morphology – techniques that were not available to Linnaeus.

In short, a genus is a group of plants (or animals) sharing a unique set of common characteristics and which have the same first name, no more and no less. As an example, *Solanum* is a Latin word for a genus of plants which includes trees, shrubs and herbaceous plants such as the familiar potato – in fact there are 1,400 species in this genus. The second word in the binomial is the specific epithet, denoting the species, and this is what sets one plant apart from others within the same genus. Specific epithets may indicate many things, from geographical origin (e.g. *japonica*, 'Japanese') to a distinguishing characteristic of colour (e.g. *alba*, 'white'), structure or habit, or might be chosen to honour a particular person, or have no particular meaning at all. For instance, as already noted, the humble potato is a member of the genus *Solanum*; its specific epithet, or species name, is *tuberosum*, which means bearing underground tubers. Another well-known *Solanum* is the tomato, or *Solanum lycopersicum* – its specific epithet literally means 'wolf-peach'.

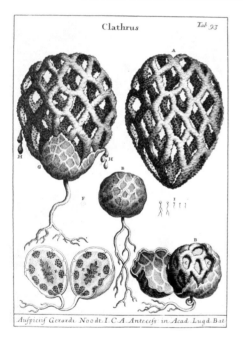

While some of the names Linnaeus gave to plants and animals have since been changed, his binomial system of nomenclature is still in use. This illustration by Pietro Antonio Micheli is of the type specimen of a fungus now known as Clathrus ruber – *the stinkhorn. A type specimen is the actual specimen designated by the person describing a species, which acts as a permanent reference.*

HIERARCHY AND RANKS

Linnaeus's full classification hierarchy, or rank system, included five levels (kingdom, class, order, genus and species). Familiar with the 'Great Chain of Being', a concept going back to Classical times and popular in the Middle Ages, which placed minerals, plants and animals in an ascending hierarchy of perfection, Linnaeus took a bold step and included humans, or *Homo sapiens* (based on the binomial and rank systems that he

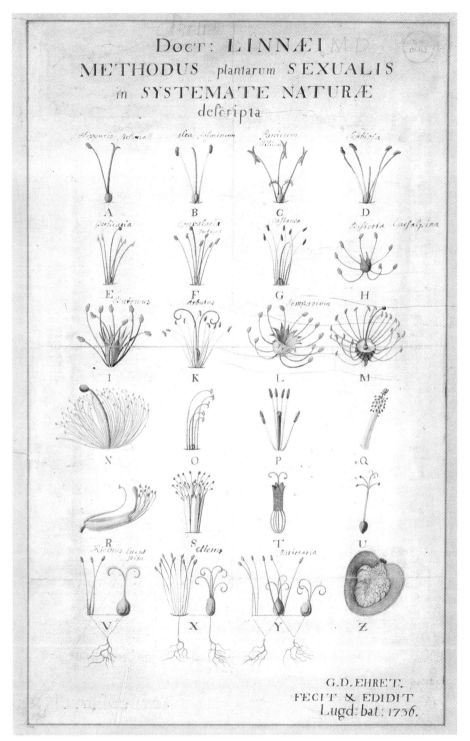

A watercolour illustration by Georg Ehret of Linnaeus's sexual system for the classification of plants from Systema Naturae, *which first appeared in 1735 but which grew to several volumes as Linnaeus developed his ideas and was sent more and more specimens.*

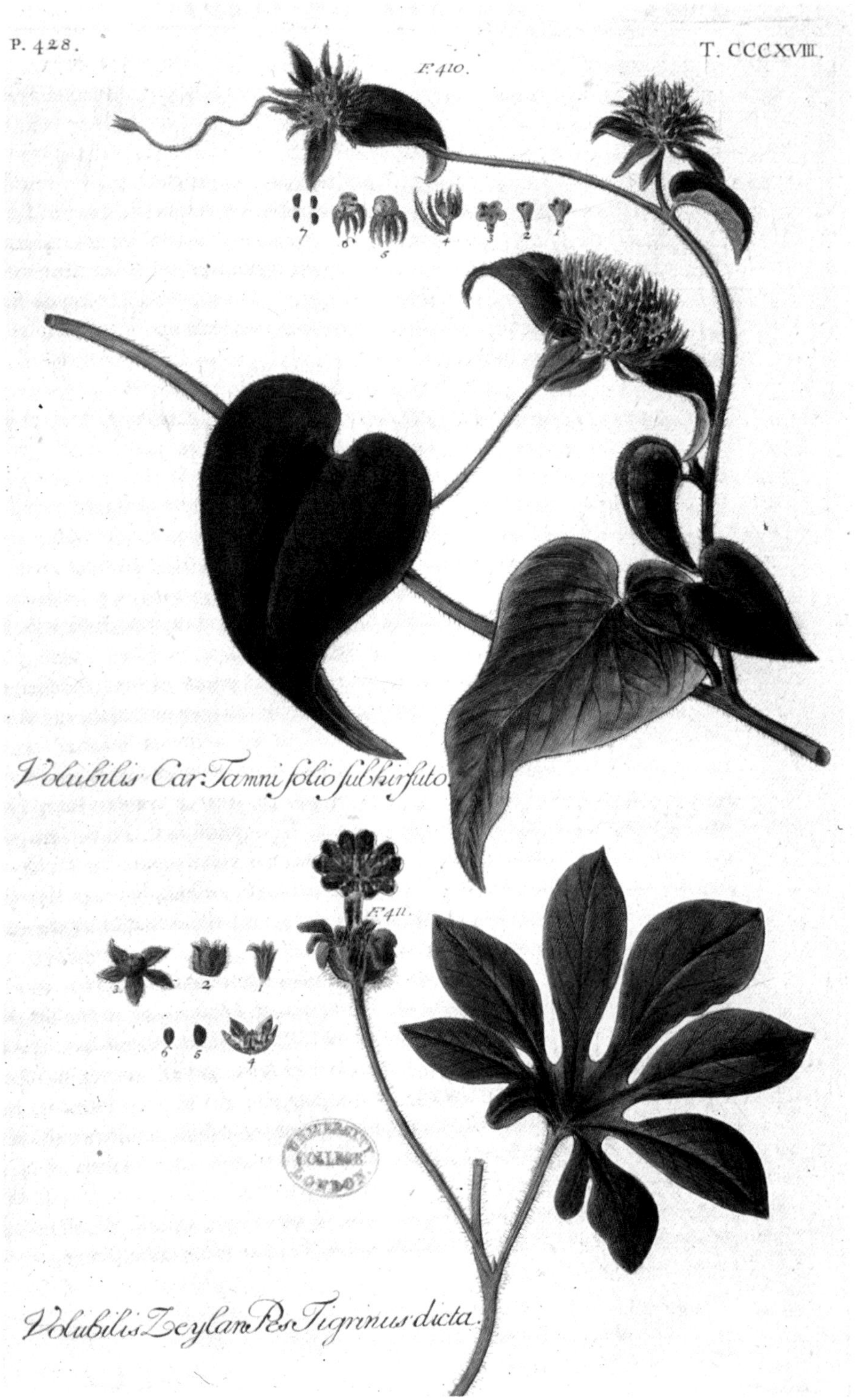

F. 410.

T. CCCXVIII.

Volubilis Car. Tamni folio subhirsuto.

F. 411.

Volubilis Zeylan. Pes Tigrinus dicta.

Illustration by Johann Jakob Dillenius in Hortus Elthamensis *of the type specimen named by* Linnaeus Ipomoea tamnifolia *(now renamed* Jacquemontia tamnifolia*) – a morning glory.*

had invented) at the top of the chain, saying that it too was an animal. Aristotle (p. 23) had also developed a similar ladder of beings, with plants at the bottom and man at the top. Linnaeus created the primates, the class of animals to which human beings, apes and monkeys belong – developing these terms in the subsequent editions of his *Systema.*

Linnaeus also made significant contributions to animal taxonomy, although he failed to achieve the clarity of his botanical work. He chose a different organ as the basis for four of the six animal classes – teeth for mammals, bills for birds, fins for fish and wings for insects. Worms (vermes), as Linnaeus called the remaining animals without a backbone, were distinguished by their external characteristics. Erroneously, rhinoceroses were classified as rodents, but he was the first to classify whales as mammals. His system became widely accepted in the 19th century.

THE LINNAEAN LEGACY

In 1762 Linnaeus had been ennobled and given the right to choose his successor, a privilege he exercised the following year, bequeathing his chair to his son, Carl Linnaeus the Younger. Linnaeus died in 1778, and, following the death of his son, the English physician James Edward Smith purchased his entire botanical collection and library in 1783. Smith founded the Linnaean (now Linnean) Society in London in 1788. The Society promoted Linnaeus's ideas, and housed, as it still does today, the original collection and a magnificent library of published works. It is now the official site for research into Linnaean species.

In its time, Linnaeus's binomial concept and other aspects of his classification system reduced confusion in the study of organisms and facilitated the advancement of botany and zoology by providing a workable method until a natural classification system could be developed. Although these artificial classifications, based on only a limited set of characters, were later replaced by more natural ones that reflected true relationships, Linnaeus had provided a simple to use system for classifying the living world and can be credited with stimulating interest in natural history in the 18th century. His binomial naming system has not been bettered to this day.

Casper Commelin, a botanist in Amsterdam, published his Plantarum Horti Medici Amstelodamensis *in 1706. It contained many exotic plants and Linnaeus used the illustrations to name specimens; this cactus is now called* Mammilaria mammilaris.

Comte de Buffon

A GRAND THEORIST

(1707–1788)

Natural history, taken in all its extent, is an immense history, it embraces all the objects with which the universe presents us. This prodigious multitude of quadrupeds, birds, fishes, insects, plants, minerals, etc, offers to the curiosity of the human spirit a vast spectacle in which the whole is so large, as it seems and as it is, so as to be inexhaustible in its details.

Comte de Buffon, Histoire Naturelle, *I, 1749*

ALONG THE SOUTH SIDE OF THE JARDIN DES PLANTES in Paris runs Rue Buffon. It is fitting that the longest axis of this garden, which today houses the natural history museum and zoo, is named for Buffon, as it was he who turned the Jardin du Roi (as it was known in his time) from a private collection for the king's pleasure into a hub for the study of natural history in its broadest sense. The Comte de Buffon was born Georges-Louis Leclerc, the eldest son of a provincial family from Montbard in Burgundy. When he was 10 years old, his mother – from whom it is said he inherited his intelligence and drive – succeeded to the large estate of Buffon, allowing her husband, Benjamin, to become the Lord of Buffon and Montbard. The inheritance opened up opportunities and the family moved to the provincial capital, Dijon, where Benjamin became a counsellor in the Burgundian parliament. Benjamin's plan for his eldest son was a career in the law, followed by a position in parliament, but it soon become clear that Georges-Louis had no aptitude for, or interest in, law – what he really liked was mathematics.

Buffon therefore switched from law to study mathematics at Angers – a backward step in the France of the day, where such careers were for the sons of the petite bourgeoisie, not of members of parliament. Along the way he changed his name to Georges-Louis Leclerc de Buffon, thus putting his claim on the family seat. The freedom of Angers suited Buffon, he wrote to a friend 'You only need leave home in order to value something and be appreciated and loved at least at the level you deserve.… I will do everything possible to stay away from Dijon as long as I can.' Buffon pursued his chosen path with energy and corresponded with the active

Buffon's engaging and populist style is reflected in this rather fanciful illustration of a giant octopus, 'la poulpe colossae', attacking a ship, from Buffon's 1805 Histoire Naturelle des Mollusques. *This organism does not exist, and the illustration is certainly based on travellers' tales of giant squid, which do exist, but are rarely seen and do not attack ships.*

mathematicians of the day, such as Gabriel Cramer of the Geneva Academy; he read Isaac Newton for the first time and also found time to botanize and take several courses at the medical school.

As well as excelling in his mathematical studies, Buffon was also a social star. After only two years in Angers, however, he became involved in a quarrel with an 'officer' and fought a duel with him, some say killing his opponent. He was forced to flee unceremoniously back to the despised, provincial Dijon, with a reputation as an unreliable hothead. He immediately left for travels around Europe with the Duke of Kingston, a young English lord who was accompanied by his amiable tutor, Nathaniel Hickman. While the three were travelling, Buffon received news of the death of his mother, who bequeathed him her fortune, providing him the means to become very rich indeed, and to enter into society at the level he desired. But his father's remarriage barely a year later put all this in jeopardy, and Buffon took his own father to court in order to secure his mother's fortune. It is unclear whether or not the suit went ahead, but Buffon recovered the money and used it to buy the family holdings in Montbard that his father had been mismanaging. Buffon intended to occupy what he considered his rightful place in the France of the Ancien Régime.

Buffon continued his studies in mathematics, applying geometry to the calculus of probability, solving the 'needle problem' – now known as Buffon's needle. Using the calculus developed by Newton he worked out the probability of a needle, thrown in the air on to a floor with parallel lines, crossing or not crossing some of the lines. His paper on the subject was sent to the Academy of Sciences and made a good impression. Buffon and his friends were now working to get him a position, a first step towards becoming part of the French scientific establishment. In 1734, Buffon was appointed by King Louis XV to the Academy of Sciences, with the strong support of the Comte de Maurepas, the minister to the navy. Buffon had come to Maurepas' attention for his work on the tensile strength of wood, which he had carried out on his estates in Montbard, now completely renovated and planted with forests.

THE KING'S GARDEN

Buffon's insistence on spending most of the year on his estates in Burgundy irritated his Academy colleagues, but allowed him to do what he was now discovering he liked best, observing and experimenting with nature. He planted trees and noted their growth and physiology, with an eye to increasing the productivity of forests and to eliminating waste. Buffon was a believer in the necessity of observation: 'In order to judge what has happened, or even what will happen, one need only examine what is happening.' He became ever more immersed in natural history, and in 1739 he requested a transfer from the mechanics section of the Academy (where mathematics resided) to the botany section. This turned out to be a stroke of good fortune – when Bernard de Jussieu was promoted, Buffon stepped into his place, and soon was actively, though discreetly through his influential friends at court, seeking the position of director of the Jardin du Roi, the King's Garden. Again thanks to the good offices of Maurepas, who had the ear of the king, he was offered the job over other candidates who were more senior and arguably better qualified. This manoeuvering and politicking earned him the lasting enmity of his colleagues, but Buffon was out to get what he wanted – position, status and money – and with this appointment, one of the highest scientific positions in France, he achieved his ambition.

George-Louis Leclerc, Comte de Buffon, was the ultimate French aristocrat.

NATURAL HISTORY, GENERAL AND PARTICULAR

Upon naming Buffon as director of the Jardin du Roi, Maurepas had requested him to write a description of the King's Cabinet – essentially a catalogue of the collections. Buffon had no intention of producing such a mundane work, leaving it to his new assistant Louis-Jean-Marie Daubenton, a medic from Montbard and a relative. Instead, Buffon's aim was no less than to publish a work that would change how people perceived natural history, the *Histoire Naturelle, Générale et Particulière* ('Natural History, General and Particular'). This was to be not simply a description of all of natural history, but a philosophy of natural history that would transcend the 'merely' descriptive or particular. This was still, after all, the age of the philosopher-naturalists. His detractors, however, thought it was too early to begin even to think of a general natural history when the particular was so little known, and were sceptical of Buffon's qualifications as a natural historian.

Fifty volumes were to be published, only 44 of which saw the light of day. The first three appeared in 1749, covering an immense variety of topics, from the history of the Earth to the natural history of animals, including man. Buffon had written a book not for his fellow academicians and scholars, but one that would appeal to the cultured public and their philosophical tendencies. He wrote for an audience he knew well – wealthy aristocrats with time on their hands and money to spend. Heavily illustrated

Great frigate bird (Fregata minor). *This engraving, hand-coloured in many of the copies of the* Histoire Naturelle des Oiseaux, *is very accurate, both in terms of the bird's appearance and its flight. In the mating season the male inflates the crop region to a red balloon.*

and written in a flowery and ornate style, Buffon's *Histoire Naturelle* was an immediate and triumphant success. The first edition sold out in six weeks and the book became the most widely read work of the 18th century – it was *the* book to talk about in the salons, much to the annoyance and frustration of Buffon's academic colleagues in the Academy. One fumed that the book 'did not succeed particularly well with educated people' and that 'women, to the contrary, attach importance to it'. They spitefully reacted to the man, who they felt was ostentatious and self-serving, as much as to his writings.

The public popularity of Buffon's work was a major impetus for the establishment and growth of many specialized collections and cabinets of objects. His writings created a vogue for natural history – not only reading about it, but collecting and displaying it as well. Such private collections in turn stimulated more research into the subject, and opened this emerging profession to people of all social classes. Buffon has been credited with 'having made natural history a popular pursuit' and stimulating public interest so that those who could afford it 'wanted to own a natural science *cabinet* the way people used to want to own a library'.

It would be easy to accept the criticisms of Buffon's academic contemporaries and dismiss the *Histoire Naturelle* as a purely popularizing work, empty and puffed up, with little real scientific value. But through his work Buffon truly changed the face of natural history in a way no academic had done before, and he knew what he was doing. The *Histoire Naturelle* contains some revolutionary ideas – ideas that today we take for granted, but which in the mid-18th century were radical indeed. He placed man as another animal, a special one who reasoned, but an animal all the same, and talked about the similarities between men and apes. He described a method for organic change through 'organic particles' – quite far-fetched, but he was struggling with ideas that were new and complex. In a later work, *Les Époques de Nature*, he even suggested that the Earth was of a great age, older than the thousands of years proclaimed by the Church. But he was careful to take the necessary precautions in his writing not to offend the prevailing orthodoxy.

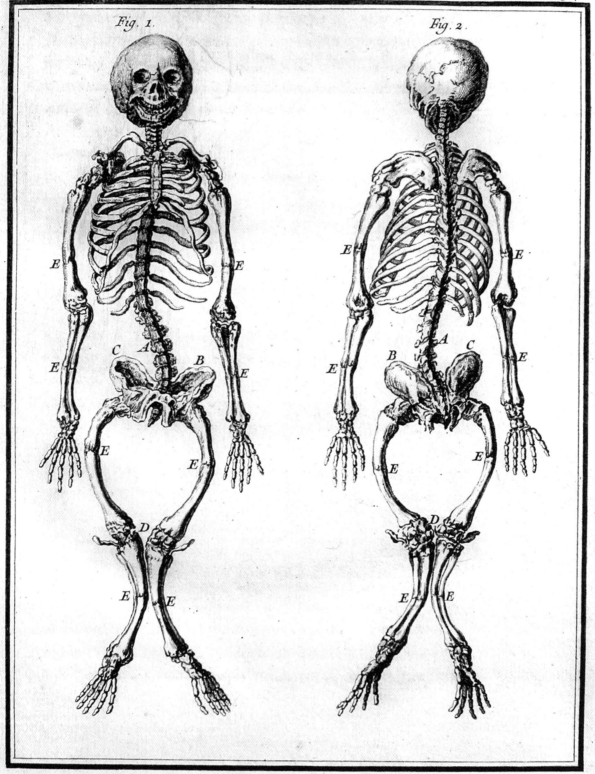

In the many volumes of the Histoire Naturelle *Buffon not only documented wild animal diversity as known at the time, but also a great deal of information about human beings. This plate shows the skeleton of a person afflicted by rickets, now known to be caused by a deficiency in Vitamin D that causes bone deformities. The depiction of humans alongside animals was controversial in the 18th century.*

Buffon's prose was so purple that the ideas themselves are almost hidden, a criticism levelled at him by his academic contemporaries, but one that surely meant that his books, and their ideas, continued to be printed. His description of age and death contains some speculation that could have been considered fairly radical, but cloaked in such language as to be almost invisible: 'All changes in nature, everything alters, all perishes; man's body is only just at his peak of perfection when he beings to decay. … Death, that so marked and dreaded change of state, is in nature nothing but the last shade of the preceding state. …We begin to live by degrees and we finish in dying as we had begun to live.' Buffon's descriptions of animals also read almost as flights of fancy: 'The exterior of the lion does not give lie to his great interior qualities; he has an imposing figure, an imposing look, a proud bearing, a terrible voice; the size is not excessive as is that of an elephant or rhinoceros … but is on the contrary, so well fit and proportioned that the body of the lion appears to be the model of strength combined with agility; as solid as sinewy, not being loaded with flesh nor fat, and not containing anything in excess, it is all nerve and muscle.' No wonder the cultured aristocratic public lapped it up – the text reads more like a romantic novel than a dry scientific treatise.

CRITICAL REACTION

Although there was opposition to Buffon's work, intellectual opinion was so divided in France at the time that his detractors were fully occupied using his work to score points against each other, rather than uniting to battle this new philosophy. However, despite containing such statements as 'Nature is but the external throne of the divine magnificence: the man who contemplates it, studies it, is elevated by degrees to the internal throne of the All-Powerful, [he is] made to adore the Creator…', *Histoire Naturelle* did not escape censure on religious grounds. The book was attacked as contradicting Genesis, thus destroying all human and moral values, and was in danger of being blacklisted. Buffon received a letter from the Faculty of Theology in Paris (the official censors), listing those things in his book that were contrary to the beliefs of the Church – in effect asking him to recant. His answer was supremely hypocritical, but did allow his work to remain in press – he believed 'very firmly all that is told [in the Bible] about Creation, both as to order of time and the circumstances of the facts', presenting his theory 'only as pure philosophical supposition'.

For the young generation of scientists, desperate to break the powerful hold Buffon had on royal influence and resources, this sort of self-serving hypocrisy was one more proof that he was an obstacle to progress. Buffon was stubborn in his

Buffon emphasized both the lion's regal bearing and personality not only in his text but also in the illustration in Histoire Naturelle. *A reader was left in no doubt as to the importance and character of the animal.*

rejection of the sexual classificatory system of Linnaeus (p. 133) – ridiculing it as based on a single character and artificial; he felt that the philosopher-naturalist's role was to explain nature, not just order it. Buffon also rejected new technologies: 'The discoveries that one can make with the microscope amount to very little, for one sees with the mind's eye and without the microscope the real existence of all these little beings.' Frustration with such suffocating of what were seen as good new ideas, coupled with Buffon's apparently unassailable position as director of the Jardin du

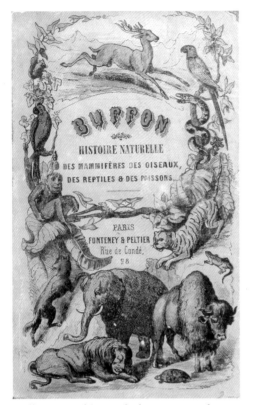

Buffon's natural history books were so popular that children's editions were also published, extending his influence to the next generation. This cover from Buffon de la Jeunesse *(2nd edition, c. 1870) has an imaginative depiction of animals living together in perfect harmony.*

Roi, his control of finances and personal arrogance, resulted in a strong desire to deliver natural history from Buffon's patronage and to transform it into a scientific rather than a literary and speculative pursuit. This was in tune with the age: in the late 18th century freedom and diversity of opinion, and liberation from the yoke of convention and tradition, were all the rage; Buffon was the last of the old school.

When Buffon died on 16 April 1788, the 19-year-old Georges Cuvier was unable to conceal his pleasure: 'This time, the Comte de Buffon is dead and buried'. The Marquis de Condorcet, the member of the Academy of Sciences who gave Buffon's *éloge* (a summing up of his career and accomplishments), used the opportunity to attack Buffon, who was now incapable of replying – the finishing stroke by his philosophical opponents. Condorcet depicted Buffon as subservient to the ruling authority, while his work was characterized as good, if rather purple prose, but terrible science, as he selected only the facts that supported his particular point of view. The reaction to Buffon's death was not long in coming, the new generation of scientists who had founded the Linnaean Society of Paris a few months earlier, in the face of strong opposition from Buffon's supporters at the Jardin du Roi, now took control. But it would be wrong to see the battle that followed Buffon's death as simply one of Linnaean versus Buffonian ideas – the intellectual situation in France at the time was more complex. The backlash against Buffon and his stranglehold on science meant that his supporters bore the brunt of a massive theoretical and institutional upheaval. This was as nothing, though, compared to the changes about to be wrought in France as a whole: on 8 August 1788, only five months after Buffon died, Louis XVI convoked the Estates General, and less than a year later the people of Paris stormed the Bastille, changing France, and French science, forever.

Georg Steller

THE DISCOVERY OF ALASKA

(1709–1746)

As long as things escape us and perish unknown with our
consent, and through our silence are counted as fabulous –
things which may be seen with little labour in the very land
where we, with all our inquisitiveness, live – it is not strange
these things, which we are prevented from observing by
the great sea that lies between, have remained to the present
time unknown and unexplored.

Georg Steller, **De Bestiis Marinis,** *1751*

GEORG STELLER WAS A PHYSICIAN, botanist and pioneering explorer who provided the first accounts of much of the natural history of the arctic regions. He was born Georg Stöller in Windsheim near Nuremberg, Germany, on 10 March 1709. Little is known of his early life and interests, but he appears to have conceived at a young age a clear plan for his career, with the aim of working in Russia.

Exploration of the North Pacific at this time aimed to achieve academic goals as well as various political, military and commercial ones. Among the controversies relating to the region were the possible existence of a sea route from Europe to Japan, China and the Indies around the northern coast of Siberia – the so-called Northeastern Passage – and the precise geographic relationship of America to Asia. Russians were prominent in this early exploration: in the 18th century Russia was changing rapidly in order to compete with other European powers. Over a period of some 50 years the governments of Peter the Great and his immediate successors poured money and resources into science in general and scientific exploration in particular, especially of the Siberian region. The Great Northern Expedition represented the largest and certainly the most expensive exploration undertaken anywhere during that century. In reality a series of expeditions, its purposes were to map Russia's arctic coastline; explore the Siberian hinterland; and undertake a number of voyages into the North Pacific. In overall charge was Vitus Bering, a Dane formerly in the Russian navy.

In 1734, three years after arriving in Russia, Steller (he had changed his name from Stöller) was appointed as a naturalist at the Academy of Sciences and accepted on to the

Petropavlovsk in Avacha (Awatscha) Bay on the east coast of Kamchatka was the start point for Bering's second expedition. Two ships, the St Peter *and the* St Paul, *left the port: only the* St Paul *returned.*

academic staff of the Great Northern Expedition. His aim was first to study the natural history of eastern Siberia and then join an expedition sailing towards Japan. Steller left for Kamchatka in winter, taking more than a year to cross the 8,000 km (5,000 miles) to eastern Siberia, stopping to collect plants at various points along the way. But before he could join up with his intended expedition, he was seduced by Bering into joining another voyage, this one seeking Northeastern America.

This was Bering's second voyage and it had taken 10 years to organize. In 1741 two ships left Avacha Bay in Kamchatka, one commanded by Bering and the other by Aleksei Chirikov, but they soon lost touch with each other and were never reunited. Both eventually, and separately, sighted America, but only the *St Peter*, with Bering and Steller, made a successful landing – at Cape St Elias (Kayak Island) after 46 days at sea. After much argument, Steller was allowed ashore for a mere 10 hours. In this brief time he became the first European to collect and describe a variety of American plants and animals, including one, the western blue (or Steller's) jay, which he recognized as being related to a common American species since he had 'seen a likeness painted in lively colours and described in the newest account of the birds and plants of the Carolinas' (Mark Catesby's *Natural History of Carolina, Florida and the Bahama Islands*; p. 124). As Steller noted, 'this bird proved to me that we were really in America'. Later, the ship anchored off the Shumagin Islands along the Alaskan Peninsula, where local Aleuts encountered Europeans for the first time.

Nearing home the ship ran aground on what is now Bering Island, some 160 km (100 miles) from Kamchatka. Nearly half the 75-man crew, including Bering, died here, mainly from scurvy: the remainder survived, largely due to knowledge gained by Steller in Kamchatka from the Kamchadal people. Indeed, Steller was the first ship's physician known to have successfully treated scurvy, antedating more famous medical and naval proponents of antiscorbutic treatments. After a harsh winter stranded on the island, the remaining crew returned to Kamchatka in a small boat pieced together from the wreck of the *St Peter*. The entire voyage had taken 15 months to complete.

Steller spent a further two years in Kamchatka and the Kuriles, exploring and cataloguing the natural history of the region. He was recalled to St Petersburg in 1744, but his journey was twice interrupted by enforced returns to Irkutsk to face trumped up charges regarding the treatment of Kamchadal prisoners. On his third attempt to return to St Petersburg he caught a sudden fever and died at Tiumen in Siberia in 1746.

Steller never published any of his numerous manuscripts, catalogues and lists detailing hundreds of plants and animals previously unknown in Europe, nor the journal of his voyage to America. Many, like the man himself, did not survive. The few that did were published posthumously or incorporated into the work of others. The former include *De Bestiis Marinis* ('Beasts of the Sea'), published in 1751, a detailed account of the animals of Bering Island. Among them were the northern fur seal, Steller's sea lion, sea otter and Steller's sea cow, a giant sirenian related to the manatees and dugongs of southern waters, and only found around Bering and Copper islands. Within 27 years, Steller's sea cow had been hunted to extinction, leaving Steller's descriptions as the only ones made by a scientist of the living animal. Steller's work, undertaken in just a few short years and under the harshest of circumstances,

A depiction of Steller taking his first measurements of the Northern or Steller's sea cow (Hydrodamalis gigas). It was a veritable behemoth, reaching nearly 8 m (26 ft) in length and weighing up to 11,196 kg (24,680 lb) on a diet of kelp. With flesh that tasted like beef and a skin tough enough to make boats from it was soon hunted to extinction.

PLATE CCCC

Many species first encountered and described by Steller were later named in his honour. Steller's eider (Polysticta stelleri) *is the smallest of the eiders and was studied by Steller on Bering Island; this painting of it is by John Gould.*

created a valuable legacy, albeit one unrecognized for many years. His were the first accounts of a world teeming with wildlife, and they provided a unique insight into the region, although it was other authors whose reputations gained immensely as a result of Steller's information. The Russian government exploited his work while simultaneously attempting to keep it secret to prevent others from doing the same. Just 60 years after Steller's birth, Russian hunters were sailing as far south as California, at the same time that Spanish missionaries were becoming established there. Eventually word leaked out. Steller's meticulous descriptions, complete with drawings, are models of observation and recording, enabling us to study many organisms today – even those driven to extinction soon after discovery.

Steller also recorded details of the Kamchadals, Aleuts and other indigenous peoples at a time when these cultures were being, or were soon to be, overrun. He recognized the link between Asian and American peoples and suggested a Mongolian origin for Americans based on cultural similarities – the first person to do so. And one of his discoveries helped shape the modern world. The Bering/Chirikov voyages established Russian sovereignty over Alaska – Steller's description of the western blue jay provided proof that Russians did, indeed, set foot in northeast America before other Europeans. Thus, Russia gained title to Alaska under the conditions of usage and claim common at the time. Eventually, of course, this region of some 1,700,000 sq. km (656,452 sq. miles) was sold in 1867 to the USA for $7.2 million – surely the bargain of the century.

Michel Adanson

A UNIVERSAL METHOD OF CLASSIFICATION

(1727–1806)

The natural method must be unique, universal and general.

S O WROTE MICHEL ADANSON IN THE *Préface istorike* of his *Familles des Plantes*, published in 1763–64. In Adanson's own description, his natural method of classification must 'have no exception', and be 'independent of our will, but model itself on the nature of beings, which is the set of their parts and of their qualities.' Through his work and writings, Adanson demonstrated that botany is not merely a science of names, it is a science of facts. His most significant contribution to botany was the establishment of modern plant families as discrete and universal groups.

Adanson was born in Aix-en-Provence in the south of France, and developed an interest in natural history at an early age. When he was 21 years old, he travelled to Africa, not as a royal botanist with all the official facilities that entails, but as a book-keeping clerk for the 'Compagnie des Indes'. Although he had learned physics, anatomy, chemistry and botany at the Jardin du Roi, Adanson now wanted to study nature through first-hand observation. He stayed in Senegal for six years (1748–54), collecting mineral samples and animal and plant specimens, noting in each case the natural context they were found in and recording any ecological and ethnological data. He learned the local names of animals and plants from the indigenous people, inquiring about their traditional uses and habits, and he also made a phonetic transcription of the Ouolof language. In Gambia, Adanson discovered the huge diversity of tropical flora and became increasingly aware of the limitations of the classification systems of Tournefort and Linnaeus (p. 133) for describing his newly collected plants. Instead, Adanson examined every part of each plant, giving priority to no one character in their classification. He addressed the basis of his 'universal method' of natural classification in a letter to the distinguished botanist Bernard de Jussieu in 1750.

Adanson returned to France personally enriched by his experiences in Africa, and a committed opponent of slavery. He began work on the publication of his collections, and in 1757 the first volume of what he intended to be a series of eight volumes appeared, entitled *Histoire Naturelle du Sénégal. Coquillages*. An English translation of this did not appear until 1759, a delay caused by the hostilities of the Seven Years War (1756–63) which was then raging intermittently in Europe, North America and

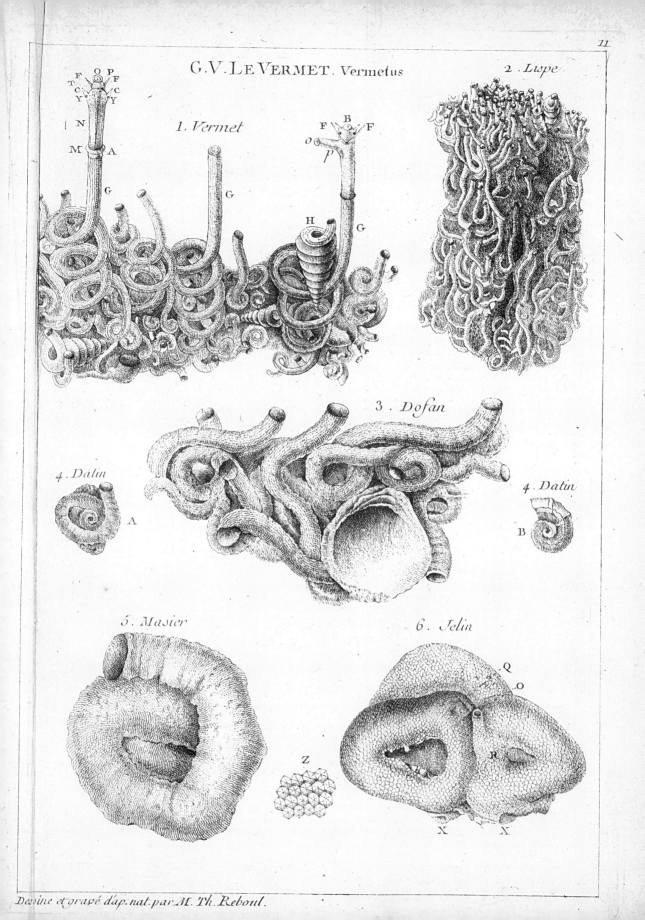

G.V. Le VERMET. *Vermetus*

1. *Vermet*

2. *Lupe.*

3. *Dofan*

4. *Datin*

4. *Datin*

5. *Masier*

6. *Jelin*

Dessine et gravé d'ap. nat. par M. Th. Reboul.

India, dragging in several countries, including France and Britain on opposing sides. Although he was elected a member of the Royal Society in 1763, Adanson only gave a summary of his findings, excluding any information that might be advantageous to the enemy.

In his book, which superficially was a description of the shells that he had collected in Africa, Adanson was actually establishing the basic principles that he would use in his new approach to botany. Adanson firmly believed that the classification of organisms required a complete description of each specimen, and a comparison with others, and should not be based on a single characteristic alone. For instance, Adanson took a great interest not only in the shell itself, but also the animal inside. In that sense he is considered as a founder of malacology (the study of molluscs), and some of the mollusc genera and species he proposed are still in use today.

In 1759, Adanson was living at the house of Bernard de Jussieu in Paris, and the two botanists worked closely together, later joined by Bernard's nephew, Antoine-Laurent de Jussieu (p. 197), in 1765. It was at this same time that Adanson was developing his ideas about his natural method, which he published in his *Familles des Plantes* (1763–64). Organized in two closely related parts, the first volume, entitled *Préface istorike sur l'état ancien et actuel de la botanike, & une théorie de cette science*, includes an historical account of old and new methods in botany and also gathered together a chronological list of botanical authors, as well as the results of recent experiments on the organization, anatomy and properties of plants. Adanson also developed his own philosophy, quoting his contribution to the natural method of classification and setting it in the context of the history of botany. In his conclusion to the *Préface*, Adanson stated that the natural method is universal because every character of a plant has to be considered, including those derived from microscopical observations.

The second volume of *Familles* dealt with Adanson's descriptions of plant families, based on his identification of their complete set of characteristics. He drew up a long list of attributes for each species, from which he deduced the similarities at the rank of genus and above. Adanson thought that each family had its own specific trait that he named 'génie': that is, members of a family possess a peculiar group of characters that help define genera and species within the family. He also noted that a particular characteristic may help define one family, but have no taxonomic value at

Adanson's classification of molluscs was considered by Cuvier (p. 202) to be superior to all previous systems, and it is one of the starting points for the modern naming of molluscs. Plate 11 of Adanson's Histoire Naturelle de Sénégal. Coquillages *shows the genus* Vermetus *and includes six species, though the sixth is in fact a polyp rather than a mollusc.*

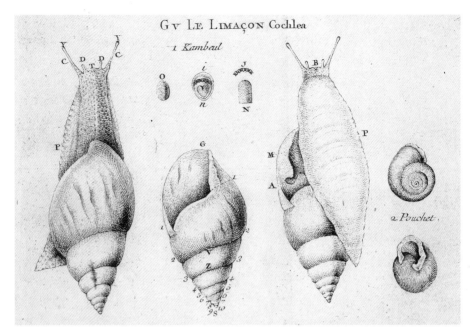

In this detail of a plate from his Histoire Naturelle de Sénégal. Coquillages *Adanson illustrates two species of* Cochlea. *Adanson believed it was necessary to study all characteristics of the creature – both shell and the animal inside it – to arrive at a natural classification system.*

all in another: the features that distinguish a daisy from a chrysanthemum, both in the same family ('Composées'), are not necessarily of any use in distinguishing a sweet pea from a bean, both in another ('Légumineuses').

Adanson's conclusions were supported by his analysis of the numerous specimens that were sent to him, but it was his personal knowledge of tropical flora and living species in their ecological context that were of particular value in his work. He also conducted his own experiments in fertilization and hybridization. Applying his principles based on the similarity of characters, Adanson proposed 58 families – the first five and the last one were what is known as cryptogams (plants with hidden sex organs, such as ferns, mosses, algae and fungi), the other 52 comprising phanerogams (plants with visible organs).

Familles des Plantes is the first book that presented a philosophical route to the elaboration of a new method of classification. It also included many innovatory ideas that were rediscovered only years later by other botanists. So why is it that Adanson's work seems to have fallen into oblivion soon after its publication? There are a number of possible reasons. First, the physical presentation of the book was not very attractive, especially Adanson's championing of the use of phonetic orthography in an attempt to standardize the pronunciation of names and their spelling (for instance, by the suppression of mute letters, or eliding letters with the same sound), which made the text harder to read and understand. Secondly, Adanson placed great emphasis on

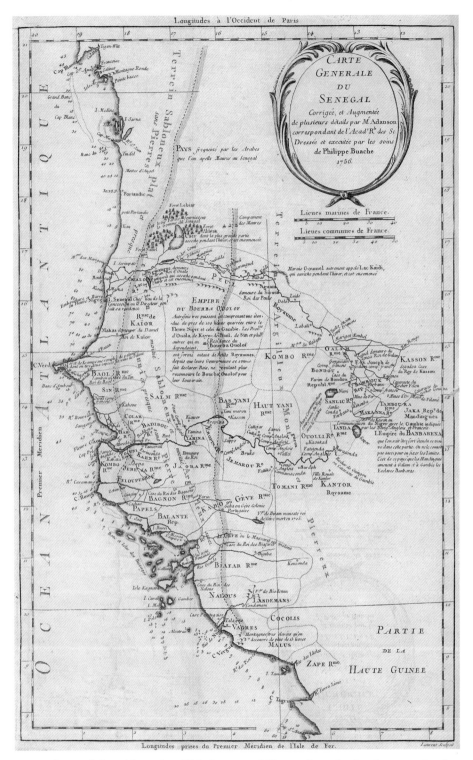

A map of Senegal from Adanson's published account of his stay there, showing the areas where he worked and travelled, with numerous ethnological and historical details added.

earlier knowledge about plants, reviving old names and using vernacular ones, while rejecting many of the name-changes of Linnaeus. He thus failed to appreciate how innovative Linnaeus's binomial system of nomenclature was, even though it was becoming widely accepted within the scientific community. Finally, in spite of his close relationship to Bernard de Jussieu, Adanson never held a high position, in particular at the Jardin du Roi, which could have helped him in promoting his ideas.

Nevertheless, Adanson had always maintained an association with the Royal Academy of Sciences (the Académie royale des sciences) and received official positions, including 'pensionnaire-botaniste' in 1782, and in 1795 he was elected a member of the newly created Institut national. Despite this, the botanical establishment consistently ignored his work and he had no students of his own to defend and promote his philosophy. His situation may also not have been helped by the fact that he was very thorough – an attitude considered by some as the mark of a foul temper.

Adanson also declared himself a philosopher and planned to create a great encyclopaedia of all knowledge of natural things, with the support of the king. On 15 February 1775, he read out the prospectus of his huge enterprise, consisting of 27 books, before the Academy. His project was rejected, however – the reviewers judging it to be beyond the capacity of one man alone. Ignoring their advice, he shut himself away through the 1780s to work on the realization of his encyclopaedic dream.

Suffering from ill health and domestic difficulties, Adanson also lost his financial support as the Revolution had suppressed the Royal Academy of Sciences and with it his academic pension; fortunately, he was helped by his servants to continue his work. In spite of his eventual nomination to the Institut, it was not until 1803 that he recovered his pension. He died in poverty, his last wish being that a floral wreath representing his 58 plant families should be laid on his grave.

Throughout his life, Adanson had wanted to encompass natural history in its entirety, and to link all its parts. His studies of the classification of molluscs and plants are probably the best-known aspects of his vast knowledge, but he meticulously observed all parts of nature, from microscopic organisms to meteorology. Although Adanson's work may not have been appreciated in his own lifetime, the first modern botanist to pay tribute to him was Henri Baillon, who defended his method in the Préface of his *Dictionnaire de Botanique*, in 1876 and set up a new journal which he named *Adansonia*, still published to this day. Finally, and appropriately for a man who learned his trade in Africa, the genus of baobab trees, found throughout Africa and of great economic importance, was named *Adansonia*.

Erasmus Darwin

EVOLUTIONARY BEGINNINGS

(1731–1802)

Dr Darwin possesses, perhaps, a greater range of
knowledge than any other man in Europe,
and is the most inventive of men.

Samuel Taylor Coleridge

ONE OF THE GREAT FIGURES OF HIS AGE, Erasmus Darwin presented a series of contradictions. At a time when London was a magnet for those seeking success and influence, he spent his life in the provinces. A part of the establishment on account of his background and profession, he supported radical thought and change. An anti-Christianity, anti-alcohol doctor with a robust approach even to his rich patients, he was invited to become physician to King George III. An unattractive man with a pronounced stammer, he was successful both in drawing-room society and in the seduction stakes. A scientist and inventor, he also became the most famous and best-selling poet of his day. But Darwin was far more than this, and his greatest contribution to natural science lies in the field of evolution.

Darwin was born at Elston Hall, near Nottingham, and was educated at Cambridge and Edinburgh, where he qualified as a physician. Returning to Nottingham, his first attempt to establish a practice failed, but after a move to Lichfield he rapidly built up an extensive clientele, eventually becoming the leading medical practitioner of the time. He relied as heavily as others on treatments then current, such as blood-letting, but also introduced novel and frequently effective approaches to medical problems. As a country doctor, Darwin had plenty of time and opportunity to observe and experiment, and possessed the intellect and curiosity to exploit both to the full.

Mechanical devices exerted a life-long fascination on Darwin. They ranged from the whimsical, such as a model spider animated by revolving magnets, to the practical. Many never got beyond sketches on the pages of his 'commonplace book' – an aide-memoire in which he recorded many of his thoughts and ideas. Thus an artificial bird powered by compressed air, a machine for copying documents and an early speaking machine remained ideas only. Some were translated into reality, though often developed and patented by others. A canal lift, a horizontal windmill and an electrostatic generator were all put to good use.

Cypripedium

The orchid Cypripedium *from 'The Loves of Plants'. Darwin compared the flower to 'a spider's bloated paunch and jointed arms' which 'hide her fine form and mask her bushy charms'.*

THE LUNAR SOCIETY

Darwin was one of a coterie of friends in the area of Lichfield and Birmingham who referred to themselves as the Lunar Society – so-called because they met for dinner and discussion on nights when the full moon provided light for the journey home. Collectively, the Lunar Society provided the chief intellectual driving force underpinning the Industrial Revolution in England, establishing some of the first factories and creating new processes, work disciplines and social infrastructure. Along with other members of the Society, Darwin supported many of the ideals emanating from pre-Revolutionary France, especially those regarding progress and the relationship of knowledge and power, and about the need for social and political change. For the Lunar Society, and Darwin in particular, science was a vehicle for such change. Later, they would become disillusioned as the French Revolution degenerated into the Great Terror, with its mobs and executions, but initially at least they looked across the English Channel for inspiration. European scientists, including those in France, were proposing theories which challenged the accepted ideas promulgated by both Church and State and nowhere more so than in natural history.

It was through his publications on natural history and agriculture that Darwin came to public notice. Two of these were notable as much for their form as for their content, since they are long poems that were part of the poetic debate about science and technology which spanned the 18th century. Although written, as Darwin says, 'to amuse', they contained numerous and often lengthy footnotes which are clearly designed to instruct. The first of these poems, *The Botanic Garden*, published in two parts in 1789 and 1791, also made him the most renowned poet in England. Another publication, *Zoonomia: or the Laws of Organic Life* (1794–96), was ostensibly a medical treatise aimed at unravelling the theory of diseases, but in it he also set out his views on evolution.

THEORIES OF EVOLUTION

During the 18th century there were strongly conflicting views on the origin of species, their ability to change or not, and how any changes might be transmitted to future generations. Were all creatures created independently of one another and immutable – a view strongly supported by the Church – or could new species arise from existing ones? Did each individual contain within it the perfect, preformed embryos of its progeny (and those embryos in turn contain their own preformed progeny, like infinite Russian dolls), or did an embryo evolve from a simple to a

Erasmus Darwin by Joseph Wright of Derby. According to the poet Anna Seward, Darwin was 'above the middle size, his form athletic', but to fellow Lunatick Richard Edgeworth he was simply 'a large man, fat and rather clumsy'.

complex structure as it approached the moment of birth? Earlier scientists such as the Comte de Buffon (p. 140; of whom Darwin was an ardent admirer) had attempted to tackle these problems but without providing wholly adequate explanations.

Darwin believed in a general progress in nature towards greater complexity and perfection, both of individual species and of the world as a whole, and the mutability of species was an evident fact for him. He followed the belief of Linnaeus (p. 133) that new species arose from existing ones by means of hybridization. He also pointed to the results of selective breeding, noting clear examples of this such as dogs and pigeons, as well as to the great changes seen in animals as they matured. It seemed obvious that not only were original characteristics passed on to succeeding generations, but that these characteristics could be changed in some way between parents and offspring, and it was even possible for entirely new characteristics to arise.

In Darwin's view, nature was a constant battle for survival, epitomized in his first law of organic life, 'eat or be eaten'. He listed three great 'wants' of organisms, which could affect change in 'the forms of many animals by their exertions to gratify them': lust, hunger and security. He also believed that acquired traits could be inherited, a view later expounded by and more closely associated with Lamarck. Once derided,

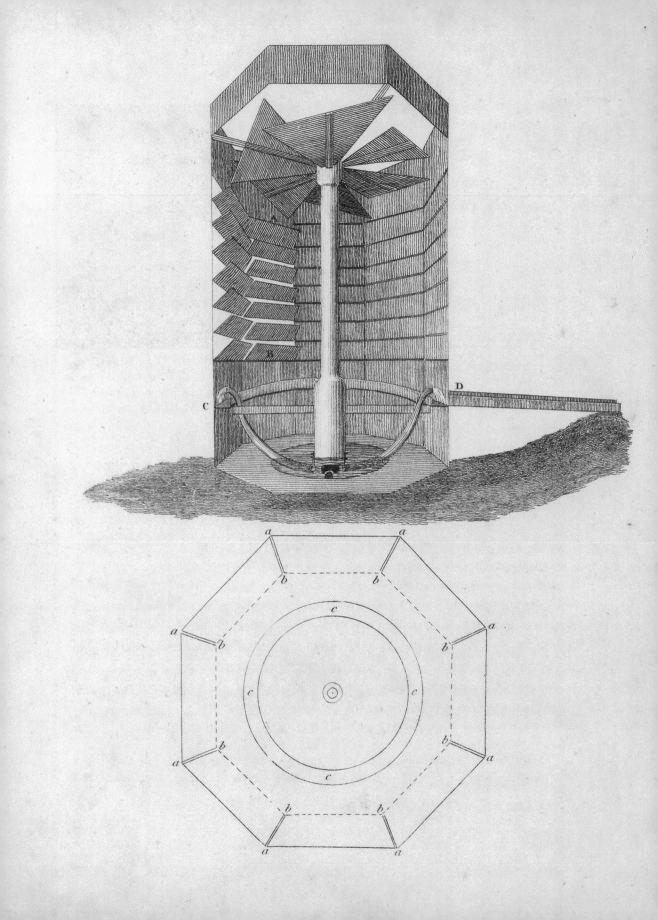

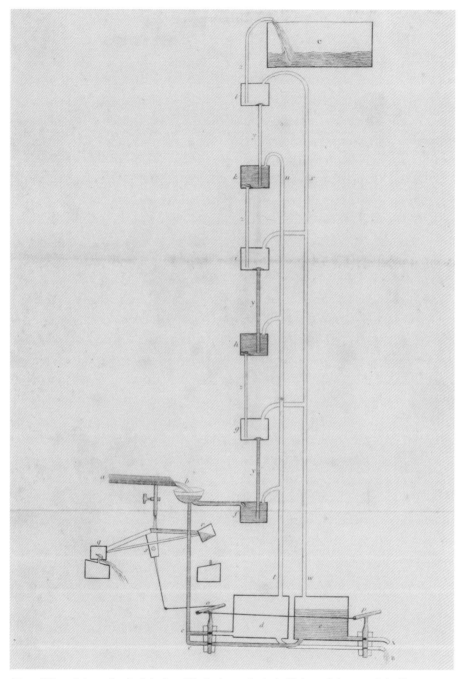

Two of Darwin's mechanical devices. His horizontal windmill (opposite) was originally intended as a drainage pump for marsh land, but that built at Wedgwood's factory at Etruria was successfully used for 14 years for grinding colours. The simple water-raising device (above) was accompanied by a lengthy explanation, part of which reads: 'This water will press the air, which was in the cistern e up the air-pipe w x, and will force the water from the small cisterns g i l into the cistern h k and great C.' Nevertheless, it worked!

this view is now recognized as being at least partially correct. Darwin thought the ability to change in response to both internal and external forces enabled organisms to become better fitted for survival and that this was the driving force of evolution, a process by which a species might 'continually improve its own inherent activity ... by generation to its posterity, world without end'.

However, challenging the idea that the world was exactly as created by God and that its order (and therefore man's place within it) was anything but a reflection of Divine Will was dangerous indeed. All thought and activity which encouraged change in the 'natural order' of society – as was happening in France – was to be avoided at all costs. Darwin was careful, therefore, to hedge his ideas about with qualifying phrases and references to God as 'THE FIRST GREAT CAUSE'. Whether this was due to a vaguely Deist belief, natural reticence or political expedience is unclear.

For Darwin, the greatest 'want' was lust, that is reproduction, which was crucial to the evolution of species, but was an area little understood at the time. At a crude scale the mechanics were obvious, but fine detail was noticeably wanting. Darwin himself originally held the (then) widespread view that the characters of offspring were determined solely by the male parent, the female merely providing nutrition and security for the embryo, but his observations caused him to change his mind and postulate that embryos were formed from 'molecules' provided by both parents. Darwin also noted that while sexual reproduction produced variation in the offspring, asexual reproduction resulted in little or none. His achievement in formulating and disseminating these concepts is all the more remarkable given the absence at this time of any knowledge of genetics. Nevertheless, he provided a remarkably clear connection between variation and reproduction, largely the basis for his grandson Charles's own work on evolution.

William Bartram

SCIENTIFIC RECORDER AND ARTIST

(1739–1823)

Continually impelled by a restless spirit of curiosity,
in pursuit of new productions of nature, my chief happiness
consisted in tracing the infinite power, majesty and
perfection of the great Almighty Creator.

THESE WORDS WERE WRITTEN BY William Bartram in his work *Travels through North and South Carolina, Georgia, East and West Florida,* published in 1791. They refer to his time spent exploring, discovering, collecting and drawing the natural history of the southeastern region of North America. For four years, Bartram travelled on foot and horseback, by sailboat and dugout canoe, through the scientifically unexplored terrain of Georgia and Florida, as far as the Mississippi River. He braved tempests, biting insects, wild bears and alligators, and the coarse and often inhumane behaviour of the traders that he sometimes travelled with. Bartram's work was to influence naturalists and poets alike, with his pioneering view of nature that conceptualized the world as an organic whole, a living unity of diverse and interdependent forms.

Bartram's great contribution to the study of natural history was his ability to combine an aesthetic appreciation of nature with an accurate recording of data, based on observations made over long periods of time. As a scientist, Bartram recognized the necessity of making such systematic descriptions and records. But it was his observations through the seasons over many years that Bartram believed brought him closer to a greater understanding of the natural world in all its complexities. He found the beauty of the wild landscape astonishing and awe inspiring, and so powerful were these encounters that he sometimes felt as if he transcended the everyday comprehension of things.

Born in 1739 into a Quaker family in Kingsessing, just outside Philadelphia, William Bartram was very much a man of his time. He was steeped in Enlightenment ideas and rational thought that permeated the household he was raised in. This was an era that was driven by science, with reason replacing dogma and superstition, and with humankind set on a continuous road to progress and improvement. The idea of applying order to the investigation of the world had become the dominant trend by

W. Bartram

the second half the 18th century. As the century came to its close, however, there was a distinct shift in thinking about the natural world. The success of Newtonian scientific method and Linnaean classification was being challenged by a new generation of writers, artists and philosophers. It was the dawning of Romanticism, a school of thought that believed that reason alone could never provide a full understanding of the world. Imagination, emotion and the experience of the senses were as important as experimentation and nomenclature. A child of the Enlightenment, William was also very much a part of the new Romanticism that was sweeping through Europe in the early 19th century.

John Bartram, William's father, was a well-known figure in horticultural and scientific circles in Europe for his trade in American seeds and plants, work for which he was appointed the King's Botanist in 1765. As a young boy William accompanied his father on plant-hunting trips up and down the east coast of the then British colonies of North America. Here he learned about plants, animals, minerals and the composition of the Earth, and on many occasions took to drawing the things he observed. William, the fifth son, was the only one of the nine children to attend the Philadelphia Academy, later to become the Pennsylvania University. His education, however, did not include any formal tuition in art. It was the colour plate books of Mark Catesby (p. 124), Sir Hans Sloane (p. 111) and George Edwards that had made their way to the Bartram house as gifts from their respective authors that made an impact on William. He studied these books and their beautiful engravings and his drawings are often directly influenced by their styles and techniques. His skills were such that the wealthy English plant collector and naturalist Peter Collinson, on receiving a drawing from William in 1767, expressed amazement, saying that he and his son 'disputed for some time whether it was an engraving or a drawing'.

TRAVELS AND OBSERVATIONS

For much of William Bartram's early adult life he struggled, almost to the point of despair, to obtain what his father called a 'temperate reasonable living'. Success eluded him in all his efforts to find a livelihood, until in 1773, at the age of 34, he made the momentous decision to abandon any further attempts to please or depend upon his family and set off on his travels, having sought patronage from a London Quaker

This drawing of Dendroica magnolia, *the magnolia warbler, is one of several sent to George Edwards in London, who reproduced it in one of his books. The drawing is dated 1757 and from correspondence it is known that it was probably executed in 1755–56, when Bartram was 16 years of age.*

The Linnaean style of natural history art provided the scientist with an excellent aid to identification, but would place the specimen out of context and in isolation. Bartram much preferred to display the interrelationship between species, as in the drawing above.

physician, John Fothergill. Bartram lived with plantation owners and traders, accompanying them on their visits to the Native American towns and settlements. His recorded observations of the Creek and Cherokee people are considered as some of the most detailed and accurate of the time.

While William was travelling, America was embarking on its own revolutionary transformation, and he was not unaffected by the turmoil. In the spring of 1776, while in Darien, Georgia, he had been active in repelling British troops attempting to cross the St Mary's River. The action was minimal, but the instability and increasing violence was enough to convince Bartram to return to Philadelphia, where he arrived home in the bleak January of 1777. Bartram's account of his travels was finally published in 1791 and was initially far more popular in Europe than America. Eight editions of the book were published in six different countries within the first 10 years, and it remains in print today. *Travels* was a scientific work that included detailed descriptions and listings of plants, animals and birds of the region. It made an important contribution to science and was recognized as such. But more than simply an academic account, *Travels* was a narrative of Bartram's wonderings, evoking images of nature written in a poetic and rhapsodic language. His lyrical descriptions of nature found great favour with European Romantic poets such as Samuel Taylor Coleridge and William Wordsworth, who borrowed heavily from his work in their poetry. Bartram's 'alligator's thunder', 'milk white fragrant blooms', 'black velvet water snakes', and the young Cherokee virgins 'disclosing their beauties to the fluttering breeze', all find their way into the poetry of the Romantics.

Bartram addressed several themes in *Travels* that challenged some of the opinions current in science and society at the time. He questioned the concept of a hierarchical chain within nature, from non-living matter up to the most sophisticated organisms, a theory that originated centuries before but had come to dominate the study of biological sciences in the 18th century. That there was a universal interconnection between all things Bartram had no doubt, but he argued that little difference existed between plants, animals and humans. For Bartram everything was infused with a universal spirit and the creator could be discerned in all things. 'Where is the essential difference', he asked, 'between the seed of peas, peaches and other tribes of plants and trees, and that of oviparous animals?' Likening the emotions of animals to those of humans he claimed that the 'filial affections of animals were as ardent, their sensibility and attachment, as active and faithful, as those observed in human nature'. Bartram continued the argument further in discussing the plant *Dionaea muscipula*, the Venus flytrap. Here was a plant that responded to stimulation and appeared to have sensibilities. It was a 'sportive vegetable' according to Bartram. 'Can we after viewing this object, hesitate a moment to confess, that vegetable beings are endued with some sensible faculties or attributes, similar to those that dignify animal nature; they are organical, living and self-moving bodies, for we see here, in this plant, motion and volition.'

American Independence

William Bartram was also an important scientific figure in the development of the new American Republic. He was well aware of the need for an independent scientific community that would no longer be reliant on Europe for either materials or the intellectual interpretation of American natural products. He recognized that in order to take control of their own science, Americans had to start naming, describing and

William Bartram, by Charles Wilson Peale.

classifying indigenous flora and fauna themselves, and by so doing would make a contribution to the building of an independent nation. Bartram was familiar with the views of the French naturalist Buffon (p. 140) and his followers, who claimed that American natural products, both vegetable and animal, had degenerated over time. Buffon explained that European species had in the past made their way to the American continent, where, due to the poor environmental conditions such as climate and diet, they had degenerated to become smaller, weaker and inferior to their European counter-parts. Buffon applied this theory also to the indigenous people of America. Bartram did not argue against the idea of environmental conditions influencing species in different regions, a theory that Humboldt was to develop in the 19th century. But that American species had degenerated was something he refuted, and did so by describing the grandeur, enormity and splendour of the flora and fauna of the continent, and its people. The Cherokee were, according to Bartram, 'the largest race of men' and one Seminole Prince was 'the most perfect human figure' he had ever seen.

Bartram dedicated a large proportion of *Travels* to discussing Native Americans, describing their appearance, lifestyle and culture, comparing them to Europeans and finding them equal. He provided detailed descriptions of their religious beliefs and practices, their mode of agriculture, their language and music. He even offered an explanation on the origins of the large mounds that were found in the region, identifying them as 'Indian'. He compared the artifacts found in them with those of living Native Americans and concluded that the resemblance was enough to suggest that early Native Americans originally inhabited the sites. His theory was dismissed at the time, but is now known to be correct. Bartram developed a great admiration for the Creek and Cherokee lifestyle and culture, particularly their relationship with nature, which confirmed many of his own views. Pantheist ideas that were in embryonic form before his travels were given substance after his encounters with Native Americans.

In his writings and his drawings Bartram strove to achieve a balance between the narrow categorizing and labelling of nature that dominated much of science at the time and a comprehension of the world as an integrated whole. To him the study of nature meant understanding how species related to and were dependent on their

Discovered by John and William Bartram in 1765, Franklinia *is now extinct in the wild; its survival in cultivation is due to William Bartram. The plant was named by William in honour of Benjamin Franklin.*

Franklinia alatamaha.   A beautiful Flowering Tree.

discovered growing near the banks of the R. Alatamaha in Georgia.

Collected & Drawn Willm Bartram. Delin.
1788.

Pages from William Bartram's journal kept during his travels in Georgia and Florida from 1773 to 1775 and sent to his patron John Fothergill in London.

surroundings, and what influence they in turn brought to bear on the local flora and fauna. Bartram introduced an aesthetic appreciation of nature that complemented the reasoned and rational study of the universe. He was left in no doubt that there was an underlying harmony to the world, and the interconnection, interrelationship and dependency between species were fundamental to his concept of nature.

By the early 19th century, William Bartram's reputation was such that he was sought after by politicians, scientists and philosophers from far and wide. He was offered the first professorship of botany at the Pennsylvania University in 1782, but never taught there. He was elected a member of the American Philosophical Society and the Academy of Natural Sciences, but took no part in their meetings. He was asked by Thomas Jefferson, then President of the United States, to participate in the Red River expedition, and although flattered found he could not accept. Many leading naturalists of the time would visit him to discuss and debate ideas on nature, and also stay at his house for long periods of time or between expeditions.

William Bartram died on a July morning in 1823 in his beloved garden. He had lived through some momentous times. His influence over the poets and thinkers of this period is unquestionable. Alexander von Humboldt (p. 224), whose view of nature was similar to Bartram's, gave expression to it when he wrote in his work *Kosmos* that nature was 'unity in diversity, and of connection resemblance and order, among created things most dissimilar in their form, one fair harmonious whole'. The term ecology was not used and environmental science was not studied until the second half of the 19th century, but their roots can be found in the ideas of the naturalists of the early Romantic Movement and in the writings and drawings of William Bartram.

Joseph Banks

VOYAGER AND PATRON OF NATURAL HISTORY

(1743–1820)

*The country where I saw it abounded with vast variety
of Plants and animals, mostly such as have not been describd
by our naturalists as so few have had an opportunity of
coming here; indeed no one that I know of even tolerably
curious has been here since Marcgrave and Piso about the
year 1640, so it is easy to guess the state in which
the nat hist of such a countrey must be.*

Joseph Banks, Brazil, 26 November 1768

BEST KNOWN PERHAPS FOR HIS VOYAGE on the *Endeavour* with Captain James Cook, Joseph Banks is widely acknowledged as having had a significant and lasting influence on natural history over the last two centuries. His travels and many enterprises won him fame and acclaim in his own day, and earn him recognition still today. Born in 1743 into a wealthy Lincolnshire family, he used his fortune and position to set out on voyages of discovery himself or to send others, identifying and making collections of plants and animals that were of both scientific and economic importance. He was also significant in establishing the king's botanical collections at Kew, now the Royal Botanic Gardens.

It is widely stated that Banks was an unenthusiastic pupil, first at Harrow and from September 1756 at Eton, and that he would rather spend time hunting than studying. His poor scholarly performance initially caused concern, but, after the Easter holidays in 1757, there was a sudden and notable change in his attitude. It was at this point that Banks's passion for the study of nature began, which would last until his death. His interest kindled by such publications as Gerard's *Herball* and his proximity to the local countryside, he began collecting plants, insects and shells along the Thames or in his Lincolnshire home at any free time during the school holidays.

In 1760 Banks went to Christ Church, Oxford, to study, but while he was in his first year there his father died, and he returned home to Revesby Abbey. Banks was 18, and being too young to inherit the family estates, his mother Sarah and uncle Robert Banks-Hodgkinson were the guardians of his fortune until he was 21. Sarah Banks moved with her two children to Chelsea, close to the Apothecaries' Physic Garden.

Nova Zelandia, prope Tigadu, Tolaga, Motuaro

Sir J. Banks & Dr. Solander 1769

Fruiting material!
ISOLECTO-TYPE SPECIMEN
Donia punicea G. Don.
Gen. Syst. 2: 467 (1832).

NEW ZEALAND 1769-70
BANKS & SOLANDER
Solander Prim.Fl.N.Zel. p. 514
Parkinson Ic. 440

Type Specimen

It was at Chelsea that Banks met Philip Miller, the distinguished gardener there, who would remain amongst Banks's most important contacts and who encouraged his studies. From 1760 to 1765 Banks divided his time between his courses at Oxford and his estates, where he occupied himself in property management and financial affairs, together with his uncle. Throughout this period he maintained his obsession with natural history and was seen as something of an oddity amongst his academic friends. His economic status afforded him a number of privileges, including obtaining the agreement of the university to bring Israel Lyons, a tutor at Cambridge, to deliver a short summer course in botany at his own expense.

After leaving Oxford following the summer of 1765, without taking his degree, Banks became an assiduous visitor to the reading room at the British Museum. His collaboration with Daniel Solander probably began at this time. Solander, a pupil of Linnaeus (p. 133), originally came to London at the request of Peter Collinson, a wealthy patron of natural history, and was working on the preparation of a systematic catalogue of the animal collections at the British Museum.

Banks was now faced with a choice – he could become a landowner living off the income from his estates, or he could follow his curiosity for the natural world. He chose both, managing his lands wisely and using some of the income to support his many interests: botany, natural history, voyages of discovery, the trading expansion of the British empire, and the diversification of the production of natural resources within the country and its colonies. This was an era of growing empires, a time of innovation and scientific discovery, when countries across Europe were competing in the race to acquire new, as yet unknown territories to extend their economic and political influence.

BANKS'S THREE VOYAGES

It was through his three epic voyages of exploration that Joseph Banks was to become one of the great naturalists. He embarked on his first when only 23 years old. This was to Newfoundland and Labrador, in Canada, on board HMS *Niger* (April 1766 – January 1767), with Captain Sir Thomas Adams. Both Banks and Lieutenant Constantine John Phipps, an old friend from Eton, joined as supernumeraries on board the *Niger*, bound on fisheries protection duty. During this journey Banks spent time collecting plant, animal and geological specimens and exploring on land when

Herbarium sheet with specimens collected in Tegadu Bay, Tolaga Bay, Motu aro Island, New Zealand by Joseph Banks and Daniel Solander during the Endeavour *voyage, 1769. This specimen is part of Banks's herbarium collection housed in the Botany Department at the Natural History Museum, London.*

A pencil drawing of Banks in later life (undated).

allowed ashore; he also tried, albeit unsuccessfully, to make contact with the Eskimos. It was a productive voyage for Banks, although he lost many living plants and seeds during a heavy gale which struck near Lisbon on the homeward journey. Despite this setback, he managed to return with a bird collection which he had gathered for the Welsh naturalist, Thomas Pennant, as well as numerous plant collections from Iceland. He also brought back many plants from the Iberian Peninsula, the Azores and South America, which he had obtained from Gerard Devisme and Domingo Vandelli in Lisbon. On his return to London, Banks had several artists (Sydney Parkinson amongst them), illustrate some of his collections.

Banks is best remembered for his second voyage, to the southern Pacific on board HMS *Endeavour* (July 1768 – July 1771), with Captain James Cook (the two had in fact overlapped in Newfoundland for a short time, though there is no record that they ever met). By the end of 1767, the Royal Society began discussing the idea of observing the Transit of Venus across the sun, with the aim of facilitating naval navigation and thereby increasing Britain's dominance over the oceans. There was much discussion about suitable persons to carry out this work, the possible locations for the observation, and finding a seaworthy vessel robust enough for the task. Banks alone was accepted as a supernumerary on the voyage, largely due to the significant sum of money he supplied to finance the expedition, which surpassed even that provided by King George III. In July 1768 he boarded the *Endeavour* with a party of eight: the botanist Daniel Solander; three artists – Sydney Parkinson, Alexander Buchan and Herman Spöring; and four servants – Peter Briscoe, James Roberts, George Dorlton and Thomas Richmond.

Owing to adverse weather conditions on the relevant days, the mission failed in its primary goal of observing the Transit of Venus and it was at this point that Cook referred to a second, secret set of orders. These were to find the suspected but as yet undiscovered land mass known as '*Terra Australis Incognita*' and to catalogue all the natural materials found there. It was this part of the mission which was to make the voyage so successful and so famous. Such was Banks's enthusiasm for the flora that he discovered in Australia that he persuaded Cook to name one of his most famous landfalls Botany Bay. During the *Endeavour* voyage Banks and Solander collected some 30,000 plant specimens, of which 1,400 were probably new to science, and over 1,000

Sir Joseph Banks's herbarium and part library in his house at 32 Soho Square, London, in a sepia painting by Francis Boott, 1820. It remained there until 1827 when it was moved to the British Museum at Montagu House.

animal specimens of all kinds, terrestrial and marine. Together with this invaluable collection, there was also an extensive graphic record, mainly by Sydney Parkinson. The resulting work comprised 18 volumes for the plants, with 269 finished drawings and 673 part-completed, and three volumes for the animals, with 298 drawings. Banks intended to publish accounts of his collections in an impressive 14-volume work, which Solander worked on after their return. However, with the death of Solander in 1782 and Banks's own increasing pre-occupation with other duties, the much-awaited work was never published in his lifetime (the beautiful artwork from the voyage was finally published in 1988).

A collection of beetles from the collection of Sir Joseph Banks, now housed in the Entomology Department at the Natural History Museum, London.

The *Endeavour* voyage was also successful in charting the eastern coast of Australia and the whole coastline of New Zealand. Banks was also interested in the many cultures encountered on the expedition, though, tragically, when the *Endeavour* first berthed in New Zealand in Poverty Bay, misunderstandings on the part of the British led to shots being fired and the loss of many Maori lives.

While Cook was to set sail on a second voyage to the southern oceans with the Admiralty, Banks prepared his own third expedition, which he led himself. This was to the Hebrides, Iceland and the Orkney Islands on board HMS *Sir Lawrence* (July 1772 – December 1772), with Captain James Hunter. While exploring the Island of Staffa near Mull, off the west coast of Scotland, Banks visited, measured and described for the first time the famous Fingal's Cave.

Before he was even 30, therefore, Joseph Banks had completed the only three voyages of overseas exploration that he would make in his life. From this time on, he was to become a patron of science, with very little time to engage in fresh adventures of his own. However, he tirelessly supported new voyages of discovery and the dissemination of knowledge relating to natural history.

KEW GARDENS

Having been presented to King George III in July 1771, Banks went on to become the king's advisor relating to the royal gardens at Kew. Under his stewardship the gardens became one of the largest botanical gardens in the world. Banks undertook the role of unofficial director and was responsible, together with William Aiton, the royal horticulturist at the time, for hugely increasing the plant collection through the importation of exotic plants, supported by an extensive herbarium (a collection of dried plants) and reference library. In 1793, for instance, as a result of three returning voyages with which Banks had contact – from Botany Bay in Australia, Vancouver in Canada and the northwest of North America, and also from Tahiti in the Pacific – he played a key role in the acquisition of new botanical specimens. Banks also initiated correspondence with William Roxburgh, the superintendent of the Botanic Garden in Calcutta (from November 1793), inviting him to send plant specimens from India to London for identification and description. For 20 years Roxburgh sent a steady flow of specimens, and through him the Royal Botanic Gardens at Kew received a rich harvest of new species.

It was during this period that Banks also developed his interest in plants of economic importance. For example, he identified Assam in India as an ideal location for the cultivation of tea to provide supplies for Britain. Half a century later this project would be realized, with Assam becoming a major exporter of tea. Banks also focused the attention of the East India Company on the production of indigo, coffee, chocolate, vanilla, cochineal and cotton – with the idea that through such initiatives Britain could obtain ready supplies of all these raw material from its colonies. At the same time, he was becoming aware of the importance and quality of Spanish merino wool, and he hoped to establish a lucrative trade in it, depriving Spain of its monopoly. Banks was also attempting to obtain the cochineal cactus and insect (which produced a scarlet dye) from Brazil, having already smuggled specimens from Honduras. He succeeded, with official French Admiralty support, in transferring two varieties of the cochineal insect from Mexico to Santo Domingo, but after some eight years of little success and many difficulties, Banks abandoned the project. In 1791 he was involved in sending two vessels under the command of Captain James Bligh to Tahiti, with the objective of collecting breadfruit and other plants. Their orders were to continue on to Jamaica, where they were to introduce many of the plants into cultivation. The horticulturist on the voyage returned to Kew with some of these plants of economic interest, as well as several native wild plants given to him in Jamaica. The plants finally arrived in Britain in 1793 and further enhanced the living collections at Kew.

In addition to all this, Banks was also President of the Royal Society from 1778 to 1820, which occupied him in diverse issues. During his presidency he suggested Botany Bay in Australia as a location for establishing a distant colony for convicts. The British government had previously sent convicts to the Americas as enforced servants, but with the outbreak of conflict there new solutions had to be found to the problem of overcrowded prisons. Two alternative destinations, the Gambia River and the Orange State in Africa, having proved unrealistic, the government acted on Banks's suggestion. He also successfully approached King George III to support Francis Masson in the botanical exploration of Madeira, the Canaries, Azores and West Indies; the resulting collections remain in the Natural History Museum, London, today.

Passion and Patronage

Through his patronage of natural history, Banks also helped support many important publications in the later 18th century. In collaboration with Solander he provided Constantine John Phipps with the classifications and descriptions of animals and plants for his official account *A voyage towards the North Pole, undertaken by His Majesty's Command, 1773*, published in 1774. Banks also supervised the engravers for John Webber's drawings from Cook's third and last Pacific voyage (1776–79). Subsequently, Banks was directly involved in the publication of Cook's own accounts of his voyage, which had ended in his death in Hawaii, successfully negotiating to obtain high-quality French paper for the illustrations. Other examples of Banks's patronage include providing funds and editorship for the printing of a catalogue and engravings of both William Houston's Caribbean and Central American plant collection in 1781, as *Reliquiae Houstounianae*, and in 1794 for *The Plants of the Coast of Coromandel*.

Banks carried his passion for nature throughout his entire life. Wherever he travelled on expeditions he would find the time to collect specimens, even in Plymouth, England, when the departure of the *Niger* to Newfoundland and Labrador was delayed in 1766. He also expanded his own collections through the efforts of fellow naturalists and friends. In a vast array of publications from Banks's own time up to the present day, he has been described in many different ways: aristocratic landowner,

A specimen of Banksia serrata *(Proteaceae) first collected in Botany Bay, Australia.*
The watercolour on paper drawing is attributed to the artist John Frederick Miller, but
the work would have been heavily based on a partially coloured sketch by Sydney Parkinson,
1773. This genus is native to Australia and was named after Sir Joseph Banks.

botanist, naturalist, explorer, scientific administrator and patron. As well as these
positive images of Banks, he has also been viewed in a more negative light, through
caricatures, burlesque poems and gossip and jokes, by people who only saw him as an
opportunistic and autocratic person, with a lust for power.

Although he inevitably experienced failures in his plans and ventures, Banks
certainly succeeded in many of his enterprises. Amongst Banks's greatest legacies was
the vast range of plants he introduced through colleagues and his position at Kew, and
the role he played in the movement of economic plants across the globe, including the
introduction of breadfruit from the southern Pacific to the West Indies and tea from
China to India. His collections of dried plants, insects and shells now reside in the
Natural History Museum in London, where they are still of great use to scientists and
historians today.

Johann Christian Fabricius

CLASSIFIER OF INSECT DIVERSITY

(1745–1808)

*The number of species in entomology is almost infinite and
if they are not brought in order entomology
will always be in chaos.*

J. C. Fabricius, Philosophia Entomologica, *1778*

I N 1668, FRANCESCO REDI DEMONSTRATED by experiment the falsity of the idea that maggots were generated spontaneously in dead flesh. But while in the 18th century knowledge of biology advanced, a credible theory of organic evolution was still lacking and it seemed that the best explanation for the origin of species was to apply the story of Genesis to all life. As Europe's power and world influence grew, however, seemingly innumerable new species began to be discovered, revealing that the Earth supported a diversity of living things far greater than previously imagined. Trying to *deal* with this multitude became a practical issue that would successfully be addressed by Johann Christian Fabricius; trying to *understand* it led to a revolution in our perception of reality, as developed by Charles Darwin and Alfred Wallace.

Fabricius was the younger son of a well-known Danish physician. Born 7 January 1745, Fabricius grew up at Tønder, where he was educated by his parents 'in a spirit of liberality and freedom'. This emphasized physical as well as intellectual development, and both proved important in Fabricius's life. From his early days he was drawn to natural history, including the study of plants and insects.

In 1761 his father became physician at Frederick's Hospital in Copenhagen, and in 1762 he arranged for his young naturalist son to go to Uppsala, where Fabricius studied with Linnaeus (p. 133) for two years. Many years later he wrote: '… this was the most important period of my life … I always look back to that period with great delight and warm feelings of gratitude towards my great master…. He properly laid the foundation of our knowledge, and imprinted on our minds the systematic order with which the study of the sciences ought to be pursued.'

THE FOUNDATIONS OF ENTOMOLOGY

By the mid-1700s, Linnaeus's new methods of hierarchical classification and binomial nomenclature began to bring order to the growing chaos. Linnaeus, however, had

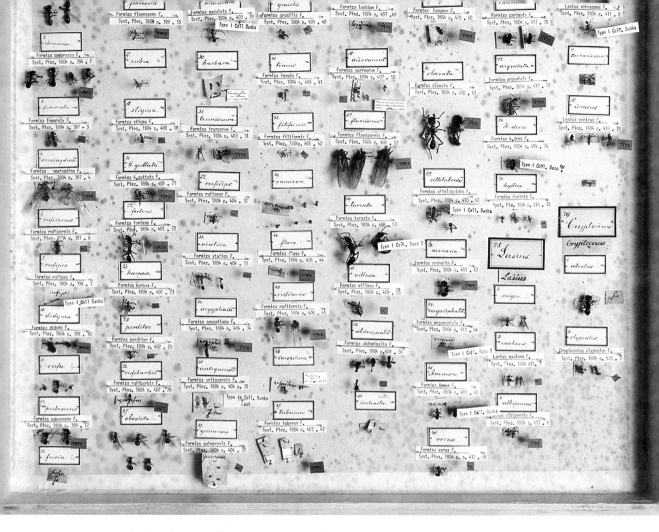

Ants in the Fabricius Collection, Copenhagen. Fabricius named many new species in all groups of insects; most specimens shown here are 'types', being the original 18th-century material on which just some of Fabricius's ant species were based. These specimens are still referred to by specialists, to ensure correct application of his names.

time only to provide a rather crude framework for the insects (Insecta), based on the number and form of the wings, and to give formal names to about 3,000 species. It was four years after publication of the 10th edition of his *Systema Naturae* that Linnaeus met the young Johann Christian Fabricius – and inspired him to take up the challenge of insect diversity.

Fabricius went on to become one of Linnaeus's greatest protégés, and the most important and prolific systematic entomologist of the 18th century. In a series of major works, notably *Systema Entomologiae* (1775), *Genera Insectorum* (1776), *Philosophia Entomologica* (1778), *Species Insectorum* (1782), *Mantissa Insectorum* (1787) and *Entomologia Systematica* (1792–94, 1798), he laid the foundations for the future of entomology.

Not only did he describe and name nearly 10,000 species (a huge number for one person, yet only 1 per cent of those now named, and probably less than 0.2 per cent of those believed to exist), but his *Philosophia* is regarded as the first general textbook of entomology, and in the *Systema* he recast the practical basis of insect systematics.

Following Linnaeus's Aristotelian methods, Fabricius emphasized adult mouth-parts instead of wings as the most important source of characters. He did this not only for practical purposes, but also because he believed that, by focusing on a feature fundamental to the biology of the entire group, a more natural classification would be achieved. His idea that the taxonomic system should reflect functional anatomy was advanced thinking for the time. His writings also reveal that he believed new species and varieties could arise through hybridization, incremental changes, environmental influences and sexual preferences. In one passage, published in 1804, he even went so far as to suggest that *Homo sapiens* appears to have evolved from 'the bigger monkeys'.

Fabricius also wrote on practical applications (e.g. on plant pathology in 1774 and horticulture in Sanders' compendium for farmers, 1784), and on politics and the Danish economy. His views were often attacked in print. An 88-page pamphlet entitled *On the Increase of Population, particularly in relation to Denmark* (1781) caused a particular stir – it is regrettable that Robert Malthus, the economist known for his somewhat gloomy vision of population growth, was apparently unaware of his work.

After Uppsala, at the age of 20, Fabricius visited Germany, then the Netherlands and Scotland, becoming an inveterate traveller. Leaving Edinburgh in autumn 1767, he spent nearly three months journeying to London by horse, studying numerous matters en route. Over the next year he met Joseph Banks (p. 173), Daniel Solander, John and William Hunter, Dru Drury, Thomas Pennant and many other London-based naturalists, with whom he formed a particularly strong bond. William Jones described him as 'a man that must please; open, free, easy, candid, unaffected'. In late 1768 he moved to Paris, then travelled widely through France and on to Italy. In spring 1769 he reached Austria, finally returning to Copenhagen only in the autumn. Subsequently, in addition to numerous trips from Denmark to London and Paris, and further journeys to Austria, Switzerland and Germany, he visited Norway in 1778 and St Petersburg in 1786. In his autobiography he mentions over 80 men of letters with whom he made contact during his travels – including Banks, Antoine-Laurent Jussieu (p. 197) and Georges Cuvier (p. 202).

Fabricius was thus a truly European 'networker'. Moreover, he was not only interested in natural history. In 1790 he travelled with his wife and daughter to Paris to see his friend the ichthyologist P. M. A. Broussonet, to study the numerous new insects gathered by French entomologists, and, following the storming of the Bastille, to witness political developments in France. He came to know several leading figures of the Revolution, including Jean Marie and Madame Roland, and attended the National Assembly and Jacobin Club. However, because of a serious accident suffered by his daughter, he and his family left Paris in the summer of 1791 and returned to Kiel. Little more than two years later his beloved daughter was dead, his friend Madame Roland had been sent to the guillotine, and Jean Marie had committed suicide.

Fabricius's travels also reflect the fact that, for many years, he and his family had lacked a truly permanent official position or home. Much of this can be attributed to the failure of the University of Kiel to make good its promises to appoint him to a professorial post. In 1768 Fabricius was appointed Professor at the Charlottenborg Institution in Copenhagen, but, on his arrival two years later, this post was transferred to the University and much reduced in value. From 1775 he was finally appointed in Kiel, but he never had the facilities and support promised, or that he expected. Increasingly frustrated, from 1789 onwards Fabricius only visited Kiel during the winter months, to give lectures to his appreciative students. From 1796 his wife moved back to Paris, where he then spent the summer months, dividing the rest of his time between Kiel and Copenhagen.

In 1768 Fabricius had helped Banks and Solander prepare for their momentous circumnavigation with James Cook, but he never visited the tropics himself. His best opportunity came during a visit to London in 1787, when a Colonel Charles Cathcart suggested he act as naturalist on a government survey of the East Indies. Fabricius was married with a young family and he tried to negotiate with the East India Company for life insurance in case he failed to return. They demurred, Cathcart sailed without a naturalist – and died in the Sunda Strait aboard HMS *Venus*. Fabricius survived another 21 years, dying in Kiel on 3 March 1808, at the age of 63 – apparently heartbroken, according to his wife, to know that Copenhagen had been bombarded by his beloved friends, the British. But by this time he

Instituted in 1941, the Fabricius Medal is awarded by the Deutsche Gesellschaft für allgemeine und angewandte Entomologie. The image of Fabricius is based on the well-known etching by G. L. Lahde.

was assured of a permanent place in the pantheon of natural historians. Although his artificial system of classification (which he adopted mainly on the grounds that it was practical) and frequent lack of detail were criticized, all acknowledged a great debt to this charming, modest and truly remarkable Dane: the man who laid the foundations of systematic entomology.

James Hutton

DISCOVERER OF GEOLOGICAL TIME

(1726–1797)

The result, therefore, of our present enquiry is that we find
no vestige of a beginning – no prospect of an end.

Quotation from Hutton's paper to the Royal Society of Edinburgh
read in 1785 and printed in the Transactions of
the Royal Society of Edinburgh, Vol I, 1788

IN THE LEARNED CIRCLES OF THE 18TH CENTURY there was already a widespread acceptance that the age of the Earth must greater than the 6,000 years calculated from the written history of the Bible. But how much older might it be and how could this age be discovered? Aristotle's (p. 23) concept of a world of infinite duration was discounted not only on theological grounds, but also because of the consensus that the Earth had been continually eroding since its formation and would eventually cease to exist. Given its present state, the Comte de Buffon (p. 140) in France and Abraham Werner in Germany both estimated an age of about 1 million years. To James Hutton this seemed absurd. He doubted that God would have created humans in a world that would waste away. In trying to answer his doubts he discovered the immensity of geological time.

SHAPING THE EARTH

The natural sciences were thriving at this time in Edinburgh. At the university, James Robertson was promoting the study of rock formations as advocated by his teacher Werner. These men believed that the Earth was gradually wasting away as erosion and occasional catastrophic events like the biblical Flood shaped its surface. Hutton, who had studied medicine after a false start in law, was now a modernizing farmer and could not accept this view. He realized that if land surfaces were not restored as well as eroded, life would decline until it reached an end. Hutton considered this to be a poor design. Instead, he argued that God had created the Earth as a well-maintained machine, constantly refreshed by repeating cycles of erosion, deposition,

Septarian nodules from the Coal formation near Edinburgh, as illustrated in Plate I of Playfair's (1802) edition of Hutton's Theory. *The cracks or 'septa' filled with calcite inside such concretions do not reach the exterior of the nodule. This led Hutton to suggest that they must be the result of fusion caused by heat rather than precipitation.*

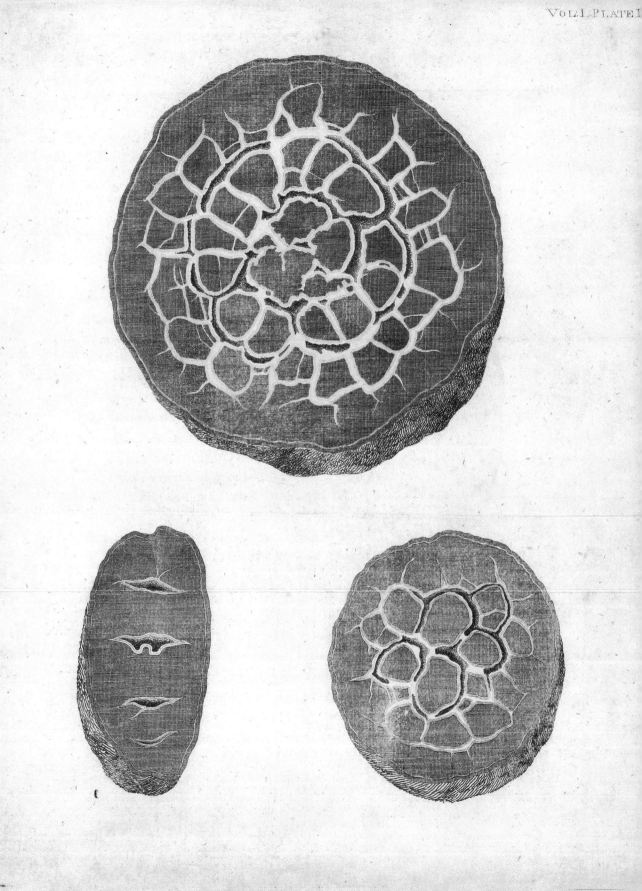

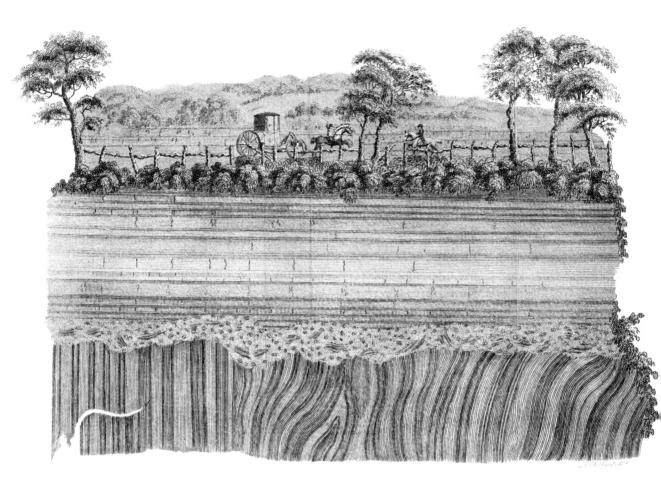

Plate III of Hutton's 1795 Theory of the Earth *shows the section at Jedburgh in the southern uplands of Scotland, illustrating his discovery of the recycling of rocks and rejuvenation of the Earth's surface by uplift. He saw that the lower schist beds were deposited horizontally before being uplifted and pushed over into the vertical position seen here. The upper surface of the schist was then eroded, before horizontal layers of sandstone were deposited on top. Further uplift, followed by weathering of the sandstone, produced the soil on top of that. The section illustrates Hutton's idea of a cyclical succession of worlds perfectly. On seeing this evidence in the field, John Playfair said 'What clearer evidence could we have had. … The mind seemed to grow giddy by looking so far into the abyss of time.'*

rock formation and uplift. As each successive cycle obliterated the previous one 'we find no vestige of a beginning – no prospect of an end'. In other words, he understood the age of the Earth to be immense but indefinite. This timescale did not alter the length of human history as set down by the Bible, nor did it change Hutton's view that life forms represented in fossils had always existed unchanged since a single creation. His interest in time allowed him to theorize that the Earth had been shaped by slow observable processes rather than catastrophes like the biblical Flood. Referring to 'natural operations' such as weathering, soil erosion, volcanic eruptions, earth movements and 'invisible processes which occur deep in the earth or under the sea', he suggested that such 'little things long continued ... would be adequate to the effects which we observe'.

POWERING THE MACHINE

In suggesting that the Earth must be a dynamic body constantly being rejuvenated, Hutton needed to identify how it worked. His answer startled his contemporaries as much as his views on time. His understanding of the latest developments in steam engines driven by latent heat led him to propose that the expansive power of heat in the depths of the Earth could uplift rocks which had formed on the ocean floor from accumulations of sediment eroded from the land. In this respect he laid the foundations for the future understanding of earth movements or 'tectonics', but his ideas on heat did not stop there.

As well as providing the energy needed to uplift and contort rocks, Hutton also proposed that heat was the mechanism that consolidated sediments to form rocks. This was extremely controversial among his so-called 'Neptunist' contemporaries led by Werner, who held that all rocks were 'sedimentary', composed of sediments laid down, compressed and cemented in the sea. This is true for sedimentary rocks, but Hutton realized that some rocks such as granite and basalt are volcanic or 'igneous' in origin. He correctly but controversially understood such rocks to have been in a molten state and observed that the heat from them altered adjacent sedimentary strata. This in its turn challenged the simple notion of Primary and Secondary rocks which had held sway since Steno (p. 87), as Hutton provided evidence to show that primary rocks such as granite and basalt could be forced up through older sedimentary rocks previously considered as always younger.

The first draft of Hutton's theory, read to the Royal Society in Edinburgh in 1785 and published in 1789, was justly criticized for lacking proof. For the next five years he dedicated himself to further fieldwork, adding the evidence he discovered to an enlarged, three-volume edition, *Theory of the Earth with Proofs and Illustrations* (1795–97). Unfortunately, this work failed to win him recognition because it was closely argued, with impenetrable theological justifications and lengthy French quotations. However, thanks to the devotion of his friend, the mathematician John Playfair, a carefully abridged and modernized version published in 1802 led some later historians to consider Hutton as the founder of modern geology.

Jean-Baptiste Lamarck

THE INHERITANCE OF ACQUIRED CHARACTERISTICS

(1744–1829)

*Suppose, for instance, that a seed of one of the meadow grasses
in question is transported to an elevated place on a dry,
barren and stony plot much exposed to the winds, and is there
left to germinate; if the plant can live in such a place, it will
always be badly nourished, and if the individuals reproduced
from it continue to exist in this bad environment, there will
result a race fundamentally different from that which lives in
the meadow and from which it originated.*

J.-B. Lamarck, **Philosophie Zoologique,** *1809*

WHEN WE HEAR THE NAME LAMARCK we perhaps think of giraffes stretching their long necks in order to eat leaves high on trees out of the reach of other browsers, an advantage which they then pass on to their offspring – this is the inheritance of acquired characters, or Lamarckian evolution. But Jean-Baptiste Pierre Antoine Demonet de Lamarck – better known as Jean-Baptiste Lamarck – was a botanist before he became a zoologist, and his interests spanned natural history. He is also usually mentioned in the same breath as Charles Darwin (p. 267), though in fact he was a contemporary of Charles's grandfather, Erasmus Darwin (p. 159). Lamarck is treated as the straw man to show Charles Darwin's true genius, a completely unfair juxtaposition.

Lamarck was the 11th and last child in an aristocratic but impoverished family from Picardy, and as befitted a younger son, he was destined by his father for a career in the Church. He reluctantly began training in a seminary, but when he was 15 years old his father died, so Jean-Baptiste decided to take up a career in the military instead. France was at war with Prussia at this time and he set off for the front, distinguishing himself in battle. When the war ended in 1763, Lamarck's regiment was stationed in Monaco, where he became fascinated by natural history, particularly botany. After four years as a soldier Lamarck left the military – the circumstances are far from clear, some say he had a tumour, others that he was not getting on with his comrades.

Returning to civilian life Lamarck began work as a bank clerk in Paris. In his spare time he studied botany and natural history, attending classes and discussions. He

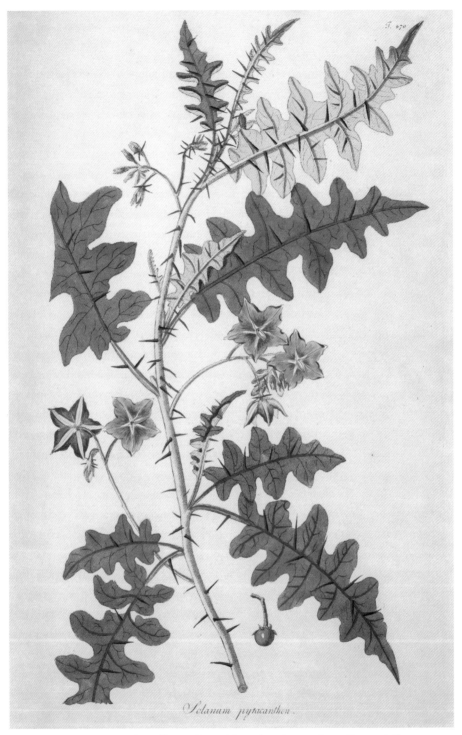

Solanum pyracanthon.

Lamarck described plants from all over the world, not just those native to France. Collectors sent seeds and plants to the Jardin du Roi in Paris where they were cultivated and classified. This nightshade, Solanum pyracanthon, *is from Madagascar, and was named for its fiery red spines.*

A formal portrait of Lamarck as professor of botany, topped by plants to symbolize his status as one of the foremost French botanists. He also invented the term 'invertebrates'.

came to the attention of the pre-eminent French naturalist of the day, Georges-Louis Leclerc, Comte de Buffon (p. 140), an ardent anti-Linnaean, and became a member of the inner circle of naturalists at the Jardin du Roi. Following in his mentor's footsteps, in his manual of the plants of France (the first ever attempted), the three-volume *Flore Française*, Lamarck cited Buffon in the introduction and severely criticized Linnaean artificial systems. For Lamarck, the philosopher-naturalist's task was to discover nature's distinct, true order; the artificial, logical classification systems erected by taxonomists like Linnaeus were of no use. Buffon was impressed and arranged for publication of the flora at the government's expense and extolled its virtues. Lamarck's *Flore Française* of 1778 – coincidentally the year Linnaeus died – was a scientific book with a difference. In it he introduced the use of common names for plants (rather than the Latin scientific names in vogue at the time, a step towards making science available to everyone) and he produced for the first time a key for identification that involved two-way choices, a dichotomous key – today commonplace, but then a novelty.

In addition to his interests in botany, Lamarck was an avid collector and seller of shells. Malacology, with botany, was a popular pastime for the 'amateur' naturalist of the 18th century, and a ready market for fossil shells meant that Lamarck could easily supplement his rather meagre income. Although he agreed with, and extolled in print, Buffon's views against artificial classifications, Lamarck did not hold with many of Buffon's later theories, such as the degradation of forms – but it was not good politics to argue with the most powerful naturalist of the day. Buffon organized an unsalaried position for Lamarck as 'correspondent' at the Jardin du Roi, and employed him as tutor to his son, thus ensuring his place in the scientific establishment in Paris.

But Buffon died on the eve of the French Revolution, and the community of French scientists split, not along revolutionary lines, but along largely 'Buffonite' versus 'anti-Buffonite' (i.e. Linnaean) lines. It is remarkable that Lamarck, a disciple of Buffon and of an aristocratic family, survived the upheaval of the French Revolution, but survive he did. In the 1793 reorganization of the Jardin du Roi into the Museum d'Histoire Naturelle, Lamarck was not given a botanical job – those went to the men who had been the 'professional' botanists of the Jardin du Roi, Antoine-

Laurent de Jussieu (p. 197) and René Louiche Desfontaines. Lamarck was transferred to zoology and appointed curator of worms – a decidedly second-class job. His situation in life was characterized in the professorial list as 'age 50, married for the second time, wife pregnant, six children, professor of the insects, worms and microscopic animals.'

NEW DIRECTIONS

Worms were not considered to be interesting – prestige was attached to the study of vertebrates or 'higher' animals. But Lamarck rose to the challenge, and completely revolutionized our understanding of these fascinating creatures. Before Lamarck, naturalists did not recognize the crustaceans (crabs and allies) as distinct from arachnids (spiders), there were just worms and not worms. Lamarck's own knowledge prior to his appointment as curator of worms was confined to their shells, but through careful and diligent study he reclassified the 'invertebrates' – a term he invented – into seven classes, all of which are still in use today. Lamarck emphasized the interconnections of all organisms, and identified what today we call homologies – structures resulting from descent from common ancestors. He saw life as organized in a series ranging from the simple to the complex, in contrast to the then prevailing view that simpler creatures were the result of degradation and thus inferior. His tree diagrams drawn to show this ladder of complexity form the basis for the paradigm in use today, albeit with radically different philosophical roots. As with many of the naturalists of the 18th century, it is easy with hindsight to see embedded in Lamarck's theories concepts far ahead of their time, but it is important to remember that we are looking through evolutionary glasses – we have the advantage of knowing that Charles Darwin articulated the mechanism that earlier generations were searching for, and we recognize glimmers of it in the work of his predecessors.

While working on zoological philosophy and his classification of invertebrates, Lamarck also developed theories of chemistry which were in direct opposition to the emerging ideas of Pierre Lavoisier and his colleagues. Lamarck felt strongly that specialization was bad, and that natural history – then including all the disciplines that today we call science – should be interdependent and seek to discover common, universal laws. He tried to make contributions to everything, and in the process developed an entirely new chemistry, which was not accepted by the scientists of the day and was soon superseded by the chemistry we know now. But Lamarck was trying to understand nature in its entirety, how it worked and where it came from. He was searching for the theory of everything, like Buffon. He characterized the science of living things as 'terrestrial physics' – stating in 1802 that 'A good *Terrestrial physics* must include all the first order considerations relative to the earth's atmosphere; next, all similar [considerations] regarding the state of the globe's outer crust, as well as the modifications and changes that it continuously undergoes; lastly [considerations] of the same kind pertaining to the origin and development of living bodies. Thus, all these considerations naturally cause terrestrial physics to be divided into three basic parts, the first of which must comprise the theory of the atmosphere, *Meteorology*, the second, that of the globe's outer crust, *Hydrogeology*, finally, that of living bodies, *Biology*.' Lamarck was thus one of the first to use the term that has today replaced 'natural history' for the study of living things – biology. The subdivision of natural history into the modern scientific disciplines had begun.

For all his good ideas, Lamarck did also have some truly eccentric ones too. He thought, for example, that life regenerated itself constantly from primordial ooze; he battled hard to set up his alternative chemistry; he argued with almost everyone. He was probably his own worst enemy. Despite his prickly nature, however, Lamarck was made a chevalier of the Legion d'Honneur, most probably in 1803, as were all the professors of the Museum at the founding of the order. He gained no further recognition, possibly because Napoleon didn't think very much of him.

Lamarck's Laws

Lamarck is chiefly remembered, however, not for his taxonomy of invertebrates, nor his invention of the term biology, nor his monumental *Flore Française*, but instead for his two 'laws' from *Philosophie Zoologique* (1809), which became enshrined as the anti-Darwinian doctrine of 'inheritance of acquired characteristics'. These laws were as follows:

First Law: 'In every animal which has not passed the limit of its development, a more frequent and continuous use of any organ gradually strengthens, develops, and enlarges that organ, and gives it a power proportional to the length of time it has been so used; while the permanent disuse of any organ imperceptibly weakens and deteriorates it, and progressively diminishes its functional capacity, until it finally disappears.'

Second Law: 'All the acquisitions and losses wrought by nature on individuals, through the **influence of environment in which their race has long been placed**, and hence through the influence of the predominant use or permanent disuse of any organ; all these are **preserved by reproduction to the new individuals which arise**, provided that the acquired modifications are common to both sexes, or at least to the individuals which produce the young' (emphasis added).

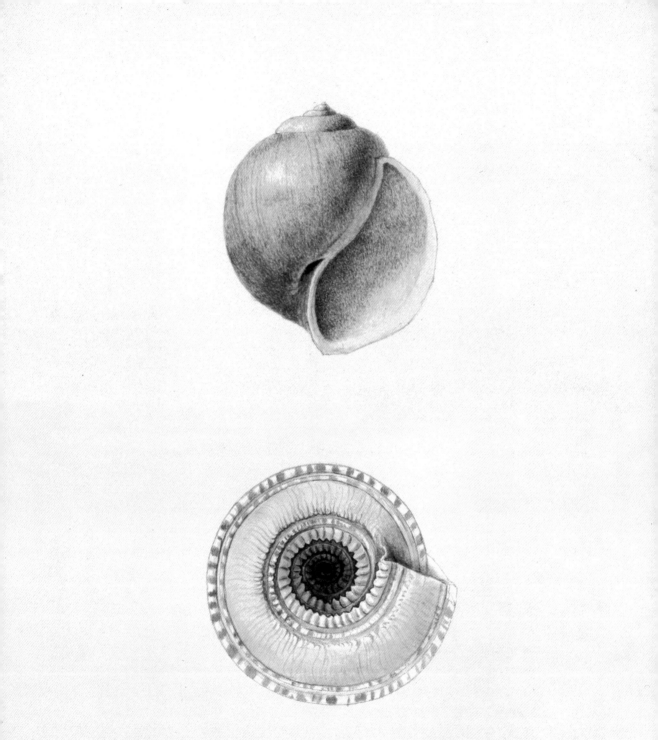

These delicate watercolours of shells (top, an apple snail Ampullaria guyanensis, *bottom, a painted sundial,* Architectona perspectiva) *were painted by Anna Atkins and were later turned into engravings to illustrate the translation of Lamarck's* Genera of Shells *by her father, John George Children. Anna was brought up by her father, who was secretary of the Royal Society, and received an unusual scientific education for the mid-19th century.*

Lamarck articulated these principles in order to explain the well-known phenomenon of what was perceived as the fitness for purpose of structures in nature – birds that lived on shorelines had long legs that allowed them to wade to hunt for food; plants growing in dry places were smaller and flowered more rapidly than those in wetter, more benign places; giraffes had long necks that allowed them to browse where others could not reach etc. To paraphrase, his laws can be caricatured as, 'giraffes stretch their necks, their children get long necks too'. Reading what Lamarck actually said, however, shows this is not what he meant. He emphasized the role of generations (to 21st-century eyes 'heredity') and environment ('adaptation') – not so strange after all.

Although Lamarck did not articulate the real mechanism for organic change, he was getting close, as was Erasmus Darwin. These natural historians were looking for a mechanistic explanation for the changes they observed in the world around them, having rejected the creationist view. In 1797 Lamarck stated, rather daringly for his time, 'life … is a physical fact, albeit somewhat complex in its principles'. By the time he was writing *Philosophie Zoologique* in 1809 he was even more definite – 'It seems, as I have already said, that time and favourable circumstances are the two principal means which nature uses in creating all its products. We know that time has no end for it, and is consequently always at its disposal' – in other words, no superior being or God is necessary, time and favourable circumstances are all that are required. These were dangerous sentiments to express publicly at the time when Napoleon and the Vatican had signed a concordat increasing the power of the Church in French life.

Lamarck's health declined in the early years of the 19th century, and he turned down the offer of a position in zoology at the Faculté de Sciences, citing chromic illness; by 1818 he was nearly blind. He died in 1829, having published the last volumes of his treatise on invertebrate zoology in 1822. Much of the way Lamarck is remembered in the English-speaking world stems from the *éloge* written after his death by the great French anatomist Georges Cuvier (p. 202). These written eulogies were used either to sanctify or assassinate colleagues – Cuvier's did the latter. The piece is subtle and cutting, and set Lamarck up as a person whose 'indulgence of a lively imagination has led to results of a more questionable kind' and as one 'whose attachments to systems so little in accordance with the ideas which prevailed in science, were not calculated to recommend him to those who had the power of dispensing favours.' A rather damning assessment, especially from one as intelligent and respected as Cuvier. Lamarck deserves to be remembered as a naturalist of great imagination and persistence, part of the panoply of 18th-century science, not as a textbook caricature set up in opposition to the science of the next century.

Antoine-Laurent de Jussieu

A NEW METHOD OF PLANT CLASSIFICATION

(1748–1836)

*[Genera Plantarum] is influential both because it was the
first accepted treatment in which all plant taxa at
and above the rank of genus were placed in a
natural sequence and clearly described, also because it
included a clear outline of the principles by which
the natural method was to be executed.*

P. F. Stevens, **The Development of Biological Systematics,** *1994*

THE YEAR 1789 IS OF COURSE FAMOUS for the storming of the Bastille in Paris on 14 July – a turning point of the French Revolution. In the history of botany it is notable as the year of the publication of a famous book by Antoine-Laurent de Jussieu, the *Genera plantarum secundum ordines naturales disposita juxta methodum in horto Regio Parisiensi exaratam*, which presented a revolutionary new method for the classification of plants.

For many botanists before Jussieu, such as John Ray (p. 92) in England, Carl Linnaeus (p. 133) in Sweden, and Pierre Magnol and Michel Adanson (p. 153) in France, the 'natural method' of plant classification had been the grail. Jussieu cannot therefore truly be said to be the 'father' of the natural method, but he did bring it a significant step closer to realization. In the guidelines he set out in his *Genera Plantarum* Jussieu did not claim to have arrived at a definitive solution, but proposed a balance between the needs of science and the practical user for a workable classification.

THE DISTINGUISHED JUSSIEU DYNASTY

Born in Lyon in 1748, Antoine-Laurent belonged to a distinguished dynasty of three generations of botanists at the Jardin du Roi, which became the Muséum d'Histoire Naturelle in 1793. First came the three brothers, Antoine (1686–1758), Joseph (1704–1779) and Bernard (1699–1777), who were all members of the Royal Academy of Sciences. Antoine de Jussieu had studied medicine in Montpellier, where Pierre Magnol, also the author of a natural classification of plant families, taught him botany. Antoine's arrival in Paris in 1708 coincided with the death of the distinguished botanist Joseph Pitton de Tournefort, and Antoine took over from him as a Professor of Botany at the Jardin du Roi. In 1716, he went to Spain to study the flora of the Iberian peninsula, accompanied by his youngest brother Bernard and the illustrator Charles-Louis Simmoneau. The journey offered Bernard an excellent opportunity to learn botany under the direction of his elders.

Bernard de Jussieu, who graduated as a doctor of medicine in 1720, can be considered the theoretician of the family. He took over from Sébastien Vaillant as a 'sous-démonstrateur de l'extérieur des plantes' at the Jardin du Roi. Antoine-Laurent de Jussieu, the nephew of Antoine and Bernard, came to Paris in 1765 and lived with Bernard for more than ten years, where he no doubt benefited from the teachings of his uncle. He became a doctor of medicine in 1770, and was appointed as assistant-botanist at the Royal Academy of Sciences in 1773, being named a professor of 'botanique à la campagne' at the newly created Muséum d'Histoire Naturelle, in 1793. His son, Adrien de Jussieu (1797–1853), took over his father's professorial chair in 1826, thus strengthening the family tradition.

From Antoine to Adrien, the Jussieus pursued the goal of the natural method of classification. While the sexual system of Linnaeus was based on the description of just one selected character, the number of stamens in a flower, for example, the natural method analyzes multiple characters from every part of the plant. In this the Jussieus were in line with the scientific thinking of the day in France. For instance, the Comte de Buffon (p. 140), director of the Jardin du Roi for 50 years, was anti-Linnaean and opposed to the artificial system. The French botanical elite, and the scientists of the Jardin du Roi in particular, were generally not in favour of the Linnaean system. While the systems of Tournefort and Linnaeus were useful in naming plants, they did not take into account the entire structure of a plant and the relationships between its different parts. What was required instead was an analysis of a large number of characters.

The Natural Method of Classification

In the search for such a natural method, Antoine-Laurent de Jussieu is given most credit. However, both his two elder relatives, Antoine and Bernard, had also promoted this method, but neither of them published writings to outline their theories and bring them to a wider audience. Bernard had many distinguished students,

The title page of Genera Plantarum, *published in 1789, in which Jussieu set out his proposed new method of plant classification. His aim was to achieve a natural method of classification – one which was based on the study and analysis of the entire structure of a plant, rather than Linnaeus's artificial system which only looked at a small number of specific parts.*

ANTONII LAURENTII DE JUSSIEU

REGI A CONSILIIS ET SECRETIS , DOCTORIS MEDICI
PARISIENSIS , REGIÆ SCIENTIARUM ACADEMIÆ REGIÆQUE
SOCIETATIS MEDICÆ PARISIENSIS , NECNON ACADEMIARUM UPSAL.
MATRIT. LUGD. SOCII , ET IN HORTO REGIO PARIS.
BOTANICES PROFESSORIS:

GENERA PLANTARUM

SECUNDUM

ORDINES NATURALES

DISPOSITA,

JUXTA METHODUM IN HORTO REGIO PARISIENSI
EXARATAM , ANNO M. DCC. LXXIV.

PARISIIS,

Apud Viduam HERISSANT, Typographum , viâ novâ
B. M. sub signo Crucis Aureæ.

Et THEOPHILUM BARROIS , ad ripam Augustinianorum.

1789.

including Michel Adanson (p. 153), the renowned botanist who also pursued a system of natural classification. One application of Bernard's ideas was in the organization in 1759 of the plants in the royal garden of Louis XV at the Trianon at Versailles. Here he presented a natural ordering of 65 groups, from fungi to conifers, creating a continuous series with very few gaps. But Bernard did not explain his method; moreover the Trianon garden was not a public garden, nor was it used for teaching purposes.

Antoine-Laurent de Jussieu first outlined insights into his new method in a memoir entitled 'Examen de la famille des Renoncules', which he presented at the Royal Academy of Sciences of Paris in 1773. He proposed that the morphological features of plants should be compared in order to organize them into groups based on the natural relationships between the specimens, thus forming families similar to 'natural' families already accepted by the botanical community (such as the umbellifers, including carrots, hemlocks and fennel). In addition, he noted that each individual character does not have an equal weight when used for comparing specimens. Thus flower colour can vary even within the same species, unlike seed structure, which remains constant throughout a genus.

In the following year, Antoine-Laurent presented a new system for ordering plants at the Royal Academy, in a lecture entitled 'Exposition d'un nouvel ordre de plantes adopté dans les démonstrations du Jardin Royal'. He then had the opportunity to illustrate his method in a practical way, proposing a rearrangement of the botanical garden of the Jardin du Roi in Paris. The garden's organization had been unchanged since its arrangement according to a system devised by Tournefort at the beginning of the 18th century, based on the form and structure of the corolla (all the petals of a flower). The new organization proposed by Antoine-Laurent was a counterpart to his uncle Bernard's at the garden of the Trianon at Versailles – in fact, Antoine-Laurent's principles came in a direct line from the teachings of Bernard. Furthermore, Antoine-Laurent's arrangement of the garden at the Jardin du Roi was both a teaching aid and an illustration of the principles of the natural method of plant classification that he was to develop later in his most influential book *Genera Plantarum*.

KEY PRINCIPLES

From a methodological point of view, there are two key elements in Jussieu's works. The first is based on the principle of continuity. His groups were characterized following the analysis and comparison of every part of every organ of a plant, resulting in relationships based on similarities of the greatest number of characters. The groups could then be arranged from the simplest to more complex organisms (from fungi to conifers). The second principle is known as the 'subordination of characters'. Jussieu pointed out that some characters in a given taxonomic group, seemed to be more constant than others. It followed therefore that not every character was of equal importance in classifying plants. Thus, characters were given a relative value, and strong, unchanged characters, or a combination of characters, were used for classification. This method is analytical and takes into account the relationships linking characters for developmental or functional reasons.

Following this second method, the vegetable kingdom was divided first into three groups, according to the presence and number of seed leaves or cotyledons in the seed, as Andrea Cesalpino (p. 63) and John Ray had already proposed in the 16th and 17th centuries. This initial

Antoine-Laurent de Jussieu, one of a great family of French botanists, in a portrait by Julien Léopold Boilly.

subdivision produced three groups: Acotyledons (plants without cotyledons, that is cryptogams and some aquatic plants: fungi, mosses, algae); Monocotyledons (plants with one cotyledon, such as lilies, orchids, wheat etc); and Dicotyledons (with two cotyledons, including beans, daisy, etc). Then, in a shift to a system based on logical deduction, 15 classes were characterized according to a small number of characteristics of the flower, such as the corolla and the position of the stamens over, under or around the pistil, creating groups respectively of epigynous, hypogynous and perigynous plants.

Finally, Antoine-Laurent de Jussieu studied 1,754 genera of plants and classified 100 families (*ordines naturales*), increasing by 36 the number described by Linnaeus and even by his own uncle, Bernard. In his study of Jussieu, P. F. Stevens wrote that 'His work is the basis of the actual classification of the genera in families, and the families in orders and classes', noting furthermore that 76 of Jussieu's names for plant families have remained in use since the publication of *Genera Plantarum*.

In 1826 Jussieu left Paris, mainly because of failing eyesight, and in 1836 he died. He had developed the first practical and robust natural classification of plants and a methodology that was to survive, at least in part, up to the present day.

Georges Cuvier

EXTINCTION AND THE ANIMAL KINGDOM
(1769–1832)

*Would there not also be some glory for men to get over
the limits of time and to rediscover by means of some
observations the history of this world and the succession
of events that preceded mankind's birth?*

GEORGES CUVIER, WHO WROTE THESE LINES in 1825 in his *Discours sur les Révolutions du Globe,* can justifiably be credited with being the first to reconstruct the faunas of lost worlds. One of the greatest scientific figures of the 19th century, his monumental works firmly established the science of comparative anatomy and laid the foundations of vertebrate palaeontology as a scientific discipline. Indeed, Cuvier examined, dissected and drew almost all the forms known in the animal kingdom at that time. He revealed the nature and diversity of the fossil bones that were being discovered in the depths of the Earth, while he also demonstrated that these remains belonged to lost species – in other words extinct animals.

Born in 1769 in the Lutheran town of Montbéliard, in eastern France (attached at that time to the duchy of Württemberg), there was nothing in the background of this son of a modest military man to suggest that he would go on to become a famous and outstanding naturalist. While he was still very young he discovered the plates of the *Histoire Naturelle* of Buffon (p. 140), but it was only during his studies in Stuttgart that Cuvier became passionately fond of entomology and botany and devoured the works of Linnaeus (p. 133), becoming an admirer of his method of classification.

In order to support himself, Cuvier took a job as a teacher to an aristocratic family in Normandy, and moved to Caen in 1788. Taking advantage of his numerous leisure hours, he occupied himself with the description of marine animals, molluscs and arthropods. His reading of Aristotle's *History of Animals* (p. 23) led him early on to elaborate a project to write a new and ambitious general natural history. At the time that Cuvier was living and working in Normandy, in Paris Lavoisier published his

The skeleton of the Egyptian sacred ibis (Threskiornis aethiopicus), *drawn by Cuvier and published in a paper by him in 1805. Cuvier was a strong opponent of the theory that animal species could change through time, and to support his view he dissected ancient Egyptian animal mummies, including ibises, to demonstrate that they were exactly the same as modern animals.*

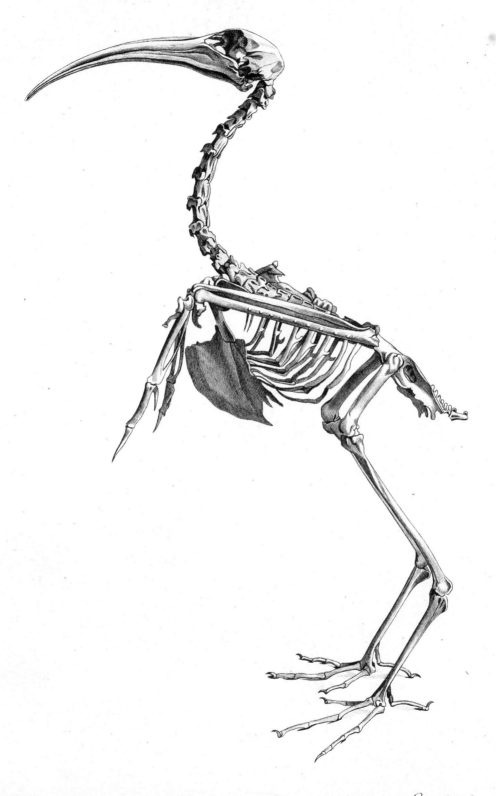

Squelette d'Ibis, tiré d'une momie de Thèbes en Egypte.

au tiers de sa grandeur.

Tab.I.

principles for a new chemistry and Antoine-Laurent de Jussieu (p. 197) proposed his new system of classification for plants in his *Genera Plantarum*. Jussieu's classification was one which reflected the reality of nature, not only demonstrating the existence of correlations between the different parts of flowers, but which also put forward the principle of subordination of characters – that not all were of equal significance in classification. Cuvier was excited by the proposals of both scientists and decided to take inspiration from their methods to reform zoology and transform it into a new science.

As Cuvier dissected and studied flat fishes in Caen, on 14 July 1789 the citizens of Paris stormed the Bastille prison. The Revolution soon swept across the whole of France, and disorders, food scarcities and the years of the Terror interrupted Cuvier's studies. He arrived in Paris in March 1795, at the invitation of the naturalist Etienne Geoffroy Saint-Hilaire, already possessing an excellent reputation as a naturalist. Within a short time, he was successively nominated as a teacher of natural history at one of the new Écoles Centrales born from the Revolution, then assistant to the professor of animal anatomy at the Muséum d'Histoire Naturelle, and finally member of the Anatomy and Zoology section of the Academy of Sciences.

At the Jardin des Plantes, Cuvier exerted his talent, ambition and power to create a cabinet of comparative anatomy, a museum devoted to the animal world. In just a few years, due to his efficient organization and with the help of a specially trained staff, this cabinet became one of the most comprehensive and famous in Europe, open to the public and displaying 16,665 zoological specimens. The British geologist Charles Lyell (p. 246) visited the museum and expressed his great admiration: 'I got into Cuvier's sanctum sanctorum yesterday, and it is truly characteristic of the man. In every part it displays that extraordinary power of methodizing which is the grand secret of the prodigious feats which he performs annually without appearing to give himself the least trouble.' The organization of the displays in the museum reflected Cuvier's ideas perfectly, with the animals arranged according to zoological classes and showing the relations between forms and functions. Cuvier's aim was to reject one of the accepted concepts of the 18th century, the 'Great Chain of Being', proposed by the Swiss naturalist Charles Bonnet, which visualized a continuity ranging from the simplest substances up to man and to celestial intelligences, in a gradual improvement of beings.

A page from Cuvier's Diarium Zoologicum *of 1788; Cuvier had made these impressively precise drawings of insects and other creatures while he was a student at Stuttgart, sketching the animals and plants that he observed around him.*

In 1812, after considerable work and study, Cuvier put forward his new arrangement for different categories of the animal kingdom. He separated it into four sub-kingdoms: Vertebrata (vertebrates); Articulata (arthropods); Mollusca (molluscs); and Radiata (such as jellyfish, sea anemones and starfish). The rejection of the concept of the Chain of Being and its replacement by Cuvier with the notion of sub-kingdoms were necessary preliminary stages in the development of a new understanding of the organization of life that reached fruition with the ideas of Lamarck (p. 190) and Darwin's evolutionary theories (p. 267).

EXTINCTION AND REVOLUTIONS

In 1800 Cuvier published *Leçons d'Anatomie Comparée*, which presented a detailed examination of the structures and functions of animal organs. Cuvier's mastery of the principles of comparative anatomy also enabled him to study, with spectacular results, the remains of extinct vertebrates. Also in 1800 he demonstrated that the teeth of fossil mammoths from Siberia, while clearly similar to those of existing Asian and African elephants, were also different and belonged to a species unknown today and which was therefore extinct. Cuvier went on to show that the well-known skull of a huge fossil animal found in a quarry at Maastricht (today identified as *Mosasaurus*) belonged to a large marine lizard, close to a type of lizard called Varans (such as monitor lizards) but now also extinct. Closer to home, Cuvier named the remains of animals found in the gypsum strata mined under the hill of Montmartre in Paris as *Paleotherium* and *Anoplotherium*. These mammals resembled tapirs, but again belonged to extinct species. He also identified a small reptile found on a lithographic limestone plate from Bavaria, Germany, as belonging to a group of vertebrates previously unknown, the flying reptiles – he called it Pterodactyl. This ability to make comparisons between animals and to reconstruct the creatures of the past deeply impressed Cuvier's contemporaries. The great French writer Honoré de Balzac, inspired by the principles established by Cuvier, published a famous series of novels entitled *La Comédie Humaine*, creating it as a comparative anatomy of 19th-century French society.

With his colleague and friend Alexandre Brongniart, Cuvier began in 1808 the *Description Géologique du Bassin de Paris*. Their studies made decisive progress in stratigraphical palaeontology, in which fossils are used to distinguish different strata, while the alternation of freshwater and marine deposits led Cuvier to suggest that in the past there had been a series of 'revolutions' or catastrophic events on the surface of the globe that had caused the sudden extinction of existing faunas. He published these ideas in his book *Discours sur les Révolutions du Globe*.

Cuvier had studied the skeleton of an orang-outang and published a study of it, with Etienne Geoffroy Saint-Hilaire, entitled Histoire naturelle des Orang-Outangs *in 1795; this plate is from an edition of the* Règne Animal *prepared by Saint-Hilaire and Cuvier's brother, Frédéric.*

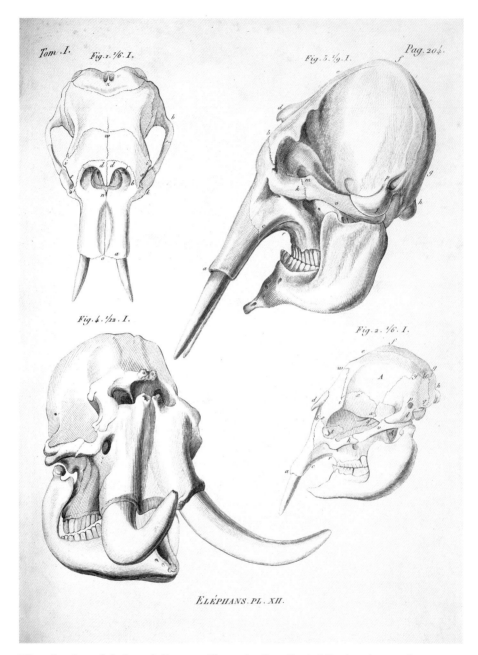

These drawings of elephant skulls are an illustration from Cuvier's Recherches sur les Ossemens Fossiles de Quadrupèdes, *first published in 1812. From his study of mammoth jawbones Cuvier demonstrated that while mammoths were similar to Indian and African elephants they were a different species, one which no longer existed today – and was therefore extinct.*

THE ANIMAL KINGDOM

Cuvier's output of published works was prodigious and reflected his very wide-ranging interests. In addition to those already mentioned, he also published *Tableau Elementaire de l'Histoire Naturelle des Animaux*, the result of lectures he gave in 1797 at the École Centrale de Panthéon. In 1812 he collected together all his papers on extinct vertebrates in the four volumes of the first edition of his *Recherches sur les Ossemens Fossiles de Quadrupèdes*, followed by a second edition in five volumes from 1821. But perhaps his greatest and most famous work appeared in 1817 in four volumes (a second edition in five volumes followed in 1829–30), the *Règne Animal Distribué d'après son Organisation*, a publication described as no less important than Linnaeus's *Systema Naturae*.

Portrait of Georges Cuvier; he received many honours from the French government for his work.

The *Règne Animal* was an attempt to create a complete inventory of the animal kingdom and to formulate a natural classification underpinned by the principles of the 'correlation of parts' (that is, all parts of an animal are functionally linked, and so from the study of single bone conclusions can be drawn about the whole animal) and the subordination of characters. In this work, Cuvier introduced clarity into natural history, accurately reproducing the actual ordering of animals. To him, each kind of animal was a unique complex of morphological resemblances, separated by unmistakable differences from all other forms.

Cuvier later directed his attention almost entirely to ichthyology. From 1820 he embarked with his colleague Achille Valenciennes on a huge *Histoire Naturelle des Poissons*, which would describe all the species known at that time. The work would have 22 volumes, 11,253 pages and 650 plates, and include descriptions of 4,055 species, 2,311 of which were new to science

At the same time as he devoted himself to his intensive and productive scientific career, Cuvier's great capacity for work and organizational skills meant that from 1800 he was also called on to fulfil many academic and administrative functions. In 1802 he was named commissary to set up new high schools, and in 1803 he was elected perpetual secretary of the Academy of Sciences, a position he held until his death in 1832; in 1809 Napoleon named him president of the commission in charge of inspecting teaching establishments in the new Empire in the Italian provinces. In 1811 he was charged with a similar mission in Holland. He also held numerous other official posts in education and natural history. Cuvier's fame brought him into contact with all the

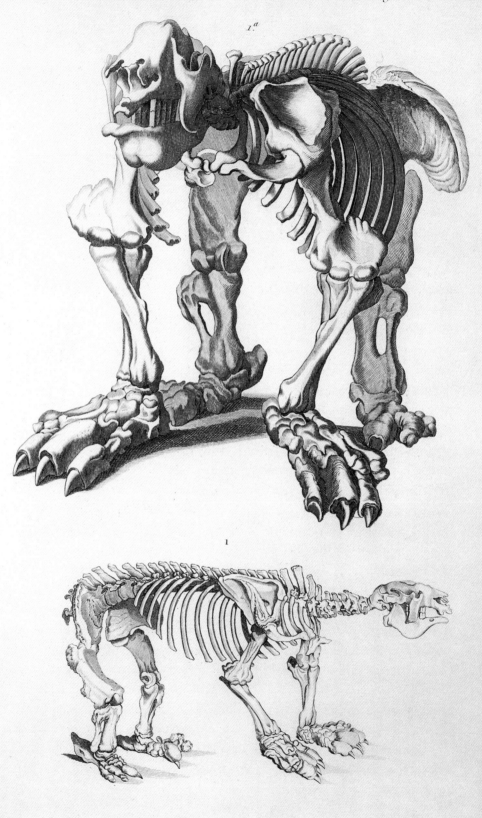

MEGATHERIUM (Megatherium)

Anaedouche sc.

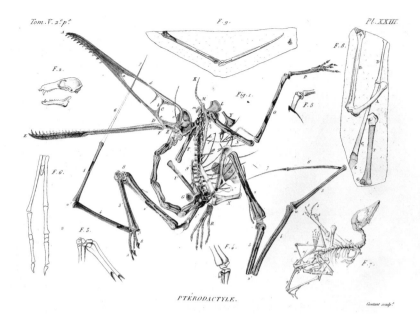

PTÉRODACTYLE.

Cuvier's skills as a comparative anatomist enabled him to identify animals both living and extinct: opposite is the skeleton of a Megatherium, *the giant ground sloth, and above are drawings of a pterodactyl skeleton – Cuvier was the first to identify and name this flying reptile.*

great naturalists of his time, at home and abroad. Though he deeply disliked travelling, he visited England twice, once in June 1818 to visit the collections of the Royal College of Surgeons in London and to see William Buckland (p. 241) in Oxford.

Cuvier's anatomical Cabinet in Paris was an obligatory visit for any foreign visitor. Richard Owen (p. 255) came in 1831 to study the display and arrangement of the collections, on which he based his own reorganization of the collections of the Royal College of Surgeons in London, and which also inspired his project to initiate a new institution dedicated to the natural sciences – the British Museum (Natural History).

Completely confident of his precise and detailed anatomical descriptions, Cuvier refused to engage in speculative theories and hypotheses. He rejected Lamarck's ideas about transformism, considering the existence of forms transitional between distinct sub-kingdoms as absolutely impossible; for the same reasons, he also quarrelled with Etienne Geoffroy Saint-Hilaire, finding the concept of the existence of a unity of plan for all living forms unacceptable. Despite his Lutheran education and beliefs, Cuvier tried to separate his religious convictions from his interpretations of nature. But he steadfastly refused to consider the antiquity of man or to admit whatsoever the possibility of the evolution of species. Paradoxically, it was the precision of his anatomical descriptions and the importance of his research on fossil bones that provided Cuvier's successors with arguments in favour of the evolutionary transformation of the animal world. Darwin himself paid tribute to the illustrious Cuvier in his *Origin of Species.*

THE 19TH CENTURY

I N SPITE OF MAJOR UPHEAVALS CAUSED BY WAR AND REVOLUTION, natural historians entered the 19th century with an amassed knowledge of the expanding world and an increasingly rational approach to understanding it. The changing nature of the living and physical world was gathering acceptance, and there was lively speculation as to how, and significantly over what time period, it had changed. Linnaeus had provided a temporary solution to the practicalities of organizing the vast numbers of new species that were being discovered, but his work was being superseded by the more natural and meaningful classifications of the great French botanists. With increasing industrialization, science – and natural science in particular – was regarded as something to be channelled, professionalized and exploited. The enthusiastic amateur remained a force in the discipline, but the professional naturalist heralded the trend towards the specialized and largely state-funded biologists of today.

Alexander von Humboldt was one of the last great amateur explorer-naturalists and his style of writing and methods of exploration were to influence Charles Darwin. Humboldt travelled extensively in Central and South America, collecting huge numbers of specimens and describing many new species and, of significance to the development of Darwin's ideas, noting the close relationship between living things and their environment, including physical factors such as climate and geology.

Contemporary with the increasingly rational and economic approach to the natural world, and somewhat contradictory to it, the Romantic Movement, often associated with William Wordsworth and Johann Wolfgang von Goethe amongst others, saw science as too restraining to the human intellect and divorced from feelings and imagination. The naturalist who perhaps represents this tendency best was the great illustrator and ornithologist John James Audubon, who saw himself as both naturalist and artist, bridging the gap between science and the aesthetic. No one could fail to be impressed by his remarkable paintings enlivened by his lyrical descriptions in his *The Birds of America*, which in many ways is unsurpassed to this day.

The Reverend William Buckland lecturing in Oxford, 1823, surrounded by fossils, drawings, maps and paintings. Buckland was a pioneering geologist, calling his subject 'undergroundology'.

The late 18th and early 19th centuries were a time when earth sciences entered what is sometimes called the Golden Age of Geology. Interest in the large-scale drama of the Earth's development was gripping society, and a number of sound and credible theories concerning the age of the Earth and its changing nature through time were becoming established. William Smith, born into modest circumstances and with little formal education, struggled to establish himself in the geological establishment. But he created the first countrywide geological map and also recognized that particular types of fossils were associated with different rock strata, and that the same sequence could be traced in rocks elsewhere – principles still used in geology today.

Fossils – now understood to be the remains of once-living creatures – were at the centre of a lively debate about how the creatures had perished and in what way they were related to organisms still living. For example, the clergyman William Buckland, who taught what he humorously called 'undergroundology' at Oxford University, developed Cuvier's Catastrophism to suggest that several such events had wiped out a

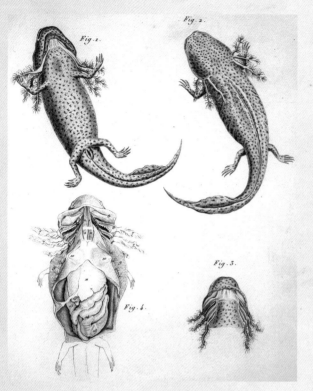

series of faunas which had become fossilized. By slotting the biblical Flood into these events, Buckland felt he had reconciled scripture and fossil evidence, although he later replaced ice as his main force of destruction. Buckland literally strode across the country with his legendary blue bag, collecting and describing many new fossil species, including the first dinosaur. He exchanged specimens and ideas with 'fossilizer' Mary Anning, who had made a commercial business out of excavating and preparing the fossils she found in the cliffs near her home in Lyme Regis, southern England. Anning was an able palaeontologist, and was the first to describe a plesiosaur and an ichthyosaur. Anning's discoveries inspired many budding geologists, including the Sussex obstetrician Gideon Mantell, who published extensively on fossils and is credited with discovering and identifying the first part of a dinosaur, the tooth of an iguanodon.

The credit for coining the word 'dinosaur' goes to Richard Owen, a critic of Darwin and a controversial figure, whose achievements go well beyond the invention of this term. A highly talented comparative anatomist and interpreter of fossils, he famously identified the giant extinct bird, the Moa, from one tiny bone and his excellent knowledge of bird anatomy. Owen's devotion to his chosen field was to manifest

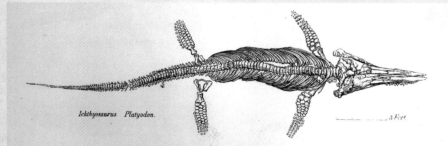

Ichthyosaurus Platyodon.

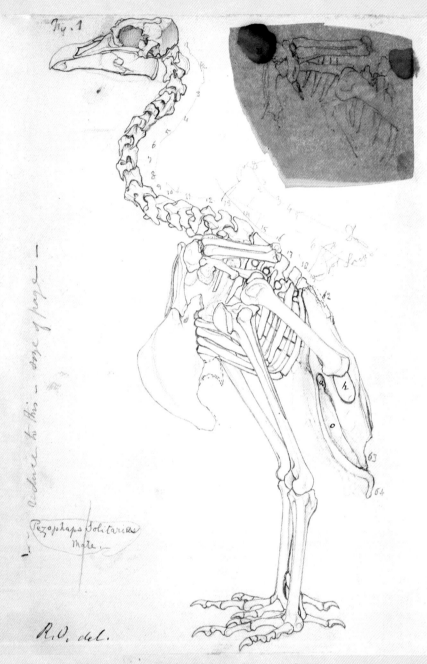

ABOVE *A drawing by Richard Owen of the skeleton of the giant flightless pigeon,* Pezophaps
solitaria, *or the Rodrigues solitaire, the closest relative of the dodo. Owen, who was the first
to examine and describe the extinct dodo, also coined the word 'dinosaur'.*
OPPOSITE ABOVE *An axolotl, or salamander* (Ambystoma mexicanum), *from* Observations de
Zoologie et d'Anatomie Comparée, *1811, by Alexander von Humboldt and Aimé Bonpland.*
OPPOSITE BELOW *An engraving of the fossil marine reptile* Ichthyosaurus platyodon, *by
William Buckland. Mary Anning, a gifted fossil collector, is credited, along with her brother,
with being the first to put together an ichthyosaur skeleton.*

itself in his promotion of the creation of a new home for the British Museum's vast natural history collections, a 'cathedral to natural history', now known as the Natural History Museum in London.

The major geological influence on Charles Darwin was Charles Lyell, who successfully challenged the belief that the Earth had been created in the way recorded in Genesis, establishing instead that it had been shaped by a process of slow change. Lyell rightly suggested that much could be learned about the Earth's history from processes going on today – an 'actualist' theory, similar to the ideas of James Hutton 50 years earlier, but more accessible. His *Principles of Geology* was a benchmark, and provided a platform for Darwin's own theories. Lyell's work established that the Earth was much, much older than previously thought, thus furnishing a sufficiently vast time scale to permit Darwin's evolutionary changes through natural selection to take place.

While Charles Darwin was contemplating his work on barnacles, and developing his ideas through the study of the collections and observations he had made on his voyage on the *Beagle*, another great naturalist was exploring and collecting in the forests of Malaysia, making observations which would bring him independently to the same conclusions as Darwin. Alfred Russel Wallace communicated his evolutionary ideas to Darwin, and the great man although at first dismayed, magnanimously offered to publish jointly. History has not been kind to Wallace, and this brilliant man was overshadowed by Darwin. In essence, Darwin and Wallace had both concluded that organisms with favourable variations survive and produce more viable offspring than their less fortunate relatives. Through many generations in a suitable environment these variations would be selected to the point that they became the norm and thus the species had changed – evolved – through a process of natural selection.

Darwin's ideas inevitably created a furore and were bitterly opposed by many other scientists, such as Richard Owen, and reached a crescendo with the debate between the Bishop of Oxford, Samuel Wilberforce, and the biologist and 'Darwin's Bulldog', Thomas Henry Huxley. For Victorian society the most controversial aspect was the concept of Man evolving from a common ancestor in the same way as all other creatures. In the United States there was no fiercer opponent than Louis Agassiz, the Swiss-born zoologist, glaciologist and geologist. Agassiz is regarded as a pioneer of modern scientific thought in America, publishing significant works on the fauna of North America and advancing taxonomy. His greatest contribution to science was perhaps his realization that any meaningful classification system should take into account the fossil record, geology, embryology, ecology and the geographical distribution of organisms, rather than being based only on superficial morphology.

While John James Audubon is primarily famous for his beautiful paintings of birds, he also embarked on a study of mammals, from which this painting of an ocelot (Leopardus pardalis) *comes, but he did not complete it.*

Agassiz's religious beliefs meant that he could not accept that nature was not shaped by any 'Grand Design' and he remained one of the last defenders of the natural theology espoused by John Ray and others almost two centuries earlier. However, his ideas were also hailed by some of his contemporaries and followers as preparing the way for evolutionary theory.

Darwin's theory was introduced to North America by Agassiz's adversary Asa Gray, who remains one of the greatest of all American botanists and after whom the herbarium (dried plant collection) of Harvard University is named. Gray not only made a huge contribution to the knowledge of North American plants, particularly of the western states, but theorized long before plate tectonics that America and Europe had once been joined together in one big land mass.

Here we close our story of the Great Naturalists, but they established the sound platform that enabled biological science to develop into the highly specialized disciplines we know today, and they continue to inspire both amateur enthusiasts and professionals. Nineteenth-century naturalists, building on the work of many others before them since antiquity, completely changed the way we view the natural world, and helped to make natural history the hugely popular and important science it is now. Their work has provided us with an understanding of the world around us, and the tools to meet the enormous challenges that we face in the future.

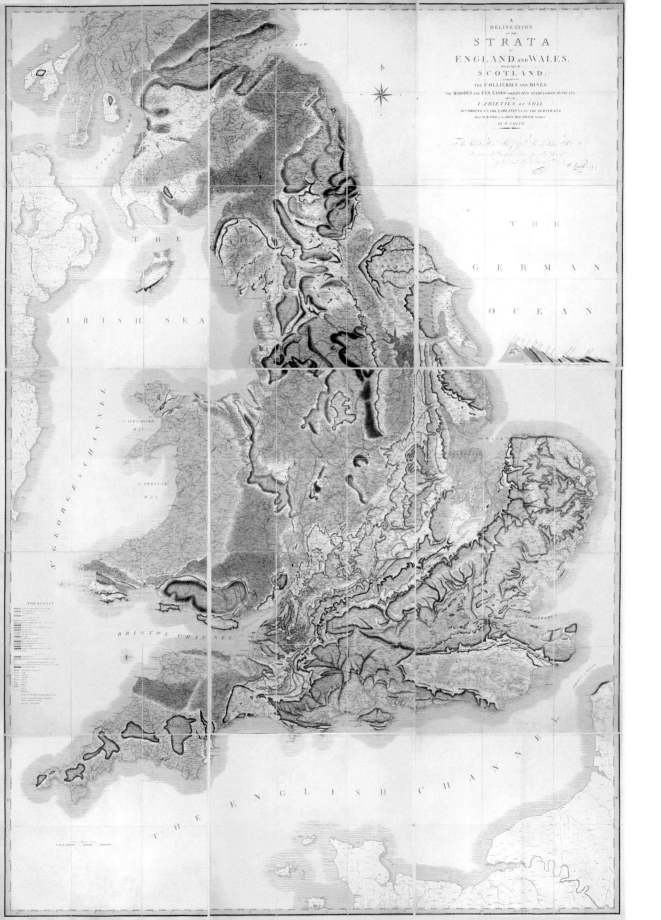

A
DELINEATION
OF THE
STRATA
OF
ENGLAND AND WALES,
WITH PART OF
SCOTLAND;
EXHIBITING
THE COLLIERIES AND MINES,
THE MARSHES AND FEN LANDS ORIGINALLY OVERFLOWED BY THE SEA,
AND THE
VARIETIES OF SOIL
ACCORDING TO THE VARIATIONS IN THE SUBSTRATA,
ILLUSTRATED BY THE MOST DESCRIPTIVE NAMES
BY W. SMITH.

THE GERMAN OCEAN

IRISH SEA

THE

FIRTH OF FORTH

ST GEORGE'S CHANNEL

CAERNARVON BAY

CARDIGAN BAY

BRISTOL CHANNEL

THE ENGLISH CHANNEL

EXPLANATION

William Smith

THE FATHER OF ENGLISH GEOLOGY

(1769–1839)

I for one can speak with gratitude of the practical lessons
I have received from Mr. Smith. It was by tracking his
footsteps, with his maps in my hand, through Wiltshire
and the neighbouring counties, where he had trodden nearly
thirty years before, that I first learned the subdivisions of our
oolitic series … I would appeal to those intelligent men who
form the strength and ornament of this Society … before we
thought of the claims of any other man, to place our first
honour on the brow of the father of English geology.

Professor Adam Sedgwick, in an address to the Geological Society of London
on the occasion of the first presentation of the Wollaston Medal for researches
concerning the mineral structure of the Earth to William Smith in 1831

O N THE EVE OF THE 19TH CENTURY, in 1796, William Smith was the first
Briton to observe that rock strata could be traced for great distances, and
that the same succession of fossil groups from older to younger rocks could
be found in many parts of England. He was soon also able to confirm his earlier beliefs
that the strata all dipped towards the southeast. He further reasoned that if the fossil
content was the same, the rocks must be of similar age, calling this the principle of
faunal succession, and related this to the principle of superposition. This had first
been proposed by Nicolaus Steno (p. 87) in the 17th century, but Smith was almost
certainly unaware of it, as at that time books and papers on geology were not easily
found. This may all seem rather elementary today, but it should be seen in the light of
contemporary teachings by the Church that the world was created in 4004 BC and that
all sedimentary rocks were the result of Noah's Flood, which they calculated took
place in 3290 BC. Fossils were interpreted as *'antediluvian exuviae'* of ancient creatures
– making them older than the rocks in which they were embedded.

William Smith was born in modest circumstances, the son of the village blacksmith in Churchill, Oxfordshire. He received only a very basic education, leaving

Smith's 1815 geological map 'A Delineation of Strata of England and Wales' contains an
enormous amount of information and is a remarkable achievement for the work of one man,
comparing favourably with later maps.

school at the age of 11. In his teens he taught himself geometry and surveying and was taken under the wing of Edward Webb, a surveyor at nearby Stow-on-the-Wold. After surveying an estate at Stowey, 16 km (10 miles) southwest of Bath, he obtained employment in the nearby coal mines. While working there he became familiar with the structure of the rocks to great depth, and a few years later, in 1799, he dictated to a friend his 'Table of the Strata near Bath', in which he listed 23 rock layers from the chalk to the coal, to which he added the most remarkable fossils found in each layer. Meanwhile, he had been engaged to plan the construction of the Somersetshire Coal Canal, a new project to carry the product of the collieries southwest of Bath to a junction with what was to become the Kennet and Avon Canal at Limpley Stoke, and thus onwards to the mills and homes of Bath.

Smith owned Tucking Mill House, Midford, near Bath, from 1798 to 1818. However, he undertook a wide range of surveying work and travelled extensively throughout England. From 1805 to 1807 he worked steadily to stop seawater flooding the marshlands of Norfolk and Suffolk and succeeded in expelling the sea from 90 parishes – more than 16,187 ha (40,000 acres). In 1808 he was commissioned to supervise the extension of the Ouse Navigation in Sussex, and over the next four years he

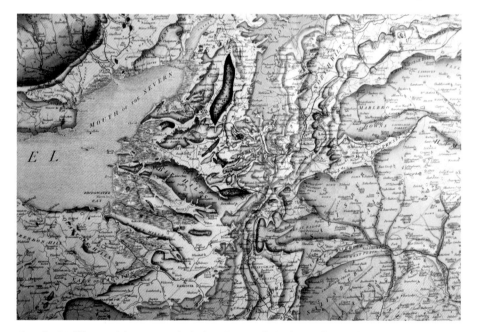

Detail of William Smith's 1815 geological and mineralogical map, for which he was awarded a prize of 50 guineas by the Society for the Encouragement of Arts, Manufactures and Commerce.

No. II.

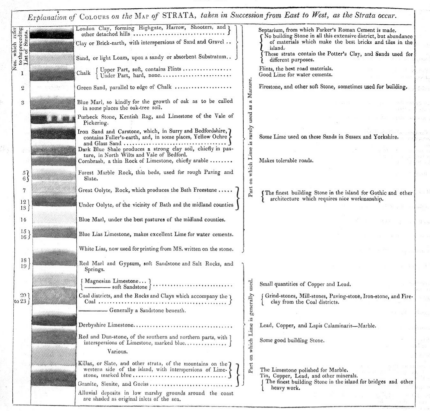

Explanation of COLOURS *on the* MAP *of* STRATA, *taken in Succession from East to West, as the Strata occur.*

Nos. which refer to the preceding List of Strata.		Stratum	Uses
		London Clay, forming Highgate, Harrow, Shooters, and other detached hills	Septarium, from which Parker's Roman Cement is made. No building Stone in all this extensive district, but abundance of materials which make the best bricks and tiles in the island. These strata contain the Potter's Clay, and Sands used for different purposes.
		Clay or Brick-earth, with interspersions of Sand and Gravel ..	
		Sand, or light Loam, upon a sandy or absorbent Substratum..	
1		Chalk { Upper Part, soft, contains Flints	Flints, the best road materials. Good Lime for water cements.
		{ Under Part, hard, none.......................	
2		Green Sand, parallel to edge of Chalk	Firestone, and other soft Stone, sometimes used for building.
3		Blue Marl, so kindly for the growth of oak as to be called in some places the oak-tree soil.	
		Purbeck Stone, Kentish Rag, and Limestone of the Vale of Pickering.	
		Iron Sand and Carstone, which, in Surry and Bedfordshire, contains Fuller's-earth, and, in some places, Yellow Ochre and Glass Sand	Some Lime used on these Sands in Sussex and Yorkshire.
		Dark Blue Shale produces a strong clay soil, chiefly in pasture, in North Wilts and Vale of Bedford.	Makes tolerable roads.
		Cornbrash, a thin Rock of Limestone, chiefly arable	
5}6}		Forest Marble Rock, thin beds, used for rough Paving and Slate.	
7		Great Oolyte, Rock, which produces the Bath Freestone	{The finest building Stone in the island for Gothic and other architecture which requires nice workmanship.
12}13}		Under Oolyte, of the vicinity of Bath and the midland counties	
14		Blue Marl, under the best pastures of the midland counties.	
15}16}		Blue Lias Limestone, makes excellent Lime for water cements.	
		White Lias, now used for printing from MS. written on the stone.	
18}19}		Red Marl and Gypsum, soft Sandstone and Salt Rocks, and Springs.	
20}to 23}		{ Magnesian Limestone... }	Small quantities of Copper and Lead.
		{ ———— soft Sandstone }	
		Coal districts, and the Rocks and Clays which accompany the Coal	{Grind-stones, Mill-stones, Paving-stone, Iron-stone, and Fire-clay from the Coal districts.
		———— Generally a Sandstone beneath.	
		Derbyshire Limestone...............................	Lead, Copper, and Lapis Calaminaris—Marble.
		Red and Dun-stone, of the southern and northern parts, with interspersions of Limestone, marked blue.............	Some good building Stone.
		Various.	
		Killas, or Slate, and other strata, of the mountains on the western side of the island, with interspersions of Lime-stone, marked blue..............................	The Limestone polished for Marble. Tin, Copper, Lead, and other minerals. {The finest building Stone in the island for bridges and other heavy work.
		Granite, Sienite, and Gneiss	
		Alluvial deposits in low marshy grounds around the coast are shaded as original inlets of the sea.	

Part on which Lime is rarely used as a Manure.

Part on which Lime is generally used.

Part on which Lime is generally used.

Explanation of the colours on the 'Map of Strata', an element of Smith's Memoir to the Map and Delineation of the Strata of England and Wales, with part of Scotland.

extended it a further 11.2 km (7 miles) inland, from Sheffield Bridge to the Balcombe Road near Cuckfield. He also submitted a plan to the Clerk of the Peace at Lewes for a branch to join near Crawley the projected Grand Southern Canal, which, had it been constructed, would have linked Chatham and Portsmouth Dockyards, avoiding the English Channel at a time when England was at war with France. In 1809, in the process of searching for materials to construct locks and bridges, he visited a quarry near Cuckfield, and was shown by the quarryman what he described as 'very large bones'. One of these was identified in 1979 by Dr Alan Charig of the Natural History Museum as the thigh-bone of an iguanodon. So, although he had no idea what they were, Smith was one of the first to handle dinosaur bones, a decade before the eminent geologist and doctor, Gideon Mantell.

Smith had produced a geological map of the district near Bath in 1799 and a 'General Map of the Strata in England and Wales' in 1801, the first geological map of the country. However, his widespread travels in the course of his work (up to 16,000 km/10,000 miles a year on horseback or in horse-drawn vehicles) allowed him to observe the geology to such an extent that he was able in 1815 to publish his greatest masterpiece, the 'Delineation of the Strata of England and Wales, with part of Scotland; exhibiting the Collieries and Mines, the Marshes and Fenlands originally overflowed by the sea, and the Varieties of Soil according to the variation in the substrata'. On a scale of 5 miles to the inch, this magnificent map measured 6 ft by 8 ft 6 in (1.8 by 2.6 m). A unique feature of the map was the darkening of the colours on the boundaries to emphasize where one type of rock ended and another began. Twenty different tints were used, and it took up to eight days for an artist to colour in a single copy. Around 400 were made and fewer than 100 are known to survive. Smith believed the map to be so important to the economy of the country that he bankrupted himself in paying for its production and spent ten weeks in a debtors' jail. Another remarkable publication was his 'Geological Section from Snowdon towards London' (1817), coloured to correspond with his 1815 map. This included the heights of mountains obtained from the Trigonometrical Survey, and showed the varieties of strata and other observations across the whole stretch.

Following his bankruptcy, Smith went with his nephew, John Phillips, to live in Yorkshire. Between them they produced geological maps of many counties. Smith used his knowledge of geology to improve the water supply of Scarborough, a popular seaside resort with a large summer influx of visitors. He blocked up springs to trap water in natural reservoirs in the rocks above the town and constructed a huge artificial reservoir, the largest covered receptacle for water in England. The circular design of the new Scarborough Museum (The Rotunda), was his suggestion, in order to display its exhibits better. He was also employed for six years as land steward by Sir John Vanden Bempde Johnstone, who owned a large estate at Hackness, near Scarborough. Smith wrote numerous papers on the local geology and gave a series of lectures to several important societies; he was himself the inspiration behind the founding of a number of philosophical societies, which encouraged the popularity of fossil-collecting.

Fossil tooth of an extinct animal from Whitlingham, Norfolk, from Strata Identified by Organized Fossils *by William Smith.*

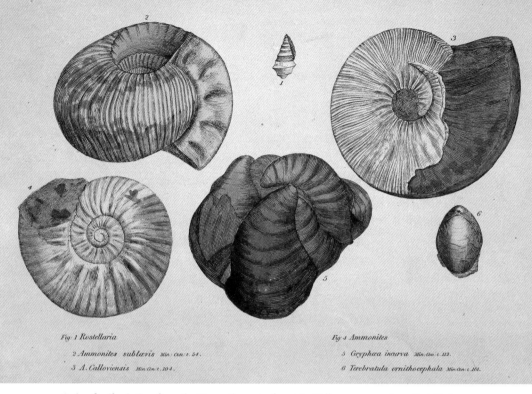

Fig 1 Rostellaria

2 Ammonites sublævis Min: Con: t. 54.

3 A. Calloviensis Min: Con: t. 104.

Fig 4 Ammonites

5 Gryphæa incurva Min: Con: t. 112.

6 Terebratula ornithocephala Min: Con: t. 101.

Index fossils, dating from the Upper Jurassic, found in Kelloways stone, from Smith's Strata Identified by Organized Fossils. *Smith intended this as a sort of handbook to enable anyone to identify fossils in the field and therefore also the stratum in which they were found.*

William Smith had been nicknamed 'Strata Smith' early in his career, from his enthusiastic efforts to show the value of geology in the improvement of land, both by drainage and by irrigation. Socially privileged members of the newly formed (1807) Geological Society were reluctant to recognize his knowledge and achievements, probably because of arrogance and snobbery, but in 1835, totally unexpectedly, Smith received an honorary Doctorate of Laws from Trinity College, Dublin. In 1838, he was appointed by the Government to serve on a small commission to choose the stone for the new Palace of Westminster, working with Sir Charles Barry (the architect of the building) and Henry Thomas De la Beche (head of the Geological Survey).

He died, probably of influenza, on 28 August 1839. It is a disgrace that, despite both his great achievements in geology and his works that so often were of benefit to people and communities, he is buried in an unmarked grave at St Peter's, Marefair, Northampton. His portrait, painted in 1837 by Hugues Foureau, hangs in the offices of the Geological Society of London in Burlington House and Lord Ducie erected a monument to him in the village of his birth, Churchill, where the inhabitants still proudly remember him. In 1977 the Geological Society instituted the William Smith Medal for Applied Geology, and the Society holds an annual William Smith Lecture.

JUDITH MAGEE

Alexander von Humboldt

A VISION OF THE UNITY OF NATURE

(1769–1859)

*The principal impulse by which I was directed was the
earnest endeavour to comprehend the phenomena of physical
objects in their general connection, and to represent nature as
one great whole, moved and animated by internal forces.
Without an earnest striving to attain to a knowledge of
special branches of study, all attempts to give a grand and
general view of the universe would be nothing
more than vain illusion.*

Alexander von Humboldt, **Kosmos,** *1845–62*

WHEN CHARLES DARWIN MADE HIS FIRST EXPEDITION to the tropical forests of Brazil during his voyage on HMS *Beagle* in 1832 he wrote to his friend John Henslow, 'I formerly admired Humboldt, I now almost adore him'. This was fine praise from one of the greatest and most influential naturalists of all time. Some 30 years before Darwin, Alexander von Humboldt had travelled to South America, conducting the first scientific exploration of what are now Venezuela, Colombia, Ecuador and Peru, travelling also to Mexico and Cuba and then to the United States. As a result of this expedition, Humboldt pioneered a new branch of science that he called plant geography; he also provided an accurate location of the Earth's magnetic equator, confirmed that the Earth's magnetic field changes with latitude and laid the foundations of subjects such as climatology and oceanography. Underlying all Humboldt's study was his view of the natural world as an organic whole – a living unity of diverse and interdependent life forms rather than some mechanical structure. He developed this universal concept of nature beyond anything that was professed at the time, heralding the study of ecology and environmentalism.

A basalt rock formation in northeast Mexico, with Humboldt and Bonpland in the lower left corner, designed after a sketch by Humboldt. Humboldt described these columns as rising 30 m (100 ft) in height and noted their similarity to formations at Vivarais in France and Antrim in Ireland, suggesting that the same geological forces had operated in different continents and at different periods to create this effect.

View of Cajambe, designed after a sketch by Humboldt. Cajambe was, according to Humboldt, the second highest peak of the Cordilleras after Chimborazo. He described it as one of the 'eternal wonders which nature has used to mark the divisions of the surface of the earth'.

Alexander von Humboldt was born in Berlin in 1769 into a minor aristocratic family and was educated by private tutors and then at universities at Frankfurt an der Oder and Göttingen. Here he studied under several outstanding tutors who were committed to the ideas of the German philosopher Immanuel Kant. Kant dismissed the Linnaean classification system, arguing that it ignored the integrative and unifying processes interlinking complex natural phenomena. Humboldt readily absorbed these ideas and came to recognize, and attach greater importance to, the complex connections and relationships of species within nature rather than their mere surface characteristics and descriptions.

While studying at Göttingen, Humboldt met Georg Forster, who was probably the greatest single influence on Humboldt and his 'guiding star', as he referred to him. As a child Humboldt had been inspired by tales of the great voyages of discovery by men such as Louis-Antoine de Bougainville and by the three voyages of Captain James Cook. Georg Forster had accompanied his father, Johann Reinhold Forster, on the second of Cook's voyages as the assistant naturalist. And it was with Forster that Humboldt gained his first taste of scientific exploration in 1790, when they travelled together along the Rhine to the Low Countries and then through France to England. Humboldt found in Forster a kindred spirit. They were both excellent linguists and shared the same wanderlust, enquiring minds and a love of nature and science; both were committed republicans and held strong liberal and humanist views; and both were sympathetic to the German Romantic Movement, the influence of which is identifiable in their styles of travel writing.

Humboldt became the leading scientific figure in German Romanticism and the only scientist to write for the dramatist Friedrich Schiller's journal, *Die Horen*. He was also invited into the exclusive literary circles in Germany and became a lifelong friend of Goethe, dedicating the German edition of his 'Essay on the Geography of Plants' to him. The Romantic influence on Humboldt can be seen in his understanding of nature: he argued that in order to comprehend the inner realities of things it was necessary to combine an aesthetic appreciation of nature with rigorous empirical investigation – the accurate recording of data through measuring, collecting and observation.

Fired by his travels with Forster, Humboldt was now determined to devote his life to scientific exploration. In 1791 he enrolled at the Freiberg Mining Academy in Saxony with the intention of learning as much practical science as possible to equip himself for his intended travels. With his training complete, Humboldt became an inspector of mines in the Prussian Department of Mines, a post he retained for five years. He spent his time conducting experiments in animal electricity, investigating geological stratification and pursuing research in botany, subterranean climates and terrestrial magnetism. By the end of this period he had acquired an extensive knowledge in all areas of natural history, had become skilled in experimentation and was a more than competent investigator with a powerful and agile intellect.

TRAVELS TO SOUTH AMERICA

Humboldt's father had died when Alexander was just nine years old, and when his mother also died in November 1796 he came into his inheritance. This provided him with financial security and independence and he resigned his post at the Ministry of Mines the following February, beginning immediately to prepare for his travels. It took two years of disappointments, arising from misconceived plans, the Napoleonic wars and bad luck, before Humboldt finally managed to accumulate all the scientific equipment he considered essential for his long journey. The number and range of scientific instruments he took with him was enormous, and everything was the most technically up to date. He had equipment to take measurements of anything he desired, from gases, liquids and solids, to variations in magnetism and electricity in the atmosphere. There were instruments that helped him make astronomical observations and apparatus to conduct relatively complex experiments in the field. Humboldt spent the months before his travels living in Paris, and it was here that he met Aimé Bonpland, whose own plans of travelling as the botanist on a French expedition under Captain Baudin had been indefinitely postponed. Bonpland agreed to join Humboldt on a journey that is now arguably one of the greatest scientific expeditions of the 19th century.

In 1799, at the age of 29, Humboldt and his travelling companion Bonpland set sail on board the *Pizarro* to cross the Atlantic bound for the New World. They had in their possession royal passports from the King of Spain that permitted them unrestricted access to the Spanish colonies of South America. Humboldt had long dreamt of one day seeing the Pacific Ocean, and now this dream was becoming reality. The entire journey was to last five years and included the first scientific exploration of the Amazon basin by Europeans. These were years of hardship, sickness and discomfort; years of intense collecting of specimens, data and observations; but also years of immeasurable pleasure wrought by the beauty and sublime wonder of nature itself.

In South America, Humboldt and Bonpland penetrated rainforests, crossed the plains and ascended the mountains of Venezuela, Colombia, Peru, Ecuador, also visiting Mexico and the island of Cuba. The two men mapped much of the land they travelled, providing the most accurate maps to date of the region, which would be of use to future travellers, traders and politicians. They charted the course of the Orinoco and Negro rivers and proved the existence of the Rio Casiquiare waterway that connected the Orinoco through the Rio Negro to the Amazon. They climbed mountains, including Chimborazo, the highest peak of the northern Andes, to within 400 m (1,300 ft) of its summit, and explored the Amazon basin, discovering plants and animals hitherto unknown to science.

Everywhere he went, Humboldt consistently took accurate measurements, temperatures and barometric readings. His studies of terrestrial magnetism were, he believed, the most important results from his American voyage and led him to locate the Earth's magnetic equator and confirm its magnetic field. His

A portrait of Humboldt by Friedrich Georg Weitsch (1806), with a specimen of a plant and a volume of a herbarium.

geological observations demonstrated that the Earth's rocks were formed by heat and ongoing violent upheaval at subterranean levels. This conclusion gave support to the Vulcanist model of rock formation, and helped Humboldt to reject the Neptunist theory that rocks were created by sedimentation deposited from the oceans – a theory he had adhered to before his travels. Humboldt and Bonpland collected between them some 60,000 botanical specimens, of which 3,000 were unknown to science. Humboldt was the first to describe the piranha fish and the first to identify and name magnetic storms; his observations of the properties of guano led to it being introduced as a fertilizer to Europe. On the basis of his accurate temperature readings of the sea, he identified the important current of upwelling cold waters along the Pacific coastline now named after him.

Humboldt was primarily a geologist, but he nevertheless provided extensive knowledge on New World fauna to the scientific world, writing essays on electric eels, piranhas and the monkeys of the forests of South America – this is Cacajao melanocephalus.

Probably the most significant result of Humboldt's researches was what he came to call plant geography. He had first written on the subject as early as 1793 in *Florae Fribergensis Specimen*, in which he looked at the influence of environment on plants. Developing these ideas during his travels in South America, Humboldt demonstrated that the effects of altitude, temperature, climate and geography are the determining factors as to where plants grow. By comparing plants growing at the same altitude, but in diverse regions of the world, he found there was a correlation between physical phenomena and vegetation. On his ascent of mount Chimborazo he defined the different zones of vegetation, recording tropical plants at the base to near arctic specimens higher up the mountain. Humboldt concluded that the Earth is made up of distinct regions, each with its own characteristics determined by the local climatic and environmental conditions; these regions combined to form a single interconnected holistic organization. Humboldt published his research on the subject in his *Essai sur la Géographie des Plantes*.

The travellers returned to Europe via the United States of America. They spent six weeks there, being honoured with a celebratory dinner organized by the leading American scientists in Philadelphia. They were also invited to the seat of government in Washington, and were personally entertained by the President, Thomas Jefferson, at his home at Monticello. Many of the travellers' exploits had already been reported in the press so that by the time they left Philadelphia on 9 July 1804, preparations for their reception in Paris were well underway.

SCIENTIFIC RESULTS

Humboldt was acclaimed as a hero and his reputation as a great international man of science never diminished. He settled in Paris and for the following 30 years dedicated himself to publishing accounts of his South American travels and the results of his investigations. The work extended to 30 volumes and included not only natural history but also political economy, a history of the discovery of America, ethnography and his research on the art, monuments and cultures of pre-Columbian civilizations.

Although a lifelong republican, Humboldt was also courted by royalty; in 1805 he was appointed Royal Chamberlain at the court in Potsdam and given an annual pension. But it was not until 1827 that Humboldt returned to the city of his birth, Berlin, and then only after a royal summons. That same year he received an invitation from the Russian tsar to undertake an expedition to the Urals. Humboldt readily accepted, and in April 1829 his expedition party set out from Berlin for St Petersburg. Now aged 60, Humboldt's travels took him across the Urals as far as the Chinese border at Baty, in modern Kazakhstan. The return journey was across the Kazakh steppes to the Caspian Sea and then on to Moscow and back to St Petersburg, arriving home in Berlin just after Christmas. As in all his work Humboldt identified the importance of collaboration between scientists in different regions of the world and he was often instrumental in maintaining such collaboration. Following his Siberian travels, he proposed the setting up of a chain of geomagnetic observation stations around the world, each making recordings on identical instruments. By 1839 such stations were in operation from St Petersburg to Beijing, across Europe and America, and at key locations in Britain's overseas territories.

The 19th and 20th centuries witnessed a growing move towards specialization in science and education that was contrary to Humboldt's universalist approach. Humboldt's interest in, and knowledge of, such a broad spectrum of science was the key to his holistic concept of nature. He recognized the mutual connection between all branches of science; studying one specific branch revealed its laws which in turn

Rhexia sarmentosa *from* Voyage aux Régions Equinoxiales; *originating from Ecuador and Peru, this plant is one of over 36 species of* Rhexia *discovered by Humboldt and Bonpland in the course of their South American travels.*

RHEXIA grandiflora.

indicated the 'existence of some other higher and more general law'. Humboldt stated that the 'view of nature should be general, grand and free' and that the essential part of his work was to make known 'the intimate connection of the general with the special', since despite the diverse phenomena in nature there was an underlying unity.

Kosmos, Humboldt's last great work, was published between 1845 and 1862, the last volume of five being completed by others from his notes and published after his death in Berlin on 6 May, four months before his 90th birthday. As the subtitle explains, *Kosmos* was a 'physical description of the universe'. Humboldt had contemplated the subject since his early 20s and the work encapsulates his whole understanding of nature and the underlying forces that operate within it. It recognizes the interrelationship and mutual dependence of diverse physical phenomena and the impact these have on all living organisms.

Humboldt's liberal and humanist sympathies are reflected in his writings. He openly condemned slavery and the barbaric treatment of indigenous people that he witnessed in South America. He had a lifelong commitment to the idea that science in itself brought progress and therefore such knowledge should not only be made available to everyone but was in fact the 'common property of all classes in society'. He successfully fused his scientific data and analysis with an aesthetic appreciation of nature, and by so doing found a much wider audience for his works than most. Humboldt was also an accomplished artist and illustrated much of his work with splendid drawings of botanical and zoological specimens, landscapes and ethnographic portrayals of people and artifacts.

Alexander von Humboldt possessed an extraordinary breadth and depth of interest in science incomparable in his day or since. He insisted that his researches and the conclusions drawn from them were possible only through the rigorous collection of primary data, recorded accurately and directly from observations of nature. He inspired a whole generation of scientists, many of whom came to excel in their own specialist fields of study. Charles Darwin, writing to Joseph Hooker in 1845, stated that 'I never forget that my whole course of life is due to having read and re-read as a youth [Humboldt's] *Personal Narrative*'. His impact on science as a whole is evident in diverse disciplines ranging from geology, physical geography, zoology to botany. By establishing a branch of botany known as plant geography he gave birth to plant ecology in the 20th century. He also laid the foundations for subjects such as climatology, oceanography and meteorology, and he provided future scientists with a method of working that remains fundamental to anyone engaged in the biological sciences today who is concerned for the biodiversity of the planet.

ROBERTA J.M. OLSON

John James Audubon

ARTIST, NATURALIST AND ADVENTURER

(1785–1851)

The sky was serene, the air perfumed, and thousands of
melodious notes from birds unknown to me urged me to arise
and go in pursuit of those beautiful and happy creatures.
Then I would find myself furnished with large and powerful
wings, and cleaving the air like an eagle, I would fly off and
by a few joyous bounds overtake the objects of my desire....
Many times indeed have such thoughts enlivened my spirits;
and now, good reader, the task is accomplished. In health
and in sickness, in adversity and prosperity, in summer and
winter, amidst the cheers of friends and the scowls of foes,
I have depicted the Birds of America, and studied their habits
as they roamed at large in their peculiar haunts.

J. J. Audubon, **Ornithological Biography,** *1831–39*

ARGUABLY ONE OF THE GREATEST AMERICAN NATURALISTS and water-colourists, John James Audubon had one foot in the natural sciences and the other in art, defying categorization. In both his written and painted work, including his greatest triumph, *The Birds of America* (1827–38), he combined a naturalist's curiosity with an artist's eye and a poet's expressiveness, ensuring his uniqueness in the pantheon of natural history. His writings – letters, journals and books – are filled with vivid stories that actively engage his audience with the birds whose lives he observed, researched and brilliantly documented.

Born the illegitimate son of a French sea captain in Saint Domingue, Audubon (his father's name) was first named Jean Rabine after his mother. When he was three, his father sent him to France, where he was renamed Jean-Jacques Fougère (fern) – to placate the French revolutionary authorities and to help disguise his illegitimacy (he was legally adopted in 1794). It was here that he began drawing birds. In 1803 he left France, in order both to oversee the family's property at Mill Grove, Pennsylvania, and to avoid conscription into Napoleon's army. Upon his arrival in America, he immediately identified with its wildlife, becoming a champion of his adopted country and a citizen in 1812. Uninterested in practical affairs, Audubon hunted and drew

birds, fashioning himself as a dashing woodsman like his hero Daniel Boone. Searching for an occupation, he attempted various entrepreneurial ventures, moving around the fringes of the fast-disappearing American wilderness. A charismatic adventurer at heart, Audubon could fence, sing, play the violin as well as the flute and other woodwind instruments, dance, ride a horse, hunt and draw.

From the beginning, Audubon was keenly aware of his predecessors in the field, and, in the spectrum of natural history, the time was ripe for his study. He first drew birds from the illustrations in Buffon's *Histoire Naturelle* (p. 140), inscribing them *Buffon*. His decision to publish a comprehensive book about North American birds was influenced by Alexander Wilson's *American Ornithology*, published in 1808–14. A meeting between the two in 1810, when Wilson was selling subscriptions for his illustrated survey, was pivotal. Although Audubon showed his watercolours to Wilson without 'the least idea of presenting the fruits of my labour to the world', this encounter was the beginning of the idea of publishing them based on Wilson's template. Always seeking to prove his credentials as a field naturalist and ornithologist, Audubon tried unsuccessfully to penetrate the scientific community in Philadelphia. By 1819–20 he had decided to follow his passion, seriously gathering material for his ambitious project. His inspired vision became a magnificent obsession, defining his life.

THE BIRDS OF AMERICA

For Audubon, birds represented a parallel universe to human experience, and he carried La Fontaine's *Fables* as a guide. His years drawing portraits to support his family and studying birds enabled him to capture the individuality of each species in an arresting, often cinematic, image. He engaged birds with a hunter's intensity, because hunting was the cultural framework from which his encounters with birds emerged. Audubon progressed from pastels over graphite outlines to complex mixed media. Having a talent with materials, he experimented with a wide variety – collage, watercolour, gouache, pastel, ink, oil paint, water-soluble glazes and adhesives, metallic pigments and chalk – to become one of America's most innovative draughtsmen. He began drawing from dead specimens but always longed to animate them back to life, which his art finally accomplished. In an article in the *Edinburgh Journal of Science* (1828), Audubon described his method of drawing birds. Since he often sketched from

The Carolina parakeet (Conuropsis carolinensis), *the only parrot native to the United States, was sighted for the final time in 1920. Today it lives on in Audubon's elegant S-curve composition. Through a brilliant layering of pigments, he has suggested the textures of their feathers, and their iridescence by meticulously outlining each barbule of every feather in sparkling graphite.*

recently dead specimens posed in life-like attitudes, he employed a mounting system to achieve animation. It consisted of a board with a grid pattern of lines from whose surface projected thin wires on which he positioned his subject. Whenever possible, Audubon preferred to draw from life, as with a broad-winged female hawk: 'I put the bird on a stick made fast to my table. It merely moved its feet to grasp the stick ... but raised its feathers.... I passed my hand over it, to smooth the feathers.... It moved not.... Its eye, directed towards mine, appeared truly *sorrowful*, with a degree of pensiveness which rendered me at the moment quite uneasy. I measured the length of its bill with the compass, began my outlines, continued measuring ... and finished the drawing without the bird ever moving once.... The drawing being finished, I raised the window, laid hold of the poor bird and launched it into the air....'

Audubon conceived of *The Birds of America* as a visual odyssey through the lives of North American birds. Although he was criticized for not employing Linnaean order, Audubon organized his images organically, giving the birds the semblance of life and evoking the experience of observing them in nature. While Audubon considered his studies of environmental interaction to be highly individualistic, they reflect an anti-systematic trend that emerged in the 18th century, as seen in the work of William Bartram (p. 165). Nevertheless, *The Birds of America*, of which approximately 120 complete copies are extant, and the companion *Ornithological Biography*, remain unequalled in scale and scope.

The genesis of the publication of *The Birds of America* is a fascinating saga of entrepreneurship, compulsive dedication and collaboration. Failing to find an engraver in Philadelphia, Audubon sailed for England in 1826, arriving in Liverpool, where he exhibited his drawings to great acclaim. Travelling to Edinburgh, he engaged as his printmaker William Home Lizars, whose colourists went on strike after the tenth plate, forcing Audubon to go to London in search of another engraver. There he found the brilliant Robert Havell, Jr, who became his ideal collaborator. Thereafter, the transatlantic project was a family affair, involving both men's nuclear and extended families. Its success depended on Audubon's dizzying schedule of travel in America and Europe in quest of specimens and subscribers, punctuated by eight Atlantic crossings and lengthy periods of residence in England to supervise the production of the plates.

Havell produced the prints by a complex process of engraving, etching and aquatint, followed by hand-colouring, in an attempt to duplicate Audubon's original

American white pelican (Pelecanus erythrorhynchos)*: Audubon described its pouch as 'thin, transparent, elastic, rugous, highly vascular, and capable of being expanded like a net.' After seeing a hundred at a time, he wrote, distinguishing it for the first time from the European variety, 'that it never descends from on wing upon its prey, as is the habit of the Brown Pelican....'*

In this portrait by Lance Calkin, Audubon is dressed like a bohemian gentleman, to appeal to potential English subscribers.

watercolours, marking an unprecedented achievement in printmaking. Their serial sale via subscription demanded exhausting production and marketing campaigns. Ultimately, each subscriber paid approximately $1,050 (roughly £560) for 435 hand-coloured prints issued in 87 parts of five prints each, a high price in its day. The double-elephant-size set contains images of 1,065 life-size birds representing 489 species. This edition is considered the most spectacular colour folio print series ever produced, and is one of the world's pre-eminent natural history documents. Superbly conceived and executed, it eclipsed all others and is acknowledged as the finest work of coloured engraving involving aquatint in existence. It is also one of the last, for around the year 1830 lithography began to replace engraving in art book production.

Without institutional backing, Audubon became a marketing machine. For Europeans, this buckskin-wearing American embodied the noble frontiersman Natty Bumppo in James Fenimore Cooper's *The Pioneers* (1823). To attract additional subscribers, he staged successful exhibitions of his watercolours throughout Great Britain, charging admission to finance the project. Of one exhibition, a London critic wrote: 'Their plumages sparkle with nature's own tints; you see them in motion or at rest, in their play and in their combats, in their anger fits and their caresses, singing, running, asleep, just awakened, beating the air, skimming the waves or rending one another in their battles ... a vision of the New World.'

All of Audubon's 435 known original preparatory watercolours for *The Birds* are held by the New-York Historical Society, which purchased 434 of this unique treasure by subscription from the naturalist's remarkable widow, Lucy Bakewell Audubon, in 1863; the final example was given to them in 1966. The 435 watercolours are preparatory for 433 of the 435 plates; none are known for plates 84 and 155. In these dazzling drawings Audubon's innovations are apparent. He not only rendered the birds life-size, but also captured them with all the drama of their avian life, enhanced with anthropomorphic anecdotes.

Audubon's *Ornithological Biography* (1831–39), which served as the text for the sumptuous folio plates, was based on accounts in his journals The five-volume work was a groundbreaking contribution to the fledgling science of ornithology. It contained the first extensive and accurate accounts of the behaviour of living birds, as opposed to mere scientific description, although it contained that too, together with information based on dissection. As a work of natural history written in a clear, lively and personal style it was aimed for a general audience. In its pages Audubon included observations not only of avian behaviour but also of the landscape, people and culture of America during the nation's springtime. The final manuscript was copied and edited by Lucy, who was the central organizing force of his life, as well as his amanuensis. The other unsung hero of these companion volumes was William MacGillivray, the disciplined Scottish naturalist and friend of Charles Darwin, who helped with the more scientific aspects of avian anatomy, scientific vocabulary and English grammar.

A seven-volume octavo edition of *The Birds of America* (1840–44) was then published, with the plates arranged in systematic order. It combines the *Ornithological Biography* text (descriptions of the anatomy, habits and localities of the birds) with 500 hand-coloured lithographs by J. T. Bowen at one-eighth the size of the originals (reduced with the camera lucida). The octavo's more affordable price and smaller size made it a moneymaker. Between 1840 and 1870 around seven editions were printed.

Northern bobwhite (Colinus virginianus) *and red-shouldered hawk* (Buteo lineatus). *Rendered with great immediacy as though embedded with the birds and from the hawk's point of view, this highly explosive scene is Audubon's only example in which the prey species constitutes the primary subject. His frontally foreshortened immature hawk surprises the covey of 18 quail.*

As Audubon's health declined, his artist sons (Victor Gifford and John Wood-house) became closely involved in the publication of their father's illustrations of mammals. The three volumes, initially entitled *The Viviparous Quadrupeds of North America*, remained incomplete, but were published in stages between 1845 and 1848. The author of the text was Audubon's friend, the naturalist the Reverend John Bachman.

SCIENTIFIC AND ENVIRONMENTAL HONOURS

A complex and often contradictory self-made man and a legend in his own time, Audubon was awarded many honours, including election to England's prestigious Royal Society and the Linnaean Society. He is considered America's first great water-colourist, and his ability to bring together science and art reveals the range of his genius. However, it is only in the last hundred years that his name has become linked with efforts to preserve America's wildlife and wilderness.

In November 1829 Audubon presciently wrote: 'When … I reflect that all this grand portion of our Union, instead of being in a state of nature, is now more or less covered with villages, farms, and towns …; that the woods are fast disappearing under the axe by day, and the fires by night …; when I see the surplus population of Europe coming to assist in the destruction of the forest and the transplanting of civilization into its darkest recesses – when I remember that these extraordinary changes have all taken place in the short period of twenty years, I pause, wonder, and although I know all to be fact, can scarcely believe in its reality.' In 1841, alarmed by these changes, Audubon approached Daniel Webster, Secretary of State, to 'establish a Natural History Institution to advance our knowledge of natural science with me at the head of it.' Regrettably his request was not successful. After his last expedition to the western United States in 1843, Audubon began losing his eyesight and by 1847 could no longer paint. Soon he experienced a rapid decline in his health, and then dementia; he died in 1851.

Today, Audubon's awareness of ecological issues and his appreciation of the natural environment find expression in the organization 'Audubon', formerly the National Audubon Society. His passion for birds that engendered *The Birds of America* has ensured his celebrity and immortality. Audubon also succeeded in ways that surpassed his great-est ambitions. He had hoped to draw the birds of America for a publication of great size, beauty and scientific import, but he accomplished much more. His name has become synonymous with not only a love of birds and nature, but also the preservation of the environment, a result that would have pleased him immensely.

William Buckland

FIRST TO DESCRIBE A DINOSAUR

(1784–1856)

The documents of geology record the warfare of ages
antecedent to the Creation of the human race, of which,
in their later days, the geologist becomes the first
and only historiographer.

William Buckland, Geology and Mineralogy, *1836*

ALTHOUGH HE WAS NOT A RADICAL THINKER, Reverend William Buckland's career influenced many of the important developments in geology, palaeontology and archaeology of the 19th century. He was also the first person to publish a scientific description of a dinosaur. His success came from a rigorously open-minded approach to evidence observed in the field.

In 1801 Buckland went to Oxford University to study theology so that he would have a living as an Anglican clergyman. However, he already had geological interests, which he pursued by attending lectures in mineralogy, chemistry and anatomy. By 1810 he was part of a wider network of geologists encouraged by the formation of the Geological Society in 1807, and had started to go into the field to gather evidence for the succession of geological strata using the methods pioneered by William Smith (p. 219). Buckland used this information to produce stratigraphic charts, which between 1811 and 1821 were modified and elaborated as he gathered new data in Britain and made trips abroad, enabling him to attempt correlations with mainland Europe.

By the time the position of lecturer in mineralogy became vacant at Oxford in 1813, Buckland was the obvious candidate. He had no intention of confining himself to the chemistry and physics of rocks merely as materials, however, but immediately introduced the study of their context and history – geology – to the curriculum. His lectures were a huge success and within five years the university made him its first Reader in Geology, and thus the first official professional geologist in Britain. His inaugural lecture justified the university's trust in him. He spoke of how geology could be reconciled with the Bible and offered nine geological 'proofs' to suggest that the world must have been overwhelmed by catastrophic flooding, which at this time he correlated with Noah's Flood. His proofs included the evidence of landforms, fossil faunas from caves and superficial deposits of clay, sands and gravels, as well as rocks transported far from their original source, now known as erratics. Such phenomena made Buckland and other European geologists doubt James Hutton's theory (p. 186) that present landscapes can be explained solely as the product of slow geological processes acting over a vast period of time. Buckland was unusual among 'catastrophists', however, in thinking that they could be attributed to a single event, and he set out to prove his case.

Buckland published his first book *Reliquiae Diluvianae* ('Remains of the Flood') in 1823. The first part describes his excavations at Kirkdale Cave, Yorkshire, where he found an animal community consisting of extinct species, such as mammoth and woolly rhinoceros, as well as animals such as hyenas and lions which are no longer present in Europe. Using modern analogues and a careful analysis of the condition of these bones, he was able to show that the remains had been accumulated by hyenas that had used the cave as a den. This brilliant study of an ancient ecology was the first of its kind. It demonstrated that all the animals represented by the remains had once lived together in the area. Having proved that the bones had not been transported from elsewhere and deposited together by the Flood, Buckland had to explain how the animals had become extinct, resting his case on the fact that the bones were lying in a waterlain silt which he attributed to the Universal Deluge before human times.

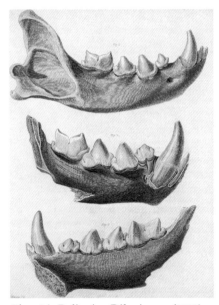

Plate 4 in Reliquiae Diluvianae *(1823) compares the jaw of a modern Cape hyena (top) with the larger jaws of the extinct hyena species found at Kirkdale Cave.*

In the second part, Buckland reviewed further evidence of bones in caves and superficial deposits in Britain and Europe and also described other evidence of landforms and erratics to support his view of a violent catastrophe, the Universal Deluge, which had occurred before human history. Even as he was writing *Reliquiae*, Buckland had evidence to suggest that there might have been more than one catastrophe, and these must have occurred in deep geological rather than biblical/human time. He had taken an interest in the giant fossils being found by Mary Anning (p. 250) and kept in close touch with her. In 1824, prompted by his friend Georges Cuvier (p. 202) and Gideon Mantell's discoveries in Sussex, he published the first scientific description of what Richard Owen (p. 255) was later to call a dinosaur. The fossils included half a jaw and bones acquired by Buckland from workmen extracting slate from just

William Buckland teaching: his use of maps, charts, illustrations and specimens reflect his insistence on working from the evidence. The lectures and field trips were popular, although Buckland's eccentric sense of humour was not always appreciated.

Part of a diagrammatic section through the Earth's crust, from a plate in Buckland's Geology
and Mineralogy *(1836), summarizing his work on the succession of strata and the distinctive
communities of plants and animals indicative of the influence of changing climate on ecology.*

above the Jurassic limestone at Stonesfield, Oxfordshire. He called the fossil *Mega-
losaurus* meaning giant lizard. Now known to be a meat-eating dinosaur dating to
181–169 million years ago, Buckland described its sharp serrated teeth and predicted
its bulky body.

As his work on the succession of geological strata and fossils in Britain and on
the continent continued, he found more evidence for a succession of past worlds
with distinctive ecosystems, summarizing this work in the first figure of his book
Geology and Mineralogy considered with reference to Natural Theology, published in 1836.
This hugely popular work provided the context which would encourage others to
think about the evolution of plant and animal species, but Buckland, who believed
in successive creations, now turned his attention to a new theory that offered an
explanation for the catastrophic phenomena he had documented in *Reliquiae* and
other scientific papers.

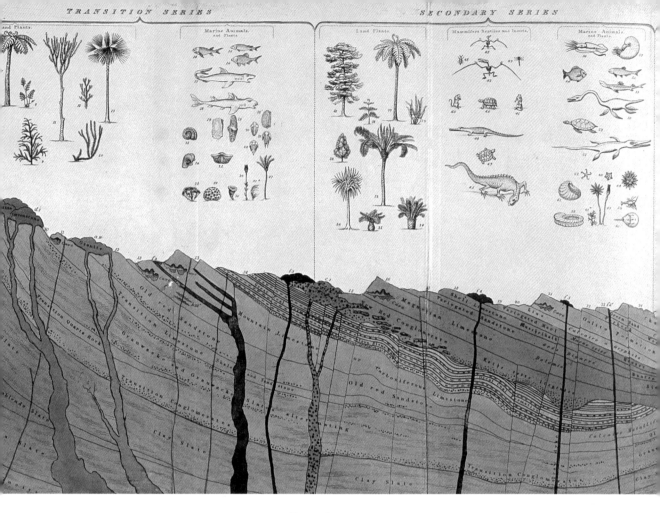

ICE AGES

Having heard Louis Agassiz's (p. 261) theory that ice had once covered much wider areas of the Earth, Buckland accompanied him to Switzerland in 1838 to look at the action of glaciers. The two men then visited Scotland, where they found abundant evidence of the many processes of erosion and deposition associated with glaciation. Buckland was now certain that he had found the true cause of the phenomena he had so accurately described but previously attributed to the Deluge. Setting aside his earlier interpretation he planned a new edition of *Geology and Mineralogy*, but did not achieve this.

In 1845 Buckland was appointed Dean at Westminster Abbey, but continued to lecture at Oxford. Although ill health dogged his latter years, he had already achieved a great deal. Geology was established as a university discipline, and the occurrence and effects of ice ages had been recognized. Although he himself believed in successive creations, he had also inadvertently provided a basis for evolutionary theory by demonstrating climatic and ecological change through time.

Charles Lyell

ADVOCATE OF MODERN GEOLOGY

(1797–1875)

... no causes whatever have from the earliest time
... to the present, ever acted, but those now acting

Charles Lyell, letter to Roderick Murchison, 15 January 1829

B Y THE TIME CHARLES LYELL went to Oxford University in 1816, geology was beginning to emerge as a subject in its own right, although its theoretical basis was still grounded in religion and philosophy. In a career which was to distinguish him as a great reformer rather than an innovative genius, Lyell severed this connection and established the fundamental principles which remain the basis of modern geology.

DEVELOPING CONVICTIONS

While studying classics and mathematics at Oxford University, Lyell was also able to attend lectures in geology given by William Buckland (p. 241), from whom he learned the importance of travel, fieldwork and facts, all of which he pursued until the end of his life. However, although Buckland taught him a lot, Lyell had also read an account of James Hutton's ideas (p. 186), which made him doubt his teacher's explanation that the formation of some landforms and the extinction of animals were caused by a catastrophic event such as the biblical Flood. His own observations suggested that Hutton's theory was more probable and this view was strengthened when, in 1821, he went on a field trip to Sussex with the eminent English geologist Gideon Mantell.

Here in the Weald, Lyell saw evidence of a Huttonian cycle of ancient life. A delta which had supported life had been submerged and covered by the deposition of chalk; this mass of new rock had then been uplifted and denuded to form the present landscape. Lyell was excited by what he saw. Whilst reluctantly practising law to earn a living, he studied geology and visited the continent. By 1829 he knew that he wanted to establish geology as a subject based on facts rather than references to the Bible and had started writing.

Frontispiece of Lyell's Principles of Geology *Vol. I (1830), showing what is now known to be a covered marketplace but was then called the temple of Serapis, near Naples, Italy. Holes in the columns made by marine molluscs in the last 2,000 years show the building has been submerged by the sea and then uplifted. For Lyell, this demonstrated the action of processes described in his book.*

T. Bradley. Sc.

Present state of the Temple of Serapis at Puzzuoli.

London, Published by John Murray, Albemarle St. June. 1830.

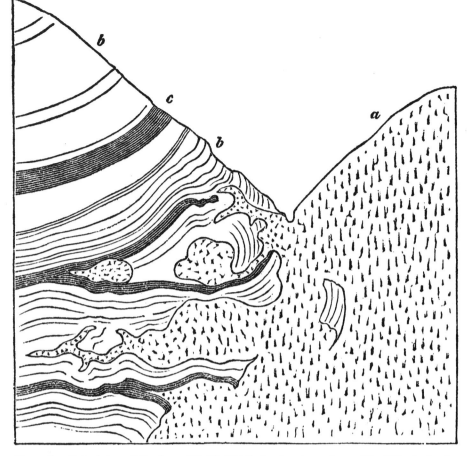

Figure from Principles of Geology *Vol. III (1833) showing the section at Glen Tilt, Scotland, where Hutton showed that granite (a) is an igneous (volcanic) rock which could be forced through and into older sedimentary rocks like limestone (b). Lyell added the term metamorphic to describe the sedimentary rocks altered by heat from such intrusions (c).*

Lyell's three-volume *Principles of Geology* was published between 1830 and 1833. Its full title set out its content and intent: '*an attempt to explain the former changes in the earth's surface by reference to causes now in operation*'. Lyell opened volume I with a history of geology which showed how the absence of clear laws to define the operation of nature's forces had held up its development. Reinvigorating Hutton, he claimed that no special or catastrophic causes are needed to explain the nature of the Earth. The processes which can be observed operating today have always acted over a vast period of time. These, he said, are the 'alphabet and grammar of geology … the key to the interpretation of all geological phenomena.' The principle that the present is the key to the past subsequently became known as 'uniformitarianism'.

The first volume of *Principles* was well received, but alarmed many who thought it would open the door to Lamarck's ideas on the transmutation of species (p. 190). Lyell

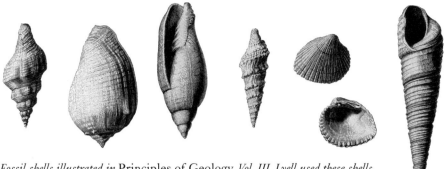

Fossil shells illustrated in Principles of Geology *Vol. III. Lyell used these shells to distinguish geological formations dating to the Miocene period of the Tertiary epoch.*

himself opposed these ideas and devoted his second volume to refuting Lamarck. While he offered no views on the origins of species, he considered that extinctions could occur gradually without catastrophes. In this he provided the first thorough consideration of how organisms may or may not become fossils, emphasizing how differential preservation could bias the fossil record. Applying these principles, the final volume describes the composition of the Earth's crust and discusses the relative ages of rock. Although he did not accept the possibility of evolution, he understood that fossils showed changes through time and could be used to distinguish strata of different ages. Applying this principle he sub-divided the rock formations of the Tertiary epoch (65–1.6 million years ago) into three periods, which he named Eocene, Miocene and Pliocene, meaning early, middle and late.

IMPACT

Lyell's rejection of transmutation prevented charges of religious heresy and allowed widespread acceptance of his views, revolutionizing the practice of geology. It was among the books which Charles Darwin (p. 267) read on his voyage on board the *Beagle*. Describing himself as one of Lyell's 'zealous disciples', Darwin was typical of a generation of natural historians in saying that *Principles* altered 'the whole tone of one's mind, & therefore when seeing a thing never seen by Lyell, one yet saw it partially through his eyes'.

Lyell revised *Principles* through 13 editions as he travelled and made further contacts in Europe and North America. It was both a major source of income and a dialogue with his contemporaries. Although he found it personally difficult to accept the idea of evolution, he had provided a framework for it. Lyell actively encouraged both Darwin and Alfred Wallace (p. 277) and published his own investigations into the evidence that humans had existed alongside certain extinct mammals in *The Antiquity of Man* (1863). Here he finally accepted evolution by natural selection as the revolution he had himself inadvertently begun by reforming geology.

Mary Anning

FOSSIL HUNTER

(1799–1847)

Miss Anning, as a child, ne'er passed
A pin upon the ground;
But picked it up, and so at last
An ichthyosaurus found.

J. W. Preston, 1884

NOT FOR NOTHING WAS MARY ANNING CALLED the princess of palaeontology, in recognition of her extraordinary talent in extraordinary circumstances. The daughter of a carpenter or cabinet maker, she was born into a dissenting family in Lyme Regis, southern England, in 1799. As a sideline, her father Richard collected and sold 'curiosities' from the cliffs: these fossils had many names, such as ladies' fingers, snake stones, devil's toenails, vertiberries (bits of backbone) and Bezoar stones (because of their alleged resemblance to the gallstones of Bezoar goats). After a fall from a cliff, and with consumption, Richard died in 1810, leaving his wife and two children (another seven died in infancy) in near destitution. They were on parish relief, at around three shillings a week, for the next five or so years.

A less promising start could hardly be imagined. But from the beginning Mary was exceptional. At the age of 15 months she was struck by lightning. The nurse holding her died, but she survived. According to her nephew, she had been dull before but afterwards became lively and intelligent. She and her brother Joseph had joined her father on fossil-hunting expeditions, and now, after her father's death, she helped her mother to develop what became the family business in fossils.

It is hard for us to think ourselves back into the mental world of the 1810s and the 1820s. In some circles, far from the rural poor of Lyme Regis, the concept of deep time was just beginning to take hold. In 1795 James Hutton (p. 186) found 'no vestige of a beginning – no prospect of an end'. Others elsewhere were reaching similar conclusions. But for most, the Bible remained the authority on chronology, as on most else, and to suggest otherwise was blasphemy. The best explanation given for fossils was that they were creatures buried in the Flood; and that even if such creatures were now unknown in one part of the world, they would probably have survived in another. It was even suggested that they might have been left around by God as a test of faith.

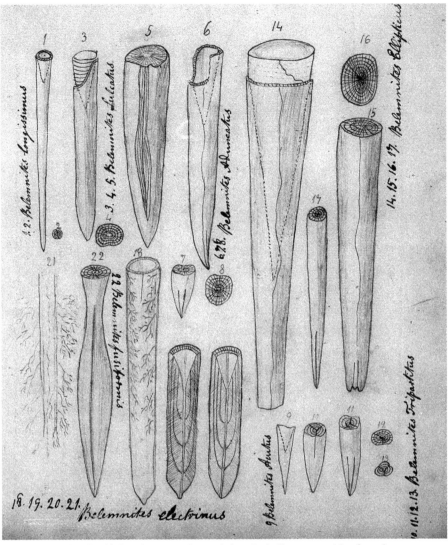

A drawing of fossils of belemnites – marine cephalopods similar to a squid – from the manuscripts collection of Mary Anning. The cliffs of Lyme Regis, where Anning lived, were rich in such fossils.

We now know that the Lower Jurassic cliffs of Lyme Regis were laid down in a somewhat muddy sea around 200 million years ago. At the bottom of the food chain were such organisms as oysters, barnacles and crinoids; in the middle were molluscs, including belemnites and ammonites; and at the top were fish and the great marine or airborne reptiles: ichthyosaurs, plesiosaurs, pliosaurs and pterodactyls. When they died, their remains sank to the bottom of the sea, where, from lack of oxygen, many were preserved. With tectonic plate movement over millions of years, they were compressed and their traces survive, like fillings in a sandwich, in the layered cliffs of the West Dorset coast.

Mary Anning had no formal education, and would have absorbed the conventional wisdom about the world around her. But in the course of odd jobs, she learned to read and write, however erratically, and when she was 14 was lent the first book she read on geology. This may have been her introduction to understanding the special character of the cliffs around Lyme. The list of her discoveries between 1811 and 1830 is impressive by any reckoning. With her brother Joseph she put together the first ichthyosaur, and later discovered two others. Among other creatures she found two plesiosaurs, one cephalopod, one pterodactyl and a fossil fish (then interpreted as a transition between a shark and a ray). The cephalopod came complete with its

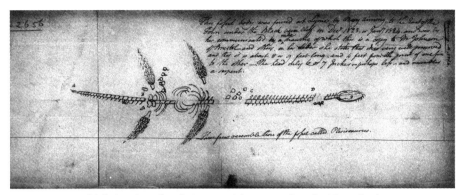

*ABOVE A pen and ink drawing of a plesiosaur, with annotations, by Mary Anning, 1824.
A remarkable fossil collector, Anning was the first, with her brother Joseph, to put together an
ichthyosaur, and the first to discover a plesiosaur.*
*OPPOSITE A painting of Mary Anning on the beach at Lyme Regis by B. J. Donne, 1847. Despite
her lowly social status and the fact that she was self-taught and a woman in a man's world, she
became a celebrity in her lifetime.*

supply of fossil ink, which one of her friends used for sketching. In addition she found
a quantity of coprolites which she was the first to identify as fossil faeces.

Mary was no mere collector, however. She saw where others failed to see, and
almost by instinct could discern the presence of a fossil on the cliff surface. Once a
fossil had been located, she took extraordinary pains in extracting or directing its
extraction without damaging it. One of her greatest skills, not always evident among
museum curators, was in putting fossil specimens together. As Lady Silvester
recorded on 17 September 1824, when Mary was only 25: 'The extraordinary thing in
this young woman is that she has made herself so thoroughly acquainted with the
science that the moment she finds any bones she knows to what tribe they belong.'
Similarly, in his *History of Lyme Regis* of 1834, George Roberts referred to her 'great
judgment in extracting the animals, and infinite skill and manipulation in their development'. In short she understood how they actually worked.

She also had luck. With the discovery of deep time, geology became the queen
of the sciences. As the search for fossils in Lyme Regis and elsewhere developed,
so people – usually wealthy gentlemen amateurs – indulged their curiosity by and
through collecting. Academic arguments over Earth history also developed. There
were those, conspicuous among them William Buckland (p. 241), who sought to
reconcile geological with biblical chronology. There were the Catastrophists, who saw
the Earth's history in terms of a series of relatively sudden events or discontinuities.
There were the Vulcanists, who believed the Earth was born from volcanoes, and the

Neptunists who believed it had crystallized from a primordial ocean. Last were the Uniformitarians, following James Hutton, William Smith (p. 219) and Charles Lyell (p. 246), who saw all change as gradual, and greatly influenced Charles Darwin (p. 267).

In spite of her many handicaps, ranging from her lowly origins to being a woman in a man's world, Mary Anning became a celebrity in her lifetime. Lady Silvester also wrote of her: 'It is certainly a wonderful instance of divine favour – that this poor ignorant girl should be so blessed, for by reading and application she has arrived to that degree of knowledge as to be in the habit of writing and talking with professors and other clever men on the subject, and they all acknowledge that she understands more of the science than anyone else in the kingdom.'

With knowledge came self-confidence, and a measure of scientific scepticism. Thomas Allen, an amateur geologist who had bought fossils from Anning, commented on her disputes with Buckland 'whose anatomical science she holds in great contempt'. Buckland was nonetheless a lifelong friend. She saw off Gideon Mantell, a doctor and natural historian, who described her as 'a prim, pedantic vinegar-looking thin female, shrewd and rather satirical in her conversation'. Later, her friend Anna Maria Pinney wrote that Mary felt that 'the world has used her ill and she does not care for it, according to her account these men of learning have sucked her brains, and made a great deal by publishing works, while she derived none of the advantages….'

It is indeed remarkable that the discoveries she made and fossils she sold rarely carried her name, instead carrying those of their owners or donors. In her lifetime only two of the species she identified were named after her, by the Swiss scientist Louis Agassiz (p. 261). Even if she enjoyed the attentions and company of the rich and famous, she never lost her Dorset accent, and only left Lyme Regis once to visit London. Indeed she regarded her visitors with some amusement, writing in a letter to Lady Murchison in 1828, 'I do so enjoy an opposition among the big-wigs'. In the words of Anna Maria Pinney, 'She frankly owns that the society of her own rank is become distasteful to her, but yet she is very kind and good to all her own relations, and what money she gets by collecting fossils goes to them or to anyone else who wants it.'

During her lifetime she neither expected nor received professional recognition. But in her last years her eminence won her a modest pension. After her death Henry De la Beche, by then President of the Geological Society of London, read out an unprecedented tribute to her in his presidential address. All those who wrote about her testified to her intelligence, toughness, independence of mind, and sometimes prickly but always generous nature. In her lifetime, and still more afterwards, she became something of an icon. And so she remains.

DAVID WILLIAMS

Richard Owen

CHAMPION OF COMPARATIVE ANATOMY

(1804–1892)

*Its forelimbs being composed of essentially the same
parts as the wings of a bird are homologous with them; but
the parachute being composed of different parts, yet
performing the same function as the wings of a bird, is
analogous to them.... But homologous parts may be, and
often are, also analogous in the fuller sense, viz. As
performing the same functions ... the pectoral fin of the
flying fish is analogous to the wing of the Bird, but, unlike
the Dragon, it is also homologous with it.*

Richard Owen, Archetype and Homologies of the Vertebrate Skeleton, 1847

IT HAS BEEN SAID OF SIR RICHARD OWEN that he lived too long. He died 89 years old, outliving his wife (who died in 1873) and his only son (who committed suicide in 1886); he also outlived Charles Darwin (who died in 1882), the man who was indirectly responsible for his downfall. Owen outlived many of his own ideas too. Yet more recently, some of Owen's theories have been revived and reworked, and he is now acknowledged for his contribution to comparative biology.

In the mid-1800s Owen introduced, promoted and studied what was then called 'homological anatomy', the study of comparative anatomy. He prepared the groundwork in a lengthy report to the British Association for the Advancement in Science in 1847, which he published as a book in a slightly modified form a year later, entitled *On the Archetype and Homologies of the Vertebrate Skeleton*. At first his ideas met with great popular success. But in the late 1850s and 1860s, 'homologizing' declined, being superseded by the new Darwinian biology created in the wake of Darwin's *Origin of Species*, and spearheaded and vigorously promoted by Thomas Henry Huxley. Sir Richard Owen thus straddled two very distinct eras, one of his own making ('homological anatomy'), the other (Darwinian biology) his undoing.

Owen was born on 20 July 1804, in Lancaster, England. His father died when he was just five years old and a year later he was enrolled at Lancaster Grammar School. He began his training in medicine in 1820, apprenticed to a Lancaster surgeon. It was during these years, dissecting cadavers, that he acquired his interest in anatomy.

Fig. 3.

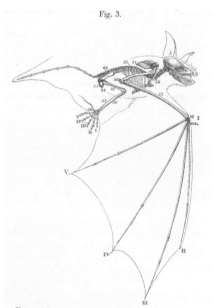

External form and skeleton of the wing of the Bat.

Drawing of the wing of a bat from Owen's book On the Nature of Limbs *(1849). In a series of drawings Owen illustrated the forelimb of a number of vertebrates. The homologues (the different parts) are numbered for comparison – so the* scapula *(51), the shoulder blade, is present in all vertebrates and while different is 'essentially' the same.*

Rather than complete this apprenticeship, Owen entered the University of Edinburgh medical school in 1824. There seemed to be much that displeased the young Owen about the Edinburgh medical school too, and rather than finish his studies he took advantage of the lessons given by the anatomist John Barclay. Barclay suggested a further apprenticeship with the eccentric and controversial surgeon John Abernethy. Abernethy was able to help Owen gain access to the Royal College of Surgeons, of which he was at that time President, in 1826, and also got him appointed Assistant Conservator.

Owen's task was to catalogue the vast number of anatomical specimens in the Hunterian Collection. This collection had been bought in 1799 by the Government, six years after the death of its owner, John Hunter. It was handed over to the Royal College of Surgeons with the proviso that a catalogue of the specimens was made, a museum created to house them and a lecture series initiated to promote them. Owen's task was made more difficult as the previous assistant, Sir Everard Home, had destroyed much of its documentation for fear of being discovered a plagiarist. Yet even if the documentation had existed, the challenge would still have been daunting. In spite of this, Owen managed to complete the catalogue by 1830, became the College's Hunterian Professor of Comparative Anatomy and Physiology in 1836, and began his first series of Hunterian lectures a year later. In 1849 he became the Conservator of the collections, remaining there until 1856, when he was appointed Superintendent of the natural history collections at the British Museum.

Recognizing that these natural history collections required a separate building – if not a separate existence – Owen patiently began to detail the many reasons why a new museum was needed. Eventually, after more than 20 years of persistent endeavour, a museum for natural history was built in South Kensington, London, opening to the public in 1881 as the British Museum (Natural History). Today it is known simply as the Natural History Museum. Owen remained in charge (as Superintendent) until

1884, when he retired with a knighthood to Sheen Lodge on the Richmond Estate. It was only after Owen's retirement that a Director was appointed, the first one being Sir William Henry Flower. A statue of Owen still stands in the main hall of the Museum.

HOMOLOGUES AND ANALOGUES

Owen was first and foremost a brilliant anatomist (he was described as the 'British Cuvier'; p. 202) and many of his scientific achievements were detailed and impressive anatomical monographs, beginning with the now classic *Memoir on the Pearly Nautilus*, published in 1832. He studied many vertebrate groups and published on 'fishes', 'reptiles' – he invented the name Dinosaurs for a group of extremely large and, in his view, distinguishable 'reptile' fossils – birds and mammals, including *Lectures on Comparative Anatomy and Physiology of the Vertebrate Animals* (1846), *A History of British Fossil Reptiles* (1849–84), *On the nature of Limbs: A discourse delivered … at … the Royal Institution* (1849), *Palaeontology, or a systematic summary of Extinct Animals and their geological relations* (1860) and *On the Anatomy of Vertebrates* (1866–68).

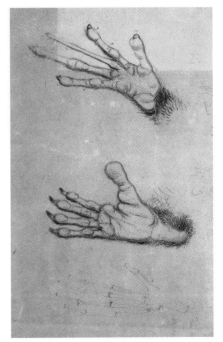

A turning point for Owen came when he attended part of the famous debate in 1830 in Paris, in which Georges Cuvier and Etienne Geoffroy Saint-Hilaire tangled over the meaning and extent of relationships among animals (and their fossil remains). For Saint-Hilaire, detailed comparisons among animals betrayed a general 'unity of plan'. This notion became his *'théorie des analogues'* (theory of analogues) – the commonality exhibited by the different parts of different organisms. Cuvier, in turn, resisted many of Saint-Hilaire's more far-fetched comparisons, and was more interested in the functional aspects of animal design. Thus, it has been said, Saint-Hilaire and Cuvier fought about form and function, and their relative importance.

Owen would have been impressed by both the functional arguments of Cuvier and the 'unity of design' arguments of Saint-Hilaire. With respect to the latter, Owen began to understand the means by which 'common plans' were discovered: the *'théorie*

Drawings of the 'hand' of an Aye-Aye from Madagascar (Daubentonia madagascariensis); *from a watercolour by Joseph Wolf. The Aye-Aye has a modified middle finger, used to probe for food, a unique feature first described by Owen in 1866.*

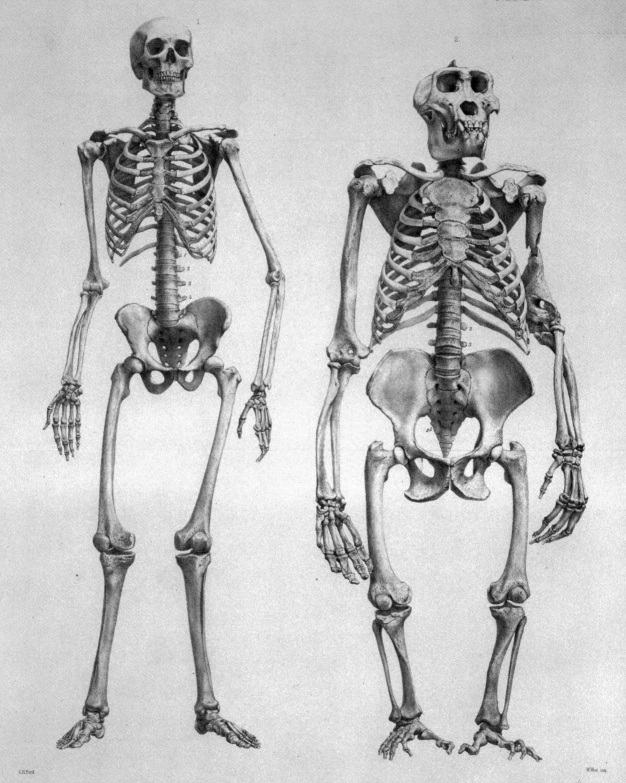

G.H. Ford

W. West. imp.

1. *Homo.*   2. *Troglodytes Gorilla.*

des analogues'. Saint-Hilaire's 'analogues' became Owen's homologues, which, in 1843, he famously defined as 'the same organ in different animals under every variety of form and function'. Thus, for example, the wing of a bat, the fore-limb of a mole and the pectoral-fin of a dugong (sea cow) are homologous, built according to the same plan and from the same 'beginning'.

Although often assumed to be a contrasting term for homologues, for Owen analogues are 'defined' solely in terms of function: legs are for walking, wings are for flying (as seen in the quote at the head of this piece, in which he is discussing the gliding lizard or 'Dragon', *Draco volans*). Hence, homology and analogy can be applied in four permutations. For example, according to Owen, the forelimb of a man and monkey are both homologous and analogous, while the forelimb of a man and the wing of a bird are homologous but not analogous.

Owen's intention was for all homologues of all organisms to be discovered, in order that the various parts of different organisms could be related one to another. Such was the general aim of 'homological anatomy' as he understood it. Nevertheless, for organisms to be built on the same plan, along the same lines and to have the same 'beginnings', led Owen to consider what it might be that underlies the structure of living creatures. To this end, Owen created his archetype, an 'image', so to speak, of the most generalized animal, the 'type' that all such creatures were 'related' to. Owen only ever presented a vertebrate archetype, but had intended to pursue the archetype of the other 'great' groups of organisms. While others had discussed archetypes before (Owen gave credit to Joseph Maclise, another medical man), it was Owen's insight to find the inter-relation between his re-definitions of homology, modifying its use from Saint-Hilaire's '*théorie des analogues*', with their derivation from a common source, the archetype. Owen considered homologues to be empty of meaning without reference to, and interpretation from, the archetype.

DARWINIAN EVOLUTION

Owen, of course, would not have been completely prepared for the events at the dawn of a Darwinian worldview. Nevertheless, in the *Origin of Species* – and leaning heavily on Owen's studies and ideas – Darwin wrote:

Drawing of a human (Homo sapiens) *and gorilla* (Gorilla gorilla) *skeleton, published by Owen in 1866. While he recognized many similarities in their skeletons, it was in the hippocampus – a part of the brain – that he saw the uniqueness of the human: the brain of man had one, that of gorillas did not. This inspired Thomas Henry Huxley into one of his many battles with Owen, arguing that both have a hippocampus; Huxley won.*

Naturalists frequently speak of the skull as formed from metamorphosed vertebrae; the jaws of crabs as metamorphosed legs, the stamens and pistils of flowers as metamorphosed leaves... Naturalists, however, use such language only in a metaphorical sense; they are far from meaning that during a long course of descent, primordial organs of any kind ... have been converted into skulls and jaws. Yet so strong is the appearance of a modification of this nature having occurred, that naturalists can hardly avoid employing language having this plain signification. In my view these terms may be used literally....

Thus, Owen's archetype became Darwin's ancestor, and the steady drift away from comparative anatomy and comparative biology began.

Owen's final days were spent at Sheen Lodge, the property given over to him by Queen Victoria in 1852. By the time of his death, Owen's reputation had dwindled away and his presence had all but vanished, being written out of history by the new generation of Darwinian biologists.

It was thus with some irony that the task of summarizing Owen's scientific achievements fell to Huxley, Owen's most persistent and eloquent foe. In an essay contributed to *The Life of Richard Owen*, Huxley wrote a lengthy review of the history of anatomy and morphology since its beginnings ('to the general public, to the great majority of whom anatomy is as much a sealed book as the higher mathematics'), mentioning neither Owen nor his achievements until he set out the distinction between the twin concepts of 'homology' and 'analogy', concepts that were clarified by Owen, being his major contribution to the fundamentals of comparative anatomy. Huxley had evidently struggled with his task. In a letter to Joseph Hooker on 4 February 1894 he wrote: 'I am toiling over my chapter about Owen, and I believe his ghost in Hades is grinning over my difficulties. The thing that strikes me most is, how he and I and all the things we fought about belong to antiquity. It is almost impertinent to trouble the modern world with such antiquarian business.' Summing up Owen's achievements, he also wrote 'I am not sure that any one but the historian of anatomical science is ever likely to recur to them'. True, it was the historians who first addressed Owen and his contributions, initially from the narrow Darwinian perspective, later from a more considered view, but in the mid- to late 20th century Owen was re-discovered by comparative biologists, who re-examined his contribution to science and began to utilize, develop and clarify the concepts of homology and analogy, acknowledging Owen's efforts as a major and important advance in comparative biology. Perhaps, even today, the significance of Owen's contributions has yet to be fully appreciated.

DAVID WILLIAMS

Jean Louis Rodolphe Agassiz

EXAMINATION, OBSERVATION, COMPARISON

(1807–1873)

*I have devoted my whole life to the study of Nature, and yet a
single sentence may express all that I have done. I have
shown that there is a correspondence between the succession
of Fishes in geological times and the different stages of
growth in the egg, – that is all.*

Louis Agassiz, 1862

LOUIS AGASSIZ IS RIGHTLY CONSIDERED A PIONEER and innovator in the
fields of comparative biology, palaeontology and the natural history of the
United States. He was an extraordinary anatomist, creating new areas of
research in systematics and palaeontology (especially of fishes), and a gifted teacher.
Often described as a pious, stubborn 'creationist' – the man who resisted the Darwinian theory of evolution to the end of his life – he was regarded as an extremely effective
and inspiring lecturer, influencing many loyal and talented students to continue his
researches. In fact his teaching methods gained attention and some notoriety, so much
so that long after Agassiz's death the poet Ezra Pound found virtue in his approach.

Pound used as his source an account of Agassiz's teaching by one of his students,
Samuel Scudder, who became a leading entomologist and palaeoentomologist; this
has since been called the 'ordeal with the fish'. Agassiz gave Scudder a fish to study.
After some days, Agassiz asked him what he saw. Scudder was not sure what Agassiz
wanted. Then Scudder realized: '"Do you perhaps mean", I asked, "that the fish has
symmetrical sides with paired organs?"' Agassiz was pleased, so Scudder asked, 'What
next?'; Agassiz replied, 'Look at your fish'. Thus Pound concluded in his *ABC of
Reading*: 'The proper METHOD of studying poetry and good letters is that of contemporary biologists, that is careful first hand examination of the matter, and
continual COMPARISON of one slide or specimen with another.' Agassiz exemplified the practice of comparative biology – for him everything worth knowing lay
within the specimen to hand.

Agassiz was born on 28 May 1807 in Motier-en-Vuly, Switzerland, the fifth child
of Rodolphe Benjamin Louis, a church minister, and Rose Mayer; their four other children died in infancy. After schooling at home, Agassiz studied at the universities of

Zurich and Heidelberg; he received his doctorate from Erlangen in 1829 and his degree in medicine from Munich in 1830. While studying for his doctorate, Agassiz was given the opportunity to examine the fishes collected from the Amazon by Johan Baptist von Spix, who had died before he could study them himself. Agassiz published his account of these fishes in 1829. He also began to study the fishes in Switzerland, and in 1842 his *Histoire Naturelle des Poissons d'Eau Douce de l'Europe Centrale* appeared. A little later, Agassiz began to work on fossil fishes. This was to result in the classic five-volume *Recherches sur les Poissons Fossiles*, published between 1833 and 1844.

In 1831 Agassiz travelled to Paris to study with Georges Cuvier (p. 202), who allowed Agassiz to use his material on fossil fishes. Their relationship was brief, however, as Cuvier died in 1832; Agassiz left Paris in September that year to become Professor of Natural History at the University of Neuchâtel in Switzerland, where he remained for the next 13 years. Here Agassiz developed his views on geology and palaeontology, particularly his controversial theories on glaciation, which, following Cuvier's catastrophism, he thought had once covered the entire Earth in an 'Ice Age'.

Agassiz's first trip to the United States was in 1846, and he returned two years later after accepting a position at Harvard. It was here that he created the Museum of Comparative Zoology, which opened to the public in 1860 and where Agassiz remained, serving as its director, until his death in 1873. In 1857, just before his directorship began, Agassiz started yet another ambitious project, the *Contributions to the Natural History of the United States of America*, a part publication that ceased in 1862, with only four of the ten proposed volumes in print. Volume 1 contained his *Essay on Classification*, an account of his views on how to account scientifically for the diversity of living organisms and their distribution around the globe. The *Essay* was published as a book two years later in 1859, the same year as Darwin's *Origin of Species*, which would completely overshadow Agassiz's book and diminish its influence.

THREE-FOLD PARALLELISM

Yet earlier, Agassiz had made some startling discoveries. In the first volume of the *Recherches sur les Poissons Fossiles* Agassiz wrote of the relationship between comparative anatomy (systematics – the discovery of relations among organisms, both those still living and those extinct), embryology and geology, thereby suggesting a 'three-fold parallelism'. For Agassiz, the three-fold parallelism was of great significance. In his *Essay on Classification* he wrote that 'the phenomena of animal life correspond to one another, whether we compare their rank as determined by structural complication with the phases of their growth, or with their succession in past geological ages;

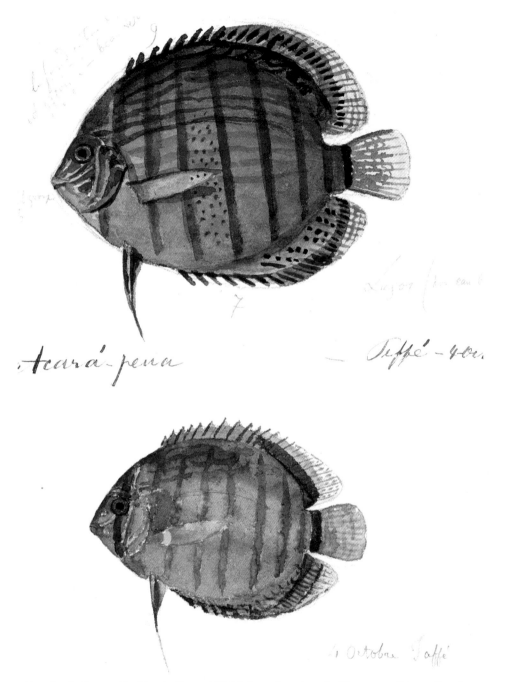

Drawing by Jacques Burkhardt of two cichlid fishes, collected on the Thayer expedition to Brazil from 1865 to 1866. Burkhardt was Agassiz's personal artist and during this expedition he completed some 2,000 watercolours.

whether we compare this succession with their relative growth, or all these different relations with each other and with the geographical distribution of animals upon the earth. The same series everywhere!'

Ideas about the apparent relation between comparative anatomy and the embryological development of individual organisms can be traced back to Johann Wolfgang von Goethe and Johann Herrmann Ferdinand von Autenrieth in the late 18th and early 19th centuries – and some would claim even further back, to Aristotle (p. 23). Nevertheless, Agassiz believed he had developed the theory by adding the relationship of the geological record, declaring in 1862, albeit rather humbly, that 'I have shown that there is a correspondence between the succession of Fishes in geological times and the different stages of their growth in the egg, – this is all'.

The significance of the three-fold relationship was absorbed into the evolutionary literature, especially by Ernst Haeckel, who as early as 1863 wrote that '...the threefold parallelism between the embryological, systematic and palaeontological development of organisms, this threefold step-ladder, I think is one of the strongest proofs of the truth of the theory of evolution'. The remark caused Agassiz to write

A group photograph of some of the Thayer expedition members, including William James (brother of novelist Henry), seated on the ground, the artist Jacques Burkhardt in the centre (with the white beard) and Thayer himself (third from left).

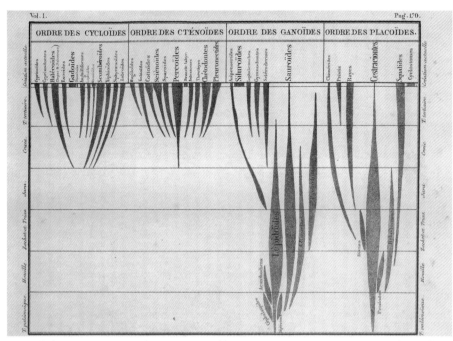

An early branching diagram from Agassiz, published in 1844, representing the 'genealogy' of fishes. The diagram links together fossil and recent taxa.

'Das ist mein Resultat!' in the margin of his copy of Haeckel's *Natürliche Schöpfungs-geschichte*. Agassiz's efforts were given a more profound interpretation by Joseph Le Conte, a student and friend of Agassiz. He believed that Agassiz was the person who had laid the foundations for the theory of evolution, through the parallels he drew between the stages of embryonic development of organisms and the order of appearance in the fossil record. 'No one', Le Conte noted, 'was reasonably entitled to believe in the transformation of species prior to the publication of the work of Agassiz.'

Earlier, on the question of the distribution of species, Agassiz had written that:

> *The greatest obstacles in the way of investigating the laws of the distribution of organized beings over the surface of our globe, are to be traced to the views generally entertained about their origin. There is a prevailing opinion, which ascribes to all living beings upon earth one common centre of origin, from which it is supposed they, in the course of time, spread over wider and wider areas, till they finally came into their present state of distribution. And what gives this view a higher recommendation in the opinion of most men is the circumstance, that such a method of distribution is considered as revealed in our sacred writings.*

Thus, while Agassiz's firmly held religious beliefs influenced his ideas, the arguments were rather more to do with *origins* than *causes* – and, whatever he might have thought was the primary cause for organisms' existence, he was not above challenging the biblical account. Agassiz thus proposed a way of looking at the world through

265

evidence, evidence from comparative anatomy, embryology, palaeontology and geography. Explaining the correspondence between these different sources of evidence was of little significance. It was *finding* the correspondence that determined how the natural world was ordered.

Agassiz was celebrated as a leading scientist of his day in America. In 1857, Henry Wadsworth Longfellow celebrated Agassiz's birthday with a poem, 'The fiftieth birthday of Agassiz', which may sum up Agassiz's beliefs as opposed to his approach:

> *And Nature, the old nurse, took*
> *The child upon her knee,*
> *Saying: 'Here is a story-book*
> *Thy Father has written for thee.'*
> *'Come, wander with me,' she said,*
> *'Into regions yet untrod;*
> *And read what is still unread*
> *In the manuscripts of God.'*

In 1865 Agassiz had the opportunity to return to an earlier interest, mounting the Thayer expedition to collect fishes in Brazil (named after Nathaniel Thayer who underwrote the trip and the curation of the specimens). The expedition left New York in mid-1865, returning in 1866 with some 34,000 specimens (William James, brother of the author Henry, was on board as a volunteer; William went on to write *Varieties of Religious Experiences*). Agassiz's purpose on board was clear: 'I am often asked what is my chief aim of this expedition to South America? No doubt in a general way it is to collect materials for future study. But the conviction which draws me irresistibly, is that the combination of animals on this continent, where the faunae are so characteristic and so distinct from all others, will give me the means of showing that the transmutation theory is wholly without foundation in facts.' And so Agassiz's remaining years were to be haunted by Darwin.

To the end of his life, Agassiz steadfastly resisted the new Darwinian worldview – a stance that brought him into conflict with fellow Harvard academic Asa Gray (p. 286) – though it was eventually adopted by his students as well as by his son Alexander. Many therefore regarded him as a 'living fossil', failing to keep alive his vision of the order evident in the natural world, and the methods of its discovery. Yet, theories of origins and causes to one side, Agassiz's greatness rests – and remains to this day – on his insistence on evaluating *evidence* and that 'no man is fit to be a naturalist, who does not know how to take care of specimens'.

KEITH THOMSON

Charles Darwin

THE COMPLETE NATURALIST

(1809–1882)

Being well prepared to appreciate the struggle for existence
that everywhere goes on from the long-continued observation
of the habits of animals and plants, it at once struck me that
under these circumstances favourable variations would tend
to be preserved and unfavourable ones to be destroyed.

Charles Darwin, Autobiography, *1887*

I
F CHARLES DARWIN HAD NEVER PUBLISHED HIS THEORY of natural selection
(the driving mechanism of evolution) he would still be famous today for his many
other works in natural history. The first of these was his description of his voyage
around the world in HMS *Beagle* (1831–36), which is still a best-seller. Darwin was
perhaps the most complete naturalist of all time. As a student, he was described by his
uncle as being 'a man of enlarged curiosity'; that curiosity led him to change forever
the fields of science that we now call evolution, ecology and behaviour, and to make
path-breaking contributions to geology.

Not only did Darwin master the skills of observation, description and classification common to all natural history, he applied his gift of critical intelligence to almost
every animal and plant group. More than anyone else, he also extended that work into
deep analysis and theory. It was never enough for him simply to observe, he needed
always to find the explanations underlying even the most commonplace phenomena.
One example of that life-long curiosity is his elegant little book on the behaviour of
earthworms. From simple quantitative experiments on the rate at which earthworms
in his garden brought up earth to the surface, he demonstrated the crucial role that
worms play in soil formation (and the burial of the ruins of ancient buildings).

Charles Darwin was such a seminal genius in the field of biology that one constantly
wonders about the sources of his ideas. The surface facts are not impressive. He was an
indifferent student at school, spent two years at Edinburgh studying medicine (which
he disliked), and then went to Cambridge where he studied (with no greater enthusiasm) for the Church. Shortly after graduating he was invited to be a naturalist on the
Navy Hydrographic Office's circumnavigation of the world by HMS *Beagle*, under
Captain Robert FitzRoy. Behind all that, however, lay the extraordinary mental capac-

ity and drive and the highly developed skills as a field naturalist that made him deserving of that appointment. Even as a small boy, he was a passionate naturalist: 'I collected all sorts of things, shells, seals, franks, coins, minerals. The passion for collecting, which leads a man to be a systematic naturalist, a virtuoso or a miser, was very strong in me.' He later experimented seriously in chemistry (with his older brother Erasmus), and was always a dedicated field sportsman.

At Cambridge he took refuge from his studies in almost obsessive collecting of insects, especially beetles, but he also developed his lifetime fascination with logic, mathematics and philosophy. When his father, a prominent doctor, complained that 'you care for nothing but shooting, dogs, and rat-catching and will be a disgrace to yourself and all your family' he was worried about Darwin's inability to find a vocation in life, not his intelligence. High achievement was the standard for the Darwin family; Charles was, after all, the grandson of the great Erasmus Darwin (p. 159), who had been not only a leading physician at the turn of the century, but also a philosopher, a poet and a pioneering evolutionary theorist. Other influences in his early life were Alexander von Humboldt (another great naturalist and theorist; p. 224), the theologian William Paley, and the astronomer John Herschel.

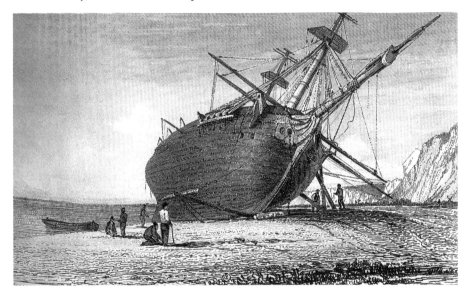

HMS Beagle *beached at low tide for repairs, Rio Santa Cruz, 16 April 1834. The drawing is by Conrad Martens, an artist on the voyage and is from* Narrative of the Surveying Voyages of HMS *Adventure and* Beagle *(1839). The voyage lasted for just over a year, from December 1831 to February 1832; Darwin suffered from sea-sickness on board ship, but also spent a lot of time on land, exploring and collecting, often for weeks at a time.*

Darwin was fortunate to have ample family funds from the estate of his mother, the daughter of Josiah Wedgwood, the pottery tycoon. By the time he returned to England from the *Beagle* voyage, he had abandoned any idea of life as a country parson and had decided to devote himself full time to research and writing. Eventually his books and investments made him a wealthy man. But he was never a well man. From early childhood, and perhaps related to the death of his mother when he was only eight, he reacted to stressful situations with a stammer, insomnia, eruptions of eczema on his hands and face, and abdominal pains and nausea. In Plymouth, waiting to set sail on the *Beagle* in 1831, he experienced palpitations of the heart. Only during the voyage itself did this strapping 6-ft tall athlete manage to avoid the crushing pressures that elsewhere in his life often left him prostrated.

THE VOYAGE OF THE *BEAGLE*

HMS *Beagle* was a tiny converted brig, only 27 m (90 ft) long. With 74 people on board, it was terribly crowded; Darwin learned to be tidy! The Admiralty had commissioned the voyage in order to establish a complete circle of measurements of longitude around the globe as a standard for cartography, and also to complete a survey of the coast of South America. FitzRoy also wanted to return to Tierra del Fuego three natives that he had taken hostage on the previous voyage of the ship (one of them was the girl Fuegia Basket). For Darwin it was the opportunity of a lifetime. He spent every available moment exploring on land, collecting and observing. Often he would strike off fearlessly for weeks at a time – across the Pampas, up the Andes. The result was an extraordinary exposure to the biodiversity of a whole continent (South America) and also to the essentially stone-age culture of the Fuegians. A special attraction for Darwin was that, after leaving the west coast of Chile, they returned to Britain via the Pacific, Australia and the Indian Ocean.

Photograph of Darwin in his study, aged 45. After the Beagle *voyage he did not travel again, and from 1842 he lived at Down House, Kent, where he developed many of his ideas in peace and privacy.*

Darwin, who had left England as a keen amateur natural historian and never ceased being a voracious collector, returned as an expert with an intellectual agenda, at first concentrating on geology. His immediate inspiration had been Charles Lyell's seminal *Principles of Geology* which he read lying in his hammock, coping with sea-sickness. Lyell's first volume was a gift from FitzRoy: Darwin's Cambridge mentor the Reverend John Stevens Henslow (Professor of Botany and Mineralogy) having advised him to read it 'but not believe it'. At the *Beagle*'s first landfall, the Cape Verde Islands, Darwin saw direct evidence for Lyell's radical views about the wholesale subsidence and elevation of land masses. He wrote to his father, who had opposed his going, 'I think, if I can so soon judge – I shall be able to do some original work in Natural History'. By the end of the voyage, and having studied the geology of the Andes intensely, Darwin was committed to writing a geology of all South America (published in 1846).

In the second volume of Lyell's work, sent out to him in 1832, Darwin read about the formation of coral atolls. Although he had not yet seen one, he devised a new theory of their formation, based on the subsidence of oceanic mountains and the offsetting growth of the fringing coral reefs. When the ship reached the Keeling Islands Darwin saw that his new view was right. It was a nice example of a scientific hypothesis because it was testable. In Darwin's theory, the coral should be hundreds of metres deep, having grown steadily as its mountain foundation subsided; dragging the bottom showed that it was.

TRANSMUTATION OF SPECIES

We may never know the extent to which Darwin had been mulling over the problem of evolution (then termed 'transmutation of species') during the voyage itself. At Edinburgh he had read his grandfather's *Zoonomia*, in which a theory of transmutation was proposed. He knew it was the inspiration for the ideas of the French zoologist Jean-Baptiste Lamarck (p. 190) that, at the time of the *Beagle* voyage, were making the concept of some kind of transmutation more acceptable. Certainly, Darwin was very interested in systems of classification that, by showing the patterns of similarities among groups of organisms, pointed to organic relatedness rather than special divine creation. Darwin, the embryo clergyman, was also interested in the problem that if the diversity of the organic world had been the result of (multiple) creation events, it was remarkably haphazard: no penguins in the Arctic; no humming birds in Africa; different species of hawk filling the same ecological role in Europe and America.

Transmutation of species seemed also to be the obvious conclusion to be drawn from the sweeping, progressive changes in life on Earth being revealed by the fossil record. He collected fossils in South America: Pleistocene armadillos and sloths that were obviously related to forms now living at the same place. His critical intelligence soon found a direct analogy between the succession of species in time, and the

One of the Galapagos Islands finches, the common cactus finch (Geospiza scandens)*, in a lithograph by John and Elizabeth Gould, from* The Zoology of HMS Beagle *(1838). It was John Gould who told Darwin that the Galapagos ground finches differed from island to island.*

patterns of distribution of living species in space – pairs of northern and a southern species, for example, of the South American rhea (an ostrich-relative).

Darwin refined his skills of observation and identification during the *Beagle* voyage, but, in the Galapagos Islands (September 1835), he seems at first not to have realized the unusual diversity of organisms on the different islands. It was a local government official who pointed out that each island had its own 'kinds' of land tortoises and mocking birds, and also the endemic tree-form *Opuntia* cactus. When Darwin got his collections back to Britain and started the difficult task of finding experts to study and describe them, the ornithologist and artist John Gould informed him that the ground finches of the Galapagos were also different species, island by island, and different yet again from the species on the mainland. Darwin's enormous *Beagle* collections were important for what they revealed about the diversity of animals and plants world-wide, but it was the Galapagos birds, tortoises and *Opuntia* that finally gave him the empirical data that he needed for what had evidently been a growing suspicion about the reality of transmutation. Within nine months of returning he began his first notebook dealing with transmutation; by 1842 a 'first sketch' of what would became the unifying theory of all biology was complete.

In the early 1800s not only were 'progression' and 'improvement' widely debated topics in economic and political philosophy, but the control of population growth was a dominant issue due to the influence of Thomas Robert Malthus. Darwin read Malthus and, 'being well prepared to appreciate the struggle for existence that everywhere goes on from the long-continued observation of the habits of animals and plants, it at once struck me that under these circumstances favourable variations would tend to be preserved and unfavourable ones to be destroyed.' Geology was also centrally important. Darwin's theory was one of slow gradual change, so time would be required, millions of years of time. The Earth had to be far older than the 6,000 years claimed by the more extreme contemporary biblical literalists.

Perhaps because of the enormity of what he was attempting, Darwin knew that he needed peace and privacy in which to work, so in 1842 he and his wife Emma Wedgwood (his first cousin) moved with their new baby and his new theory from London to

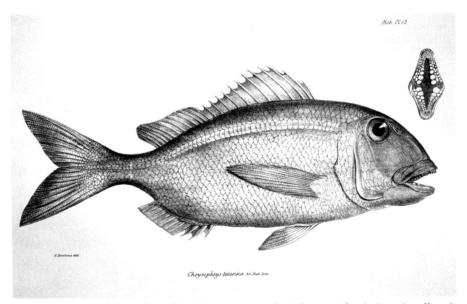

The fish Chrysophrys taurina *collected by Darwin in the Galapagos Islands. Darwin collected avidly throughout the voyage, returning home with an enormous number of specimens and a determination to be a natural historian.*

Down House, near Bromley in Kent. There, for the rest of his life, he could think and write out his dangerous thoughts in isolation from the normal cares of the world and the cold resisting stare of the scientific and political establishment. From his 'ship on the Downs' he developed an enormous correspondence with experts all over the world who willingly sent him information on every subject, from the dispersal of seeds over long distances across salt water to the life histories of jellyfish. Often with the help of his children, he conducted experiments on the reproduction of plants in his greenhouses and studied variability in pigeons by rearing dozens of different varieties, and never tired of observing every living thing for new insights into behaviour and ecology.

This was natural history on a grand scale, involving the synthesis of almost all of contemporary biology into evidence for his theories. The pattern of working alone continued all his life, but, while essentially a recluse in terms of public affairs, he developed a close group of influential friends, who, like Thomas Henry Huxley, became almost his disciples. Joseph Hooker, the director of Kew Gardens, for example, had no qualms about passing on to Darwin specimens from the national collections. During his years at Down, as greedily as he had once gone after beetle specimens in the Cambridgeshire Fens, Darwin avidly collected the information that he had such a unique ability to turn into new ideas. As to the two general approaches towards discovery in science, deductive reasoning (arguing from general principles to explain particular circumstances) or (perhaps the more common way for a naturalist) induction (assembling facts from which to distill general laws), it is clear that Darwin varied his approach to suit his needs.

The personal cost of all this intense cerebration on controversial subjects was great; his situation was not helped by the fact that his beloved wife Emma remained to her death a devout Christian while he progressed uneasily from agnosticism to atheism. When he lived in London, working on geological matters, his health mostly continued strong, as it had been (except for continual sea-sickness) during the months of wonderful freedom on the *Beagle*. There is an almost incomprehensible contrast between the young Darwin who explored on horseback for weeks across the Pampas and climbed the Andes, and the invalid recluse of the later years. It is possible that he had contracted some tropical disease (Chaga's disease is a favourite candidate), but the correspondence between ill health and mental pressure is striking. As he told Hooker, writing on transmutation was like 'confessing to a murder'. When his beloved daughter Annie died in 1851, he was so distraught that he could not attend the funeral. Her death was the final blow in Darwin's loss of religious faith.

NATURAL SELECTION

Darwin might have been tempted to publish on natural selection as early as 1844, but that year Robert Chambers published (anonymously) his *Vestiges of Creation* espousing strong Lamarckian evolutionary views. This was a time of social revolution in continental Europe and, while a popular success among political liberals, the book was thoroughly savaged by its scientific reviewers and its ideas judged dangerous by the political establishment. Darwin knew that he would have slowly and carefully to build a constituency among authoritative people like Lyell and Huxley before publishing his own ideas. In that sense Chambers' work was a useful stalking horse for Darwin. Perhaps it was also a precipitating factor in causing him to immerse himself in a detailed study of the reproduction, anatomy and classification of barnacles, a subject that had fascinated him since the *Beagle* years and that, in a sense, allowed him to work out the implications and consequences of his theories for practical zoology.

Darwin also knew that having an elegant theory was never going to be enough to establish the causes of evolutionary change. He did not have what we now call the 'smoking gun' – direct evidence of the transmutation of one species into another. Instead he would have to persuade his audience with the logic of his 'one long argument' and overwhelm them with a weight of evidence about the phenomena of variation, heredity and selection. Here his vast knowledge of natural history came to the fore and, in fact, *On the Origin of Species by Means of Natural Selection or the Preservation of Favoured Races in the Struggle for Life* (1859) was really just a distillation of the much longer compilation of evidence entitled *Natural Selection* that he never finished. Writing the *Origin* was precipitated by the bombshell of a letter that he received from the naturalist Alfred Russel Wallace (p. 277), announcing that he had also discovered natural selection. Depressed, Darwin was only persuaded by friends from abandoning the whole venture.

The elements of Darwin's theory of 'natural selection', brilliant in their simplicity, were laid out in the first four chapters of the *Origin*. Darwin first documented the well-known power of selective breeding to produce new races of organisms. Next, he demonstrated the variability of natural populations and the heritability of important parts of that variation (as opposed to features that come and go during a single lifetime through, for example, exercise or will power). Then he posited the constant operation of a 'struggle for existence' in nature arising from the potential of all populations to 'increase at a geometrical ratio' unless checked. If only a very small number of the offspring of any species ever survived to maturity, then nature would favour those variations best suited to particular conditions, producing not just races but new species. 'As man can produce and certainly has produced a great result by his method-ical and unconscious means of selection, what may not nature effect?' Most of the time, natural selection would serve to weed out undesirable variants; sometimes it would be the agent of change. A parallel phenomenon was 'sexual selection', involv-ing the choice of the best mates, and accounting, for example, for elaborate sexual dimorphisms like the male peacock's tail. A great deal of supporting evidence came from his knowledge of the geographical distributions of organisms, which he used to refute the old idea that living diversity had arisen from multiple 'centres of creation'. The diversity of living and fossil organisms, in his view, was the result of continuous branching processes contingent upon time and place.

A strength of the *Origin* is that Darwin anticipated and answered the possible objections of critics. The geological record was imperfect but the Earth had to be extremely old to provide the time for evolution to create a diversity of species and whole new structures like the eye ('from the simple apparatus of an optic nerve') or a wing (from a limb). He even offered up a test: 'If it could be demonstrated that any complex organ existed, which could not possibly have been formed by numerous, successive, slight modifications, my theory would absolutely break down. But I can find no such case.'

ORCHIDS AND EARTHWORMS

Throughout his life, natural history was not only the greatest stimulus to his intelli-gence but also the great healer. And, after the *Beagle* voyage, he never again needed to travel to find his inspiration; it was right there in his garden and the delights of the English countryside. After the *Origin* came out, to great acclaim amongst the scien-tific class, Darwin retreated to his roots in natural history and the study of orchids; inevitably this also became a major book. Something of a pattern developed, after having put himself through the mental turmoil of producing a difficult book like the *Origin,* he would regroup by immersing himself in painstaking observations of, for example, the behaviour of ants or the biology of climbing plants.

The *Origin* does not contain material on the most contentious of all issues, the evolution of humans, but next Darwin tackled this and produced his enormously influential *The Descent of Man* (1871), using the same technique of arguing logically from amassed natural history data. 'The sole object of this work is to consider, firstly, whether man, like every other species, is descended from some pre-existing form.' As this was before the human fossil record was well developed, his views, then still

Drawing of a kiwi by Darwin from a letter sent by him to Lord Hill on Zoological Society of London notepaper in 1851. Darwin charmingly sketches the bird 'resting on his beak, wading in a great pool and running forth in a quest of cockroaches or bugs or anything else he can catch'.

controversial, depended heavily on comparisons with the apes and monkeys. Darwin did not hesitate, however, to look to selection for the evolutionary origin of language, social behaviour, systems of morals and even the origins of religion. A lot of the book is about his ideas on sexual selection, which he saw as the origin of human racial differences. At every point he was concerned with demonstrating that all aspects of human-ness are part of a continuum of gradual organic evolution. It was his most difficult book, for both author and reader, and he knew that he would be 'denounced by some as highly irreligious'. Nonetheless, 'The birth both of the species and the individual are equally part of that grand sequence of events, which our minds refuse to accept as the result of blind chance (rather than) ordained for some special purpose.'

One of Darwin's greatest delights was his children. He not only used them as assistants in his many experiments, they were also a handy set of subjects for his groundbreaking study *The Expression of Emotions in Man and the Animals* (1872). After 1875 he retreated even more into his domestic isolation at Down and essentially retired from controversial areas of science, finally enjoying a period of great contentment. Still never straying far, he demonstrated the extraordinary breadth of his interests and his intense powers of observation and analysis in books on subjects as disparate as *Insectivorous Plants* (1875), *Climbing Plants* (1875), *Different Forms of Flowers on Plants of the Same Species* (1877) and *Power of Movement in Plants* (1880), and finally sent his earthworms book (*Formation of Vegetable Mould through the Action of Worms*) to press in 1881.

Darwin, a man who, as he said of himself, had 'unbounded patience in long reflecting over any subject,' refused most honours during his lifetime. But he was buried in Westminster Abbey among the greats like Newton, having done as much or more to revolutionize biological science as Newton had the physical sciences.

SANDRA KNAPP

Alfred Russel Wallace

THE PROBLEM OF THE ORIGIN OF SPECIES

(1823–1913)

*The next two days were so wet and windy that there was no
going out; but on the succeeding one the sun shone brightly,
and I had the good fortune to capture one of the most
magnificent insects the world contains, the great bird-winged
butterfly,* Ornithoptera poseidon. *I trembled with
excitement as I saw it coming majestically towards me,
and could hardly believe I had really succeeded in my
stroke till I had taken it out of the net and was gazing, lost
in admiration, at the velvet black and brilliant green of
its wings, seven inches across, its golden body,
and crimson breast.*

Alfred Russel Wallace, **The Malay Archipelago,** *1869*

A NATURALIST'S NATURALIST, Alfred Russel Wallace was a consummate collector and an unparalleled observer of nature. His name is usually associated with that of Charles Darwin, with whom he co-published the first public articulation of the theory of evolution by natural selection. He is often seen as being in the shadow of Darwin, and, because his name has not become as well-known as that of Darwin, even badly treated by the scientific establishment of the day. His influence on natural history goes far beyond the simple, if profound and visionary, elaboration of a theory of organic change – he changed the discipline completely through his fieldwork and observations, and through his many collections that became the evidence base for the new theory, and that continue to be important to biologists today.

Wallace was the fifth and penultimate child of an upper-middle-class family who had fallen on somewhat straitened times due to bad speculations and investments in the heady early years of the 19th century. He thus never had the luxury of being able to pursue his interests unencumbered by the need to earn his living, unlike the gentleman naturalists of the day. The Wallace family moved often, from Usk in Monmouthshire, to London, to Hertford. Alfred was only able to keep in schooling by teaching the younger boys, but never did particularly well and had no pretensions to an academic future. At 14 he left school for good, and went to live with his older

Wallace's Standardwing (Semioptera wallacei) *was collected on Bacan Island in the northern Moluccas by Ali, who pointed out its 'four long white plumes [which] give the bird its unique character'. These are swivelled and erected during courtship displays and are only found on male birds. Wallace described this behaviour, allowing the artist to portray the plumes accurately.*

brother John near Regent's Park in London. Here he began to develop his taste for the science of natural history, going to London Zoo and attending lectures at the 'Hall of Science', off Tottenham Court Road. In the summer of 1837 he was apprenticed to his eldest brother William, a surveyor.

Wallace as a young man in 1848, just before he set off on his great adventure collecting in the Amazon basin.

It was whilst working with his brother that Wallace's interests in the natural world were really kindled, and, almost unknowingly, he developed skills that would prove so useful later on. He surveyed with William for six and a half years, learning about the geology of Britain, the basic rules of geometry and trigonometry, and how to repair delicate equipment. Much of the work was the result of the Tithe Act – the land was measured in order that its owners would pay the correct tithe (tax) for the upkeep of the local church – but some was related to the General Enclosures Act, which disturbed Wallace greatly. As a consequence of this Act, access to common land was now denied to the poorest in society, awakening in Wallace a sense of injustice that never left him. His later campaigns for land national-ization and his passionate belief that everyone had a fundamental right to share in the Earth's riches grew from his observations as a young surveyor in Wales. Wallace read voraciously – Charles Lyell's *Principles of Geology* (p. 246), John Lindley's *General System of Botany* and Alexander von Humboldt and Aimé Bonpland's *Personal Narrative of Travels* (p. 224). He began to keep a small herbarium, despite the disapproval of his brother. This time was critical to his development; he considered it the 'turning point' in his life.

Surveying jobs dried up in the early 1840s, and when Wallace's father died it was decided that he ought to make his own way with the small annuity left to him. He obtained the post of drawing master at the Collegiate School in Leicester, and there met a friend with whom he would set out on a venture that would completely change his life. Henry Walter Bates was the son of a hosiery manufacturer in the town and had a passion for beetles, with which he rapidly inspired his new friend Alfred. The young men became fast friends, collecting together, reading and discussing books – Wallace had at last found a person with whom he could talk about natural history and philosophy, a sounding board for the development of his own ideas and opinions. When Wallace left Leicester less than two years later to take up William's surveying practice in Neath, he wrote to Bates, 'I quite envy you, who have friends near you attached to the same pursuits. I know not a single person in the little town who studies any one branch of natural history, so I am quite alone in this respect.'

COLLECTING IN THE AMAZON

Together the two young men conceived a bold idea, they would leave England and go to the Amazon, where they would finance their travels by collecting and selling specimens, a sort of natural history entrepreneurship. They would also gather facts towards 'solving the problem of the origin of species', a subject they had discussed and corresponded about over several years. In April 1848, Wallace and Bates set off for South America – they had an agent in London to handle their specimens and letters of introduction from the great and good of British science, such as Sir William Hooker of Kew Gardens – and reached Pará (now Belem) in northern Brazil in late May. They needed to meet market demands in order to finance themselves and so focused on birds, butterflies and beetles – groups that were of interest to wealthy amateurs building private natural history collections.

The men collected together for a little more than a year, but separated in order to maximize both the scientific and commercial possibilities of this vast region. Bates went to the west, up the Rio Solimões to Obidos, spending 11 years in the Amazon and collecting thousands of wonderful specimens. For Wallace, however, this was not to be. He went up the blackwater Rio Negro, north towards what is now Venezuela. Here he spent four years collecting on the Rio Negro and the Rio Uaupés – amassing specimens that he thought were being sent on to his agent, Samuel Stevens, in London. But when he reached Manaus, having decided to return to England after a particularly difficult bout of malaria, he discovered

Wallace's field books contain notes and sketches of the animals he was discovering on his travels in Southeast Asia. Such naturalists' notes, combined with the specimens held in collections, are the basis of natural history.

Wallace's book The Geographical Distribution of Animals, *published in 1876, was a two-volume treatise explaining how the distribution of animals found in different continents and parts of the world can be related to their evolution. This plate illustrates native mammals of Tasmania, many of which were unique and are now extinct.*

all his work in a warehouse, impounded by Customs. His collections eventually released, Wallace found passage back to England on the ill-fated brig *Helen*. Three weeks into the journey across the Atlantic, fire broke out on board. When it became apparent that the ship was beyond saving, Wallace rushed back to his cabin and scooped up a small tin box with some drawings of fish and palms, some shirts and a few note-books before getting in the lifeboats with the crew. The rest of his collections – four years of hard work and his only path to becoming a member of the scientific establishment back home – were in the hold, and hence lost forever.

Another man might have been destroyed by such an experience, but not Wallace; as he later wrote in his account of the event: 'And now everything was gone, and I had not one specimen to illustrate the unknown lands I had trod, or to call back the recollection of the wild scenes I had beheld! But such regrets I knew were in vain, and I tried to think as little as possible about what might have been, and to occupy myself with the state of things that actually existed.' An intensely practical man, Wallace set about publishing as much as he could salvage from his notes, and planning his next collecting trip. Anyone else might have decided never to venture into the field again,

The spectacular birdwing butterflies are known only from the Wallace's Malay Archipelago region and were particular favourites of Wallace, both for their beauty and biological interest. Males are more brightly coloured than females, and the wingspan of some species reaches 16 cm (over 6 in). The golden Ornithoptera croesus *(top), described by Wallace, is a species of lowland rainforest and is considered vulnerable to extinction due to habitat destruction.* Ornithoptera priamus *(above), on the other hand, is more widespread and comes in a wide range of colour forms, ranging from green to blue.*

but Wallace obtained passage on a steamer bound for the Malay Archipelago (today Indonesia) through the good offices of Sir Roderick Murchison, President of the Royal Geographical Society. This time he would stay away for eight years and return, not empty-handed but as an acknowledged member of London's scientific elite and the 'co-discoverer' of evolution by natural selection.

BUTTERFLIES AND BIRDS OF PARADISE

He arrived in the East already an experienced collector and with the knowledge of how to operate as a naturalist in a foreign land. He retained his agent, Samuel Stevens, and knew there was a ready market for specimens of such wonders as birds of paradise and fantastically coloured butterflies. Today we look upon the collection of specimens of these animals, some of them endangered and close to extinction, as a wanton waste. But in the 19th century very little was known scientifically about such creatures of the tropics, and that information was only as a result of the few examples that had made it back to European institutions. Only by examining a large number of individuals does the variety of, and the variability within, individual species become apparent. The present state of our knowledge is built upon the study of specimens brought back by field naturalists like Wallace. He was in a land where there was much to learn.

Having once nearly died alone when he was on the upper Rio Negro, Wallace had vowed never to travel again without a companion. He took with him an English apprentice, Charles Allen, and once in the region engaged a young Malay assistant, Ali. Allen did not last the course, but Ali remained with Wallace for all his 'eight years wandering', and he ultimately took the surname of Wallace. The Malay region is composed of many islands, and Wallace travelled amongst them, catching rides in local boats (praus) one to another. The map of Wallace's travels looks like a piece of string wound around the islands; he visited many several times over in the course of his travels.

Despite the hardships of collecting in the tropics, Wallace never lost his excitement at seeing new things and making discoveries; on catching a male specimen of a new species of birdwing butterfly, he wrote 'none but a naturalist can image the intense excitement I experienced when I at length captured it. On taking it out of my net and opening the glorious wings, my heart began to beat violently, the blood rushed to my head, and I felt much more like fainting than I have done when in apprehension of immediate death.' He ultimately went on to describe this amazing insect as *Ornithoptera croesus* – the golden birdwing.

Tired of depending upon others for his travels, Wallace had his own prau built and set off for New Guinea to collect birds of paradise, then very poorly known.

He was amazingly successful, even discovering a new species, ultimately named *Semioptera wallacei* in his honour. His remarks on collecting the extremely rare King bird of paradise show that he was not just focused on obtaining specimens, but that his thoughts were also of a philosophical nature – they could even be seen as those of a conservationist, concerned with man's destruction of the planet:

> *The emotions excited in the mind of a naturalist, who has long desired to see the actual thing which he has hitherto known only by description, drawing or badly-preserved external covering – especially when that thing is of surpassing rarity and beauty – require the poetic faculty fully to express them. ... It seems sad on one hand such exquisite creatures should live out their lives and exhibit their charms only in these wild, inhospitable regions ... while on the other hand, should civilized man ever reach these distant lands, ... we may be sure that he will so disturb the nicely-balanced relations of organic and inorganic nature so as to cause the disappearance, and finally the extinction, of these very beings whose wonderful structure and beauty he alone is fitted to appreciate and enjoy. This consideration must surely tell us that all living things were* not *made for man.*

Wallace's observations of the profound differences in fauna between the eastern and western parts of the archipelago led him to describe what is now called 'Wallace's line' – the great division between the Asian and Australian faunas. This is seen at its most obvious between the islands of Bali and Lombok. Although separated only by a narrow strait, the faunas of the two are profoundly different. Cockatoos, for example, occur on Lombok and into Australia, but not on Bali. Wallace's line represents the division between two of the great continental plates, since demonstrated geologically but then only inferred from animal distributions. His careful recording of the localities for all his collections led him to make observations about distributions of animals that others had missed; he has been called the father of biogeography, the study of plant and animal distributions.

EVOLUTION BY NATURAL SELECTION

While in Southeast Asia, Wallace wrote to various friends and acquaintances, among them Charles Darwin. When he sent Darwin, whom he greatly admired, an essay entitled 'On the tendency of Varieties to depart indefinitely from the original Type', he beautifully articulated the theory that Darwin himself was thinking about – evolution by natural selection. Wallace's essay was the result of his careful observations made in the field over many years, all in pursuit of his goal on his first tropical voyage – the study of 'the problem of [the] origin of species'. Darwin, a true gentleman, arranged (or his friends arranged) for joint publication of papers at the Linnaean

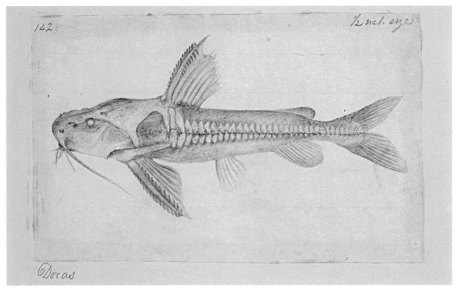

The delicate pencil drawings of fish are among the only results of Wallace's years of collecting in the Amazon that survived the shipwreck of the Helen. *This armoured catfish (*Centrodoras *sp.), locally known as caracadá, has still not been identified to species.*

Society of London on 1 July 1858, while Wallace was still abroad. The two men had come to the idea from entirely different intellectual angles – Darwin from an enormous correspondence and his gardens at Down House and Wallace from his experiences in the tropics, observing and collecting. Darwin is the name most associate with evolution by natural selection, leading some to think Wallace was hard done by. Wallace himself, however, always gave Darwin the credit for articulating the idea more completely than he had, and his book *Darwinism* did a great deal to spread the ideas and to associate them with Darwin's name.

On his return from the Malay Archipelago in 1848, Wallace found himself a valued member of the scientific establishment. He worked on his collections, and wrote extensively on many topics, from biology to land reform, but found it difficult to obtain lasting employment. His interests in spiritualism frightened some more established scientists like Thomas Henry Huxley, but Darwin eventually managed to push through a government pension for Wallace, which he accepted – although he turned down many other honours (such as fellowship of the Royal Society).

Wallace lived to see the start of the 20th century, having been a major, but modest, player in the changes that so differentiated it from the 19th. Wallace's fieldwork and careful specimen collecting laid the foundations not only for the theory of evolution by natural selection, but also for the development of the close link between field observation and study in natural habitats and theory that is the cornerstone of modern ecology and natural history.

Asa Gray

THE PLANTS OF THE AMERICAN WEST

(1810–1888)

*I have settled down to my work with enjoyment but with a
growing sense of discouragement growing out of an embarras
de richesses. It was natural to find here a great accumulation
of collections of North American plants; all needing
examination; but unfortunately, they continue to come in
faster than I can study and dispose of them. …. I begin to
think it were a happier lot to have the comparatively
completed botany of an old country to study, in which your
work 'were done when't were done', and in which, even if it
were not done quickly, you were not called on to do it over and
over, to bring the new into shape and symmetry with the old.*

Asa Gray to Sir Edward Fry, 26 February 1882

AMERICAN EXPLORATION OF THE WESTERN REACHES of the continent can
be said to have begun with the great Lewis and Clark expedition of the first
decade of the 19th century. Thomas Jefferson, third President of the United
States, sent Meriwether Lewis and William Clark to explore and collect the products
of the newly purchased lands of 'Louisiana', and to push on to the Pacific Ocean. The
Lewis and Clark expedition made possible the acquisition of the western part of the
continent for the United States, so beginning a tradition of government sponsorship
of scientific exploration of its diverse and rich lands. It was Asa Gray, however, who
catalogued the plants of the West and set them into a global context. Gray never saw
the Rocky Mountains or the giant redwoods until he was an old man, but he, more
than any other botanist, was responsible for scientific description of the plants of
these wild and beautiful lands.

In his series of publications Chloris Boreali-Americana *(starting in 1846), Gray illustrated
and explained American plants that had hitherto been misunderstood or badly represented by
other botanists.* Brazoria truncata – *named for the Brazos River in Texas and a member of the
mint family – had been misrepresented by the great British botanist Sir William Hooker. Gray
was not afraid to use his superior knowledge gained from his field collectors to disagree with the
great and the good.*

286

Tab. 5

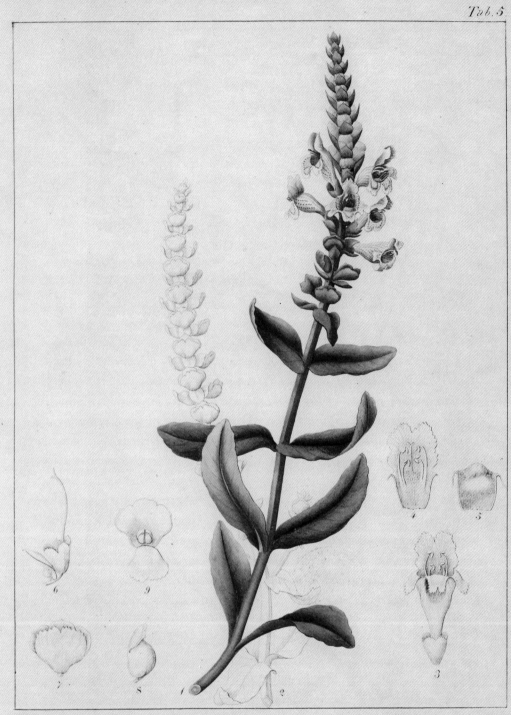

Brazoria truncata.

The New York Botanical Garden

Solanum **triflorum** *Nutt.*

det. M. Nee, 2005

Plantae Novo-Mexicanae.

№.

№ 671.

A. Fendler coll. 1847.

Solanum triflorum Nutt.

A third generation American of northern Irish stock, Asa Gray was born, if not in a log cabin like his contemporary Abraham Lincoln, in humble circumstances in a small town in upstate New York. He became interested in botany during his time as a medical student, and collected herbarium specimens, a parcel of which he left with Dr John Torrey, New York's most prominent botanist. The two men soon became friends, and Torrey invited Gray to be his botanical assistant. Gray began to write papers on the taxonomy of North American plants, and Torrey described him as having 'no superior in botany, considering his age, & any subject he takes up he handles in a masterly manner. ... He is an uncommonly fine fellow and will make a great noise in the scientific world one of these days.' Despite this glowing reference, Gray was unable to find employment as a botanist or naturalist, but rather than resting on his laurels, he wrote *Elements of Botany*, with the aim of producing a book in an American context for use in the United States. With Torrey, Gray began work on a flora, or compilation of all the plants, of North America, work that was to continue through his entire life.

Gray was then offered the position of botanist on the United States Exploring Expedition to the South Pacific, a marvellous chance to get into the field – but bickering, jealousy and delays all diminished Gray's desire to travel with an expedition he felt was improperly constituted. Fortunately, he was at the same time offered a professorship in the new state of Michigan. He took it, and missed participating in the expedition, which made scientific history – he never experienced field natural history in the way many of his contemporaries did, such as Alfred Russel Wallace (p. 277) or Joseph Hooker.

Instead, as the premises of the new university were not yet ready, he went to Europe, 'determined to get abroad and consult some of the principal herbaria'. He was beginning to set the flora of North America in a global context. While doing the tour of the great European herbaria throughout 1838 and 1839 – London, Paris, Vienna, Geneva, Berlin – he met the great and good of the European scientific world, including Charles Darwin (p. 267) and Sir William Hooker and his son Joseph. He was particularly anxious to obtain sets of North American plants from these European herbaria for his own collection; he strongly felt that specimens of American plants should be held in American institutions – a sentiment today echoed more

Herbarium specimens collected by the young men sent into the field by George Engelmann and Asa Gray formed the real basis for our understanding of the identity and distribution of the plants of the American West. This specimen of Solanum triflorum *was collected by Augustus Fendler in the region of Santa Fé, New Mexico, an area Gray was particularly keen to have explored.*

Full of energy and zeal, Asa Gray's enthusiasm for the botany of the United States pushed exploration to new heights. Clearly visible in this portrait from the mid-1860s is his determination that inspired others to regard him as a true leader.

globally in the Convention on Biological Diversity. When he returned, as the university was still not ready he was granted a leave of absence without pay for a couple of years and set to work in earnest on the flora of North America. But in 1842 he was offered another professorship in natural history, at Harvard University – where he stayed for the rest of his life.

While at Harvard, Gray continued to work with Torrey on the flora of North America, but he also began to study bundles of plants sent back from the exploration of the American West. By 1842 it was clear that to document these botanical riches properly, professional collectors were needed – 'Somebody must go into this unexplored field!' With Dr George Engelmann of St Louis, Gray organized and raised the money for a series of collectors, some more successful than others. Gray directed where they went: 'I had rather [Augustus] Fendler should go north and west of Santa Fé. New Spain and Rocky Mountain botany is far more interesting to us than Mexican'; worried about temptations: 'But will he not take gold fever and leave us in the lurch? ... I fear it'; and generally controlled everything. The botanical riches that resulted were incredible; many plants of the American West were described for the first time by Torrey and Gray.

Gray was so busy describing the new material flooding in that he fell far behind in writing his monumental Flora of North America, and decided to attempt a simpler, less 'scientific' book that could be used in the field, written in plain English rather than scholarly Latin. The result was what is now known as *Gray's Manual of Botany* – a handbook of the flowering plants and ferns of the northeastern states which is still in use today. The *Manual* combined Gray's expert and in-depth knowledge of the plants of the region with an easy style and concise descriptions, making it an indispensable field guide for both the amateur and professional.

Gray's work on the *Manual*, as well as his studies of Western botany, were not done in isolation, he was a superb organizer and his personal, informal style made people want to work with him. But he didn't get along with everyone. The Swiss zoologist Louis Agassiz (p. 261) came to Harvard, initially with strong support from Gray, but Gray later fell out with him over his religious views. Gray was a keen observer and had seen thousands of specimens, all of which convinced him of the mutability of species.

While frenetically working on new plants from the West, as well as his *Manual* and numerous other projects, Gray kept up a copious correspondence with his European friends, including Joseph Hooker, with whom he shared a fascination with plant distribution. Hooker discussed Gray's opinions with Charles Darwin, and Darwin saw in Gray a fellow empiricist who could help him with information about the plants of the Americas. In April 1855 Darwin wrote to Gray 'I have for several years been collecting facts on "Variation", & when I find that any remark holds true amongst animals, I try to test it on Plants.' He had let Gray into the secret of his research into evolution, and then asked for facts about North American plants. The two men became regular correspondents, Gray sending Darwin facts about plants, such as the 'Statistics of the Flora of North America' and his thoughts about the relationships of Pacific and Asian plants with those of North America, and Darwin sounding Gray out on his developing ideas. When the *Origin of Species* was finally published in 1859, Gray became its vigorous and principal defender in the United States – he battled against Agassiz in a series of debates held from 1859 to 1861. Gray defended Darwin's ideas with good, solid evidence gleaned from his years of study of the North American flora; it was said of him that 'Over here [in the US] they regard Gray as the greatest botanist in the world, even a little bigger than Hooker.'

Asa Gray was a truly American botanist, he was adamant that specimens of American plants belonged in the United States, he worked amazingly hard to describe and document the riches emanating from the exploration of the American West and beyond into the Pacific, and he was steadfastly pro-Union in the face of opposition from his European friends (not including Darwin!) during the American Civil War. When he finally did get to the west of America in the summer of 1872, he at last saw the magnificence of the lands that he had sent collectors to so meticulously – he collected only a little, saying 'I suspect I shan't collect much. Younger men (like Torrey! [then 75]) must do that! – I go to rest and loaf and see the plants in situ.' By the 1870s Gray was truly the father of American botany, everyone sought his advice – he helped to organize the Missouri Botanical Garden and Stanford University, and his students founded botany departments all over the United States. More than any other scientist of the 19th century he 'helped give scientific meaning to the expansion of the United States.'

a ein Schamann im 𝔇uictru

F. A. Krebs scu M.

CONTRIBUTORS

ROBERT HUXLEY is Head of Collections, Department of Botany, Natural History Museum, London.

JULIA BRITTAIN is the author of *Plant Names Explained* (2006) and *Plants, People and Places* (2006).

STEVE CAFFERTY is Collections Project Manager in the Botany Department at the Natural History Museum, London.

JILL COOK is Head of Prehistory in the Department of Prehistory and Europe, and Curator of the Palaeolithic (or Old Stone Age) Collections at the British Museum, London.

ALAN CUTLER is the author of *The Seashell on the Mountaintop*, a biography of Nicolaus Steno.

TANIA DURT is Research Assistant, Department of Botany, the Natural History Museum, London, and was previously at the Royal Botanic Gardens, Kew.

BRIAN J. FORD is Visiting Professor at Leicester University, a Fellow of Cardiff University and an Associate at Gonville & Caius, Cambridge University. He is author of *The Leeuwenhoek Legacy* (1991) and Robert Hooke's *Micrographia*, issued on CD (1998).

CHRISTOPHER J. HUMPHRIES is Merit Researcher, Natural History Museum, London, Visiting Professor at the School of Plant Sciences, University of Reading and author and editor of 14 books including *Ontogeny and Systematics* (1988) and *Systematics and Conservation, Databases: from cottage industry to industrial networks* (1994).

SANDRA KNAPP is Merit Researcher, Global Biodiversity, Department of Botany, at the Natural History Museum, London.

SACHIKO KUSUKAWA is Tutor and Fellow in History and Philosophy of Science, Trinity College, Cambridge.

H. WALTER LACK is Director of the Botanic Garden and Botanical Museum Berlin-Dahlem, Freie Universität Berlin.

DENIS LAMY is a historian of sciences at the Muséum national d'Histoire naturelle, Paris.

JUDITH MAGEE is Collection Development Manager, Library & Information Services, at the Natural History Museum, London, and is the author of *The Art and Science of William Bartram* (2007).

JOHN L. MORTON is the author of *Strata: The Remarkable Life Story of William Smith, 'the Father of English Geology'* (new ed. 2004) and *King of Siluria: How Roderick Murchison Changed the Face of Geology* (2004).

BRIAN W. OGILVIE, Associate Professor of History at the University of Massachusetts Amherst is the author of *The Science of Describing: Natural History in Renaissance Europe* (2006).

GIUSEPPE OLMI, Professor of Modern History at the University of Bologna and is the author of *Ulisse Aldrovandi. Scienza e natura nel secondo Cinquecento* (1976).

ROBERTA J. M. OLSON is Curator of Drawings at the New-York Historical Society and Professor Emeritus of Art History, Wheaton College, Norton, Massachusetts.

ROBERT PRESS is Associate Keeper of Botany at the Natural History Museum, London.

DAVID SUTTON is Researcher Higher Plants Division, Department of Botany, the Natural History Museum, London.

PHILIPPE TAQUET is Professor of Palaeontology at the Muséum national d'Histoire naturelle, Paris, and the author of *Georges Cuvier – Naissance d'un génie* (2006).

KEITH THOMSON is Professor Emeritus of Natural History, University of Oxford, and Senior Research Fellow, American Philosophical Society.

SIR CRISPIN TICKELL is the Director of the Policy Foresight Programme at the James Martin Institute for Science and Civilization, Oxford University.

R. I. VANE-WRIGHT is Scientific Associate, Department of Entomology, the Natural History Museum, London, and a Fellow of the National Endowment for Science, Technology and the Arts.

DAVID WILLIAMS is Diatom Researcher and Head of Global Biodiversity in the Department of Botany, the Natural History Museum, London.

FURTHER READING

THE ANCIENTS

Aristotle

Aristotle, *The Complete Works of Aristotle*, edited by J Barnes (Princeton: Princeton University Press, 1984)

Barnes, Jonathan, *Aristotle: A Very Short Introduction* (Oxford and New York: Oxford University Press, 2000)

Barnes, Jonathan, Schofield, M. and Sorabji, R., *Articles on Aristotle*, vol. 1 *Science* (London: Duckworth, 1975)

Gillispie, C. C. (ed.), *Dictionary of Scientific Biography*, vol. 1 (New York: Charles Scribner's Sons, 1970)

Gotthelf, Allan, 'Darwin on Aristotle', *Journal of the History of Biology*, vol. 32, no. 1 (1999), 3–30

Theophrastus

Sharples, R. W., *Theophrastus of Eresus, Commentary Volume 5: Sources on Biology (Human Physiology, Living Creatures, Botany: Texts 328-435)* (Leiden: Brill, 1994)

Morton, A. G., *History of Botanical Science* (London: Academic Press, 1981)

Theophrastus, *Enquiry into Plants*, trans. Sir Arthur Holt (London: W. Heinemann; New York: G. P. Putnam's Sons, 1916)

Theophrastus, *De Causis Plantarum*, trans. Robert E. Denger (Philadelphia: Westbrook Pub. Co., 1927)

Pedanios Dioscorides

Brubaker, L., 'The Vienna Dioskorides and Anicia Juliana', in A. Littlewood, H. Maguire and Wolschke-Bulmahn (eds), *Byzantine Garden Culture* (Washington, DC: Dumbarton Oaks Research Library and Collection, 2002)

Downs, R. B., 'First herbalist: Dioscorides (*c.* 40–80)' in R. B. Downs (ed.), *Landmarks in Science: Hippocrates to Carson* (Littleton: Libraries Unlimited, 1982), 52–54

Greene, E. L., *Landmarks of Botanical History* (Stanford: Stanford University Press, 1983), vol. 1, 218–23

Morton, A. G., *History of Botanical Science* (London: Academic Press, 1981), 70–71

Riddle, John, *Dioscorides on Pharmacy and Medicine* (Austin: University of Texas Press, 1985)

Pliny the Elder

Downs, R. B., 'The great compiler: Pliny the Elder: Natural History (23–79), in R. B. Downs (ed.), *Landmarks in Science: Hippocrates to Carson* (Littleton: Libraries Unlimited, 1982), 48–51

Morton, A. G., *History of Botanical Science* (London: Academic Press, 1981)

Green, E. L., *Landmarks of Botanical History* (Stanford: Stanford University Press, 1983), vol. 1, 223–28

Pliny the Elder, *Natural History*, trans. and introduction by John Healy (London: Penguin, 1991)

THE RENAISSANCE

Leonhart Fuchs

Arber, Agnes, *Herbals: Their Origin and Evolution; a Chapter in the History of Botany, 1470–1670* (Cambridge: Cambridge University Press, 3rd ed., 1986)

Greene, E. L., *Landmarks of Botanical History*, edited by Frank N. Egerton (Stanford: Stanford University Press, 1983)

Kusukawa, Sachiko, 'Leonhart Fuchs on the importance of pictures', *Journal of the History of Ideas* 58 (1997), 403–27

Meyer, Frederick G., Emmart Trueblood, Emily and Heller, John L., *The Great Herbal of Leonhart Fuchs: De historia stirpium commentarii insignes, 1542 (Notable Commentaries on the History of Plants)* (Stanford: Stanford University Press, 1999)

Ogilvie, Brian W., *The Science of Describing: Natural History in Renaissance Europe* (Chicago: University of Chicago Press, 2006)

Reeds, Karen M., *Botany in Medieval and Renaissance Universities* (New York and London: Garland Publishing, Inc., 1991)

Ulisse Aldrovandi

Findlen, P., *Possessing Nature. Museums, Collecting and Scientific Culture in Early Modern Italy* (Berkeley, Los Angeles, London: University of California Press, 1994)

Il teatro della natura di Ulisse Aldrovandi, Bologna (Editrice Compositori: Bologna, 2001)

Olmi, G., 'Science-Honour-Metaphor: Italian Cabinets of the Sixteenth and Seventeenth Centuries', in O. Impey and A. MacGregor (eds), *The Origins of Museums* (Oxford, Clarendon Press, 1985), 5–16

Olmi, G., *L'inventario del mondo. Catalogazione della natura e luoghi del sapere nella prima età moderna* (Bologna: Il Mulino, 1992)

Olmi, G. and Tongiorgi Tomasi, L., *De piscibus. La bottega artistica di Ulisse Aldrovandi e l'immagine naturalistica* (Rome: Edizioni dell'Elefante, 1993)

Andrea Cesalpino

Green, E. L., *Landmarks of Botanical History*, edited by Frank N. Egerton (Stanford: Stanford University Press, 1983), vol. 2, 807–31

Morton, A. G., *History of Botanical Science* (London: Academic Press, 1981)

Viviani, U., *Vita ed opere di Andrea Cesalpino* (Arezzo, 1923)

Pierre Belon

Cole, Francis J., *History of Comparative Anatomy* (London: Macmillan, 1944)

Gudger, E. W., 'The Five Great Naturalists of the Sixteenth Century: Belon, Rondelet, Salviani, Gesner and Aldrovandi: A Chapter in the History of Ichthyology', *Isis*, 22, No. 1 (Dec., 1934), 21–40

Konrad Gessner

Braun, L., *Conrad Gessner* (in French) (Slatkine: Geneva, 1990)

Pinon, L., 'Conrad Gessner and the historical depth of Renaissance natural history', in G. Pomata and N. G. Siraisi (eds), *Empiricism and Erudition in Early Modern Europe* (Cambridge, MA and London: MIT Press, 2005)

Wellisch, H. H., *Conrad Gessner: a Bio-Bibliography* (Zug: IDC, 1984)

THE ENLIGHTENMENT

Nicolaus Steno

Cutler, Alan, *The Seashell on the Mountaintop. A Story of Science, Sainthood, and the Humble Genius Who Discovered a New History of the Earth* (New York: Dutton; London: Heinemann, 2003)

Kardel, Troels, 'Steno: Life, Science, Philosophy', *Acta Historica Scientiarum Naturalium et Medicinalium* 42, 1949

Rudwick, Martin J. S., *The Meaning of Fossils: Episodes in the History of Palaeontology* (Chicago: University of Chicago Press, 1976)

Scherz, Gustav (ed.), *Steno: Geological Papers. Odense* (Odense: Odense University Press, 1969)

John Ray

Baldwin, Stuart, *John Ray (1627–1705), Essex Naturalist: A Summary of his Life, Work and Scientific Significance* (Baldwin's Books: Witham, 1986)

Keynes, Geoffrey Langdon, *John Ray: A Bibliography* (London: Faber and Faber, 1951)

Raven, Charles Earle, *John Ray Naturalist: His Life and Works* (Cambridge: Cambridge University Press, 2nd ed., 1950)

Robert Hooke

Hooke, Robert, *Micrographia* (1665), facsimile edition (Mineola, NY: Dover Publications, 2003)

Hooke, Robert, *Micrographia*, facsimile edition on CD-ROM, with introduction by Brian J. Ford (London: John Martyn and James Allestry; Palo Alto: Octavo)

Inwood, Stephen, *Forgotten Genius: The Biography of Robert Hooke* (New York: MacAdam Cage Publishing, 2005)

Jardine, Lisa, *The Curious Life of Robert Hooke*, (London and New York: HarperCollins, 2004)

Antony van Leeuwenhoek

Dobell, Clifford, *Antony van Leeuwenhoek and his Little Animals* (original edition 1932; reprint Mineola, NY: Dover, 1962)

Ford, Brian J., *The Leeuwenhoek Legacy* (Balogh Scientific Books: Champaign IL, 1991)

Ford, Brian J., *Single Lens: the Story of the Simple Microscope* (London: William Heinemann; New York: Harper & Row, 1985)

Palm, L. C. and Snelders, H. A. M. (eds), *Antoni van Leeuwenhoek, 1632–1723* (Amsterdam: Rodopi, 1982)

Sir Hans Sloane

Brooks, E. St John, *Sir Hans Sloane. The Great Collector and his Circle* (London: the Batchworth Press, 1954)

de Beer, Sir Gavin, *Sir Hans Sloane and the British Museum* (New York: Arno Press, 1975; reprint of Oxford University Press 1953 edition)

MacGregor, Arthur, *Sir Hans Sloane: Collector, Scientist, Antiquary, Founding Father of the British Museum* (London: British Museum Press in association with Alistair McAlpine for the Trustees of the British Museum, 1994)

Sloane, Sir Hans, *A voyage to the islands Madera, Barbados, Nieves, S. Christophers and Jamaica …*, 2 vols (London: 1707–25)

Maria Sibylla Merian

Merian, Maria Sibylla, *Metamorphosis Insectorum Surinamensium (Amsterdam 1705)*, facsimile (London: Pion, 1980)

Rucker, E. and Stearn, W. T., Maria Sibylla Merian in Surinam. Commentary to the Facsimile Edition of *Metamorphosis Insectorum Surinamensium (Amsterdam*

1705). Based on original watercolours in the Royal
Collection, Windsor Castle (London: Pion, 1982)

Stearn, W. T., *The Wondrous Transformation of
Caterpillars* (London: Scolar Press, 1978)

Wettengl, K. (ed.), *Maria Sibylla Merian. 1647–1717.
Künstlerin und Naturforscherin* (Osterfildern: Hatje
Cantz, 1997). Published in English as *Maria Sibylla
Merian 1647–1717. Artist and Naturalist*

Mark Catesby

Catesby, Mark, *The Natural History of Carolina, Florida,
and the Bahama Islands.* Introduction by George
Frick and notes by Joseph Ewan (Savannah:
Beehive Press, 1974)

Desmond, R., *Great Natural History Books and their
Creators* (British Library: London; New Castle: Oak
Knoll, 2003)

Meyers, A. R. W. and Pritchard, B., *Empire's Nature:
Mark Catesby's New World Vision* (Chapel Hill
and London: University of North Carolina Press,
1998)

Elman, R., *First in the Field: America's Pioneering
Naturalists* (New York: Van Nostrand Reinhold,
1977)

Jackson, Christine E., *Bird Etchings: The Illustrators and
their Books, 1655–1855* (Ithaca and London: Cornell
University Press, 1985)

Frick, G. F. and Stearns, R. P., *Mark Catesby. The
Colonial Audubon* (Urbana: University of Illinois
Press, 1961)

McBurney, H., *Mark Catesby's Natural History of
America, The Watercolours from the Royal library,
Windsor Castle* (London: Merrell Holberton, 1997)

Carl Linnaeus

Blunt, W., *The Compleat Naturalist: A Life of Linnaeus,*
with intro. by W. T. Stearn (London: Frances
Lincoln, 3rd ed., 2002)

Farber, Paul Lawrence, *Finding Order in Nature: The
Naturalist Tradition from Linnaeus to E. O. Wilson*
(Baltimore: Johns Hopkins University Press, 2000)

Frängsmyr, Tore, Lindroth, Sten and Eriksson,
Gunnar, *Linnaeus: The Man and His Work,* Uppsala
Studies in History of Science, Vol 18 (Canton, MA:
Science History Publications, 1994)

Freer, Stephen (trans.), *Linnaeus' Philosophica Botanica*
(Oxford: Oxford University Press: 2005)

Jackson, B. D., *Linnaeus* (London: H. F. & G.
Witherby, 1923)

Jarvis, C., *Order Out of Chaos: Linnaean Plant Names and
their Types* (London: Linnean Society of London

and The Natural History Museum, 2007)

Koerner, Lisbet, *Linnaeus: Nature and Nation*
(Cambridge, MA: Harvard University Press, 2001)

http://www.linnean.org

Comte de Buffon

Dujarric de la Rivière, R. *Buffon: sa vie, ses oeuvres.
Pages choisies* (Paris: J. Peyronnet, 1971)

Roger, J., *Buffon: A Life in Natural History,* translated
from the French by S. L. Bonnefoi, edited by L. P.
Williams (Ithaca, NY: Cornell University Press,
1997)

http://www.buffon.cnrs.fr/ (in French; includes the
works of Buffon)

Georg Steller

Ford, C., *Where the Sea Breaks its Back: The Epic Story
of a Pioneer Naturalist and the Discovery of Alaska*
(London: Victor Gollancz Ltd, 1967)

Steller, G. W. *Journal of a Voyage with Bering,
1741–1742.* Edited and with an introduction by
O. W. Frost. Translated by Margritt A. Engel and
O. W. Frost (Stanford: Stanford University Press,
1988)

Stejneger, L. *Georg Wilhelm Steller: The Pioneer of
Alaskan Natural History* (Cambridge, MA: Harvard
University Press, 1936)

Michel Adanson

Adanson, M., *Histoire Naturelle du Sénégal: Coquillages.
Avec la Relation d'un Voyage Fait en ce Pays, Pendant les
Années 1749, 50, 51, 52, & 53* (Paris, 1757)

Adanson, M., *Familles des plantes* (Paris, 1763)

Lawrence, G. H. M., *Adanson: The Bicentennial of
Michel Adanson's Familles des Plantes,* 2 vols
(Pittsburgh: Hunt Botanical Library, Carnegie
Institute of Technology, 1963–1964)

Nicolas, J. P., 'Adanson, Michel' in *Dictionary of
Scientific Biography* (New York: Charles Scribner's
& Sons, 1970), 1: 58-59

Erasmus Darwin

Darwin, Erasmus, *The Botanic Garden.* Part 1. *The
Economy of Vegetation;* Part 2. *The Loves of the Plants*
(London: J. Johnson, 1791 and 1789)

Darwin, Erasmus, *Phytologia; or, the Philosphy of
Agriculture and Gardening* (London: J. Johnson, 1800)

Darwin, Erasmus, *Zoonomia; or, the Laws of Organic Life,*
Parts 1–3 (London: J. Johnson, 1794-1796)

Darwin, Erasmus, *The Temple of Nature; or, the Origin of
Society* (London: J. Johnson, 1803)

King-Hele, D., *The Essential Writings of Erasmus Darwin* (Worcester and London: Trinity Press, 1968)

King-Hele, D., *A Life of Unequalled Achievement* (London: Giles de la Mare, 1999)

William Bartram

Bartram, William, *The Travels of William Bartram*, edited by Francis Harper (Athens, GA: University of Georgia Press, 1998)

Magee, Judith, *The Art and Science of William Bartram* (London and University Park: Natural History Museum and Penn State University Press, 2007)

Slaughter, Thomas, *The Nature of John & William Bartram* (New York: Alfred A Knopf, 1996)

Joseph Banks

Beaglehole, J. C., *The Endeavour Journal of Joseph Banks 1768–1771* (Sydney: The Trustees of The Public Library of New South Wales in association with Angus & Robertson, Halstead Press, 1962)

Bulletin of the British Museum (Natural History), Historical Series vols 11–13 (Complete). Catalogue of the Natural History Drawings commissioned by Joseph Banks on the *Endeavour* voyage 1768–1771 held in the British Museum (Natural History) (London, 1984)

Carter, H. B., *Sir Joseph Banks* (London: British Museum (Natural History), 1988)

Carter, H. B., Diment, Judith A., Humphries, C. J. and Wheeler, Alwyne, 'The Banksian natural history collections of the *Endeavour* voyage and their relevance to modern taxonomy', in *History in the Service of Systematics* (Papers from the Conference to celebrate the Centenary of the British Museum, Natural History 13–16 April, 1981) (London: Society for the Bibliography of Natural History, 1981)

Johann Christian Fabricius

Armitage, A., 'A naturalist's vacation. The London letters of J. C. Fabricius', *Annals of Science* 14(2) (1958), 116–31

Hope, F. W., 'The auto-biography of John Christian Fabricius, translated from the Danish, with additional notes and observations', *Transactions of the Entomological Society of London* 4 (1845), i–xvi

Jespersen, P. H., [J. C. Fabricius as an evolutionist], *Sv. Linné-Sällsk. Årsskr.* 29 (1946), 35–56,

Tuxen, S. L., 'The entomologist, J. C. Fabricius', *Annual Review of Entomology* 12 (1967), 1–14

James Hutton

Baxter, S., *Revolutions in the Earth. James Hutton and the True Age of the World* (London: Weidenfeld & Nicolson, 2003)

Cook, Jill, 'Rocks, fossils and the emergence of palaeontology', in K. Sloan (ed.) *Enlightenment. Discovering the World in the Eighteenth Century* (London: British Museum Press, 2003), 100–05

Hutton, James, *The Theory of the Earth* (original edition, Edinburgh, 1795; reprinted New York: Cramer, Stechert-Hafner, 1972)

Rudwick, M. J. S., 2005. *Bursting the Limits of Time. The Reconstruction of Geohistory in the Age of Revolution* (Chicago and London: The University of Chicago Press, 2005)

Jean-Baptiste Lamarck

Burkhardt, R. W. Jr, *The Spirit of System: Lamarck and Evolutionary Biology* (Cambridge, MA and London: Harvard University Press, 2nd ed., 1995)

Corsi, P., *The Age of Lamarck: Evolutionary Theories in France 1790–1830*. Revised and updated, translated from the Italian by J. Mandelbaum (Berkeley, Los Angeles and London: University of California Press, 1988) (first published as *Oetre il mito: Lamarck e le scienze naturali del suo tempo*. Il Mulino: Bologna, 1983)

Lamarck, J.-B., *Flore Française or descriptions succintes de toutes les plantes qui croissent naturellment en France, disposes selon une nouvelle méthode d'analyse*, 3 vols (Paris: Imprimerie Royale, 1778)

Lamarck, J.-B., 1984. *Zoological Philosophy; An Exposition with Regard to the Natural History of Animals*, translated from the French by Hugh Elliot; originally published in 1809 as *Philosophie zoologique* (Chicago: University of Chicago Press, 1984)

Laurent, G. (ed.), *Jean-Baptiste Lamarck 1744–1829* (Paris: Éditions de CTHS, 1997)

Antoine-Laurent Jussieu

Jussieu, A.-L., *Genera plantarum*. With an introduction by Frans A. Stafleu (New York: Weinheim, J. Cramer, 1964)

Spary, E. C., *Utopia's Garden: French Natural History from Old Regime to Revolution* (Chicago: University of Chicago Press, 2000)

Stevens, P. F., *The Development of Biological Systematics: Antoine-Laurent de Jussieu, Nature, and the Natural system* (New York: Columbia University Press, 1994)

Georges Cuvier

Coleman, W., *Georges Cuvier, Zoologist. A Study in the History of Evolution Theory* (Cambridge, MA: Harvard University Press, 1964)

Pietsch, T. W., *Historical Portrait of the Progress of Ichthyology from Its Origins to Our Own Time. Georges Cuvier* (Baltimore: Johns Hopkins University Press, 1995)

Rudwick, M. J. S., *Georges Cuvier, Fossil Bones and Geological Catastrophes. New Translations and Interpretations of the Primary Texts* (Chicago and London: University of Chicago Press, 1997)

Rudwick, M. J. S., *Bursting the Limits of Time. The Reconstruction of Geohistory in the Age of Revolution* (Chicago and London: University of Chicago Press, 2005)

Taquet P., *Georges Cuvier. Naissance d'un Génie* (Paris: Odile Jacob, 2006)

THE 19TH CENTURY

William Smith

Morton, J. L., *Strata: The Remarkable Life Story of William Smith, 'the Father of English Geology'* (Horsham: Brocken Spectre Publishing, 2nd ed., 2004)

Phillips, J., *Memoirs of William Smith, LL.D.* (London: John Murray, 1884; reprinted 2004 by the History of Geology Group of the Geological Society, London)

Sheppard, T., *William Smith: His Maps and Memoirs* (Hull: A. Brown & Sons, 1917, *Proceedings of the Yorkshire Geological Society*, 19. 75–253; reprinted 1920)

Alexander von Humboldt

Botting, Douglas, *Humboldt and the Cosmos* (London: Michael Joseph; New York: Harper & Row, 1973)

Helferich, Gerard, *Humboldt's Cosmos: Alexander von Humboldt and the Latin American Journey that Changed the Way We See the World* (New York: Gotham Books, 2004)

Humboldt, Alexander von, *Personal Narrative of a Journey to the Equinoctial Regions of the New Continent* (London: Penguin, 1995)

John James Audubon

Blaugrund, Annette and Stebbins, Theodore E., Jr. (eds), *John James Audubon: The Watercolors for "The Birds of America"* (New York: Villard Books, Random House and The New-York Historical Society, 1993)

Davis, Duff Hart, *Audubon's Elephant: America's Greatest Naturalist and the Making of "The Birds of America"* (New York: H. Holt, 2004)

Ford, Alice, *John James Audubon* (Norman: University of Oklahoma Press, 1965; 2nd ed. New York: Abbeville Press, 1988)

Fries, Waldemar H., *The Double Elephant Folio: The Story of Audubon's "Birds of America"* (Chicago: American Library Association, 1973; 2nd ed. Amherst, MA: Zenaida Publishing, 2005)

Low, Suzanne M., *An Index and Guide to Audubon's "Birds of America"* (New York: Abbeville Press, 1988; 2nd ed., New Haven and New York: William Reese Company & Donald A. Heald, 2002)

Rhodes, Richard, *John James Audubon: The Making of An American* (New York: Alfred A. Knopf, 2004)

Souder, William, *Under a Wild Sky: John James Audubon and the Making of the "Birds of America"* (New York: North Point Press, 2004)

William Buckland

Cadbury, D., *The Dinosaur Hunters* (London: Fourth Estate, 2000); *Terrible Lizard: The First Dinosaur Hunters and the Birth of a New Science* (New York: Holt, 2001)

Cook, J., 'The discovery of British antiquity', in K. Sloan (ed.) *Enlightenment. Discovering the World in the Eighteenth Century* (London: British Museum Press, 2003)

Rudwick, M. J. S., *Bursting the Limits of Time. The Reconstruction of Geohistory in the Age of Revolution* (Chicago and London: University of Chicago Press, 2005)

Rupke, N. A., *The Great Chain of History. William Buckland and the English School of Geology. (1814–1849)* (Oxford: Clarendon Press, 1983)

Charles Lyell

Blundell, D. J. and Scott, D. C. (eds), *Lyell: The Past is the Key to the Present*. Geological Society Special Publication (London: Geological Society, 1998)

Lyell, C., *Principles of Geology* (London: Penguin, 1997)

Rudwick, M. J. S., *The Great Devonian Controversy: The Shaping of Scientific Knowledge among Gentlemanly Specialists* (Chicago and London: University of Chicago Press, 1985)

Rudwick, M .J. S., *The Meaning of Fossils: Episodes in the History of Paleontology* (London: Macdonald; New York: Elsevier, 1972)

Mary Anning

Goodhue, Thomas W., *Fossil Hunter: The Life and Times of Mary Anning (1799–1847)* (Bethesda: Academica Press, 2004)

Lang, W. D., *Proceedings of the Dorset Natural History and Archaeological Society*, vols 60, 62, 66, 68, 71, 74, 76, 80 & 81

Tickell, Crispin, *Mary Anning of Lyme Regis* (Lyme Regis: Philpot Museum, 1996 and 1998)

Torrens, Hugh, 'Mary Anning (1799–1847)', Presidential address to the British Society for the History of Science, April 1993

Richard Owen

Camardi, Giovanni, 'Richard Owen, Morphology and Evolution', *Journal of History of Biology*, 34 (2001), 481–515

MacLeod, Roy M., 'Evolution and Richard Owen', *Isis*, 56 (1965) 259–80

Owen, Richard S., *The Life of Richard Owen*, 2 vols (London: John Murray, 1894)

Richards, Evelleen, 'A question of property rights: Richard Owen's evolutionism reassessed', *British Journal for the History of Science*, 20 (1987) 129–71

Rupke, N. A. 1994. *Richard Owen: Victorian Naturalist* (New Haven and London: Yale University Press)

Jean-Louis Agassiz

Agassiz, Elizabeth Cary, *Louis Agassiz, His Life and Correspondence* (Boston and New York: Houghton Mifflin, 1885)

Guyot, Arnold Henry, *Memoir of Louis Agassiz, 1807–1873* (Princeton: C. S. Robinson and Co., 1883)

Lurie, Edward, *Louis Agassiz: A Life in Science* (Chicago: University of Chicago Press, 1960)

Marcou, Jules, *Life, Letters and Works of Louis Agassiz* (New York: MacMillan, 1895)

Thuillier, Pierre, 'Un anti-évolutionniste exemplaire: Louis Agassiz' *Revue des Questions Scientifiques* 145 (1974), 195–215, 405–24

Walcott, Charles Doolittle, 'Louis Agassiz *Smithsonian Miscellaneous Collections* 50 (IV) (1908), 216–18

Charles Darwin

Browne, E. J., *Charles Darwin, a Biography*, 2 vols (New York: Knopf: 1995 and 2002)

Desmond, Adrian and Moore, James, *Darwin, the Life of a Tormented Evolutionist* (New York: W.W. Norton, 1991)

Keynes, Randal, *Annie's Box* (London: Fourth Estate, 2002)

Keynes, Richard Darwin, *The Beagle Record* (Cambridge: Cambridge University Press, 1979)

Herbert, Sandra, *Charles Darwin, Geologist* (Ithaca: Cornell University Press, 2005)

Hodge, Jonathan and Radick, Gregory (eds), *The Cambridge Companion to Darwin* (Cambridge: Cambridge University Press, 2003)

http://darwin-online.org.uk

http://www.darwinproject.ac.uk

Alfred Russel Wallace

Berry, A. (ed.), *Infinite Tropics: An Alfred Russel Wallace Anthology* (London and New York: Verso, 2002)

Raby, P., *Alfred Russel Wallace: A Life* (London: Chatto & Windus, 2001)

Knapp, S., *Footsteps in the Forest: Alfred Russel Wallace in the Amazon* (London: Natural History Museum, 1999)

Van Oosterzee, P., *Where Worlds Collide: The Wallace Line* (Ithaca and London: Cornell University Press, 1997)

Wallace, A. R 1869. *The Malay Archipelago: The Land of the Orang-utan and the Bird of Paradise, A Narrative of Travel with Studies of Man and Nature* (London: Macmillan & Co., 1869; facsimile reprint edition, New York: Dover Publications, 1962)

Wallace, A. R., *Peixes do Rio Negro/Fishes of the Rio Negro*, organized by M. de Toledo-Pizo Ragazzo (Sao Paulo: Editora da Universidade de Sao Paulo, 2000)

Wilson, J. G., *The Forgotten Naturalist: In Search of Alfred Russel Wallace* (Kew, Victoria, Australia: Arcadia, 2000)

Asa Gray

Dupree, A. H., *Asa Gray: American Botanist, Friend of Darwin.* (Baltimore and London: The Johns Hopkins University Press, 1959)

Gray, J. L. (ed.), *The Letters of Asa Gray*, 2 vols (London: MacMillan & Co., 1893)

Illustration page 292: Drawing of a shaman from the published account of Steller's journey to arctic Siberia. Illustrations pages 295, 299 & 300: Images from Konrad Gessner's History of Animals.

SOURCES OF ILLUSTRATIONS

a: above; b: below; c: centre; l: left; r: right

1, 3, 6 Natural History Museum, London; 9 Alamy/Visual Arts Library, London; 10 Alamy/David Sanger Photography; 13, 14, 15, 16, 19 Natural History Museum, London; 21ar Topkapi Palace Museum, Istanbul; 21cr Natural History Museum, London; 22 Bridgeman Art Library/Vatican Museums and Galleries, Vatican City; 25 Natural History Museum, London; 27 Bridgeman Art Library/Archives Charmet, Bibliothèque Sainte-Genevieve, Paris; 28 Bridgeman Art Library/Stapleton Collection, Private Collection; 31 Alamy/The Print Collector; 32, 35 Natural History Museum, London; 36 Freer Gallery of Art, Smithsonian Institution, Washington, D.C. Purchase, F1938.1; 39 Bridgeman Art Library/Accademia Italiana, London, Private Collection; 40 Courtesy of History of Science Collections, University of Oklahoma Libraries; 41 Alamy/Visual Arts Library London; 42 Bridgeman Art Library/Alinari, Biblioteca Estense, Modena; 44 University Library of Bologna; 47 Bibliothèque nationale de France, Paris; 49 Courtesy History of Science Collections, University of Oklahoma Libraries; 50al & ar Österreichische Nationalbibliothek, Vienna; 52, 53, 55, 56, 57 Courtesy History of Science Collections, University of Oklahoma Libraries; 58 Österreichische Nationalbibliothek, Vienna; 60 Corbis/Archivo Iconografico/Krause Johansen; 61a, c & b Natural History Museum, London; 62 University Library of Bologna; 65 Courtesy Sezione Botanica del Museo di Storia Naturale dell'Università di Firenze, Florence; 66, 69l & r Natural History Museum, London; 70 Bibliothèque nationale de France, Paris; 72, 73, 75, 77 Natural History Museum, London; 78 Alamy/INTERFOTO Pressebildagentur; 79 Natural History Museum, London; 80 Courtesy The Royal Library, Copenhagen; 81 akg-images; 82, 83, 84 Natural History Museum, London; 86 Courtesy History of Science Collections, University of Oklahoma Libraries; 88 Natural History Museum, London; 89 Courtesy the Institute of Medical Anatomy, University of Copenhagen; 93 Natural History Museum, London; 95 National Portrait Gallery, London; 96 Natural History Museum, London; 97 Wellcome Library, London; 98 Natural History Museum, London; 100 © The Royal Society, London; 102, 103 Natural History Museum, London; 105, 106 © The Royal Society, London; 107 Courtesy History of Science Collections, University of Oklahoma Libraries; 108 Courtesy Museum Boerhaave, Leiden/Rijksmuseum voor de Geschiedenis van de Natuurwetenschappen en van de Geneeskunde, Leiden, Netherlands, inv. PO7252; 109 Courtesy University Museum, Utrecht; 112, 113a & b, 114, 115, 117, 117 Natural History Museum, London; 119 Staatliche Museen, Berlin Kupferstichkabinett Kd/8929; 120 Germanisches Nationalmuseum, Nünrberg, Inv. Nr Hz 3/1; 121 Staatsbibliothek, Bamberg, Inv. Nr. 1 B 90; 122, 123, 125, 126, 127, 128, 129, 130, 132, 134, 136, 137, 138, 139, 141, 143, 144 Natural History Museum, London; 145 Courtesy History of Science Collections, University of Oklahoma Libraries; 147 Natural History Museum, London; 148 Courtesy History of Science Collections, University of Oklahoma Libraries; 150 Alamy/INTERFOTO Pressebildagentur; 151 Private Collection; 152, 154, 156, 157, 160 Natural History Museum, London; 161 Alamy/Visual Arts Library, London; 162, 163, 166, 168 Natural History Museum, London; 170 Courtesy Independence National Historical Park Collection, Philadelphia; 171, 172, 174, 176, 177, 178, 181 Natural History Museum, London; 183 Natural History Museum of Denmark/Photo Geert Brovad; 185 Deutsche Gesellschaft für allgemeine und angewandte Entomologie e.V., Geschäftsstelle am DEI, Müncheberg/Photo Christian Kutzscher, Deutsches Entomologisches Institut, Müncheberg; 187, 188, 191, 192, 195a & b Natural History Museum, London; 199, 201 Wellcome Library, London; 203 Natural History Museum, London; 204 Bridgeman Art Library/Bibliothèque de l'Institut de France, Paris; 207. 208, 209, 210 Natural History Museum, London; 211 From C. E. von Baer, *De ovi mammalium et hominis genesi*, 1827; 213 Courtesy History of Science Collections, University of Oklahoma Libraries; 214a Natural History Museum, London; 214b Courtesy History of Science Collections, University of Oklahoma Libraries; 215, 217, 218 Natural History Museum, London; 220 Courtesy History of Science Collections, University of Oklahoma Libraries; 221, 222, 223, 225, 226 Natural History Museum, London; 228 Staatliche Museen, Berlin; 229, 231 Natural History Museum, London; 234 The Collection of The New-York Historical Society, Purchased for the Society by public subscription from Mrs. John J. Audubon, 1863.17.26; 237 The Collection of The New-York Historical Society, Purchased for the Society by public subscription from Mrs. John J. Audubon, 1863.17.311; 238 Natural History Museum, London; 239 The Collection of The New-York Historical Society, Purchased for the Society by public subscription from Mrs. John J. Audubon, 1863.17.76; 242, 243, 244–45, 247, 248, 249l–r, 250, 251, 256, 257, 258, Natural History Museum, London; 263, 264 Archives of the Ernst Mayr Library, Museum of Comparative Zoology, Harvard University, Cambridge; 265, 268, 269, 271, 272 Natural History Museum, London; 276 Sotheby's Picture Library, London; 278, 279, 280, 281, 282a&b, 285, 287, 288, 290, 292, 295, 299, 300 Natural History Museum, London. Endpapers Natural History Museum, London

INDEX

for the Support of their Stocks, of Cattle &c.

Here are very good Mills both for grist
for sawing Lumber fit for building &c
is in this Village a very large brick Church
nished with a Cupola & Bell, & some very
t private buildings. — After breakfasting and
taking a view of the place we persued our jour
ough Pine groves the Land flat, the soil sandy
the country every where clad with green, gra
the forests & beautifull Savanahs richly pain
with various col'd flowers. a pretty yellow Ci
eautifull Citisus, Penguicula's of various col'd
ts, & Phlox of various dies, Iris, Ixia, Bartsia
an endless variety of other, gay subjects of t
itable Kingdom. & here in the Pine Forest
ust observed, that very pretty yellow Flower ze
g a Lithospermum. The next morning being
pleasant, invited us early on our way, Went o